TO SHORTEN THE ROAD

TO SHORTEN THE ROAD

Essays and biographies by
George Gmelch

Folktales edited by
Ben Kroup

Photographs by George Gmelch and others

THE O'BRIEN PRESS
11 CLARE ST DUBLIN 2

First published 1978
The O'Brien Press Ltd.,
11 Clare Street, Dublin 2, Ireland

© Copyright Reserved
ISBN 0 905140 37 0

Jacket design and layout:
Michael O'Brien, Sharon Gmelch
Jacket photos: George Gmelch
Binding: John F. Newman Ltd.
Typesetting: Redsetter Ltd.
Printed in the Republic of Ireland
by E. & T. O'Brien Ltd., Dublin

Contents

Acknowledgements 6
List of Illustrations 7
The Folktales and the Collectors 9
On the Roadside in the 1930s 17

PART 1   The Folktales of Oney Power 38
         Johnnie and Tommie 41
         Jack the Highway Robber 53
         Jack from Tubberclare 62
         Jack the Ghost 71
         The Story of the Omadhaun Laois 79
         The Fresh Loaf or the Three-legged Lamb 83
         The Firey Dragon 88
         Jack the Fisherman 97
         The Wild Sow of the Forest 103
         Jack the Bear 112

PART 2   The Folktales of John Power 125
         Buddy 126
         Jack the Cobbler — The Widow's Son from Ireland 131
         Horse, Hound and Hawk 138
         The Roarin' Bull of Orange 147
         The Wonderful Sword 156

PART 3   The Folktales of Mickey Greene 165
         The Four Kings of Ireland 168
         The Little Blue Bonnet 177

Notes 182
Glossary 184
Index of Tale Types 187
Bibliography 188

Opposite — The news makes the rounds at Puck Fair, Killorglin, Co. Kerry.

Acknowledgements

This book would not have been possible without the co-operation and help of many people. The Department of Irish Folklore at University College Dublin, successor to the Irish Folklore Commission, kindly gave permission to publish the folktales in this collection. In the same Department, Professor Bo Almqvist provided valuable comments on the text, archivists Séamus O'Catháin and Seán O'Súilleabháin answered many questions about the early collectors and work of the Irish Folklore Commission, and sound specialist Leo Corduff demonstrated the use of the Ediphone recording machine. While the Department of Irish Folklore assisted in many ways, it is not responsible for any omissions or errors of interpretation.

I am indebted to Sharon Bohn Gmelch, my wife and colleague, for editing the text and for helping in the search for period photographs. Betty Kruger and Jo Ann Somich painstakingly typed the tales from a difficult handscript. Edna Gmelch did a superb job in the printing of the photographs. A special word of thanks is due our publisher, Michael O'Brien, for his editorial advice and thoughtful suggestions. Among the many others who contributed in various ways are Lucy Berger, Vincent and Margaret Jones, Eithne Russell, Tom Furey, Linda Kent, David Smith, and the staff of the National Library.

Over the years many Travellers have provided me with a wealth of information about their traditional way of life. In particular I wish to thank Nan Donoghue, Mick and Katie Connors, Tom Connors, Biddy Connors, Neddie Connors, Nan and Paddy Maugham, Tom Connors, Luke Wall, Nellie and Bridget Delaney, and the late Mick Donoghue and Jim Connors. Of special help were Nan Donoghue and Larry Green who recounted the lives of their relatives, the storytellers. Financial support for my research on Irish Travellers, although not specifically for this project, has come at different times from the Institute of Social and Economic Research of Memorial University of Newfoundland, the University of California at Santa Barbara, and McGill University. Ben Kroup's research on Irish folktales was supported by an International Research and Exchange Grant.

Finally we come to the collectors and storytellers themselves. This book would not have been possible were it not for the dedicated work of Pádraig MacGréine and James G. Delaney who along with other collectors have preserved Ireland's oral traditions and folklore for all time. But most important of all are the storytellers Oney Power, John Power, and Mickey Green who gave their time and tales unselfishly.

George Gmelch
Dublin, March 1978

List of Illustrations

Biddy Connors, grandmother of seventy – photo by George Gmelch	page 2
Exchanging Gossip at Puck Fair – George Gmelch	4
Storyteller using Ediphone – Dept. of Irish Folklore UCD ...	11
Folklore Collector and his Informant – Dept. of Irish Folklore UCD	12
Collecting Folklore on the Roadside – C. Ó'Danachair, Dept. of Irish Folklore UCD	12
Hand Transcription of Recorded Folktale – Dept of Irish Folklore UCD	15
A Blinkered Pony – George Gmelch	16
Shelter Tents on Roadside – Jimmy Walshe	19
Roadside Camp outside Galway – C. Ó'Danachair, Dept. of Irish Folklore UCD	19
Tools of the Tinsmith – National Museum of Ireland	22
Horse Fair in the 1950's – I.A.O.S.	24
Travelling Family with Donkey and Dray – Pádraig MacGréine	26
Fortune Telling – G. A. Duncan	29
The Gladar Box – George Gmelch	31
Two travelling families in the 1930's – Pádraig MacGréine ...	36
A Campfire inside a Tent – George Gmelch	37
Campfire Chat – George Gmelch	51
Man with Mare – George Gmelch	61
Horse and Travellers take a Break – George Gmelch	70
Cooking in the Open – George Gmelch	78
A Weather Worn Travelling Woman – George Gmelch	82
A Storyteller – George Gmelch	87
A Traditional Barrel-top Wagon – George Gmelch	96
An Elderly Travelling Couple – George Gmelch	102
Girls in Trailer Doorway – George Gmelch	111
An Intimate Joke at Puck Fair – George Gmelch	124
Richly Decorated Barrel-top Wagon – George Gmelch ...	130
An Under-wagon Bed – George Gmelch	136/7
The Art of the Tinsmith – George Gmelch	146
Girl with 'Ponnie' or Handmade Tin Mug – George Gmelch ...	155
An Elderly Traveller – George Gmelch	164
Babies in a Bender Tent – George Gmelch	176

*To the Travelling People
especially Nan Donoghue,
the Connors of Holylands,
and
the Maughams of Moate.*

The Folktales and the Collectors

The title of this book, To Shorten the Road, was once a common phrase used by both Travellers and country people. It refers to the custom of telling stories to pass the time and lighten the burden of a long journey. The following account of a father and son who set out travelling together is a common event in Irish folktales. After walking several miles, the father turns to his son and requests "Shorten the road for me." "I can't shorten it shorter than it was made." the son responds, failing to understand. At this the father stops and in disgust turns back home, his son following close behind. This happens several days in a row until finally the son's wife demands, "Why are ye turning back every day an' coming back home again?" The son explains his confusion, whereupon his wife exclaims, "You amadán! You fool! Follow him again and be telling him stories. That's the way to shorten the road, to be telling him stories." When the pair set out the next morning, the son immediately begins to tell the old man a story, and "they never feel the road again until landed abroad".[1]

The folktales contained in this volume were told by the Travelling People or Tinkers of Ireland. Most of the stories were recorded from 1930 to 1932; two were collected in 1972. The tales were selected from a corpus of thirty-five Traveller folktales recorded by collectors for *Coimisiún Béaloideasa Éireann* (Irish Folklore Commission), now Roinn Bhéaloideas Éireann (Department of Irish Folklore), University College Dublin.

In comparison to the total collection of more than 40,000 folktales contained in the archives of the Department of Irish Folklore, the number of tales recorded from Travellers is tiny. That so few stories were collected seems surprising, for Travellers had a reputation as gifted storytellers. Besides, itinerant peoples by virtue of their isolation often retained folklore traditions that have long since died out among the settled community. This fact became evident quite recently in Ireland when in the course of collecting traditional music around the country folklorist Tom Munnelly discovered a number of songs among Travelling People completely forgotten by the settled population.[2]

There may have been a number of reasons why so few folktales were collected from Irish Tinkers. For one, the art of storytelling in the early part of the century was most highly developed in Irish-speaking areas and because the Gaeltachts were rapidly dwindling, collecting was naturally most intensive there. When the collecting started few Tinkers spoke Irish. Travelling on foot or bicycle while lugging a bulky Ediphone recording machine along, collectors may have been unwilling to chance a trip to a camp never knowing for sure if the Tinkers would still be there. Unlike the farmer who was certain to be at home, Travellers were always moving on. And because itinerants were not permanent residents it would have been difficult to develop the rapport needed to collect information.

Sixteen of the tales in this volume were collected by Pádraig MacGréine, a part-time fieldworker for the Irish Folklore Commission. The two remaining stories were recorded by James G. Delaney, currently a full-time collector for the Department of Irish Folklore.

While a young school teacher in County Longford, Pádraig MacGréine joined the Folklore of Ireland Society shortly after it was founded in 1926. This is how he recalls becoming involved:

> The year the Folklore Society was founded I was in Ballingeary in County Cork at an Irish course for school teachers. One evening just as the class was finishing, Fíonán MacColuim, who was a founder-member — a Kerryman who'd thrown up a civil service job in London to come back to Ireland to try to spread the language — came into the classroom to introduce the Folklore Society and point out the work they intended to do: to save as quickly as they could, folk material in the way of folktales, ballads and customs which were rapidly dying out. He said that we were the last bastion for folk culture studies in Western Europe. So the annual subscription was a pound, and I happened to have a pound in my pocket. I gave them a pound and my name and got the first edition of *Béaloideas*. And that's the way it happened.[3]

MacGréine became one of several dozen volunteer fieldworkers who in their spare time tracked down and recorded local storytellers. The focus of the Irish Folklore Commission was clearly on the recording of Ireland's oral traditions.[4] However, the fieldworkers were also instructed to collect information on other folklore topics including traditional crafts, dwellings, pastimes, folk medicines, popular beliefs, and religious traditions.

The principal tool of the early collectors was the Ediphone recording machine, the first of which was donated to the Folklore Society by the Edison Company. It was a bulky machine weighing over fifty pounds which

Despite its bulk and weight of about fifty pounds, the enthusiastic collector often carried the Ediphone to remote areas to collect folklore. In this case the storyteller is Peats Buí O Súilleabháin, a farmer from Ballinskelligs, Co. Kerry. Circa 1940.

Above — Seosamh Ó Dalaigh (left) a full-time collector with the Irish Folklore Commission recording Pádraig Sayers farmer, on the Ediphone in Dunquin, Co. Kerry, circa 1940.

Left — Full-time collector for the Irish Folklore Commission Tadhg Ó Murchadha, recording a farmer in Waterville, Co Kerry. Circa 1940.

recorded sound on fragile, wax cylinders. In the early years the Folklore Commission had only three recorders. As a result, most collectors had the use of one for only a few weeks of the year. Short items of prose and simple information could easily be taken down directly by hand, but long tales would often have to wait until the Ediphone arrived. Then the collector recorded feverishly, attempting to complete the work in the short time the machine was allotted to him. MacGréine outlines the main steps of the work, beginning with the actual recording.

> I would tell the narrator to hold the voice box close to his mouth... then when the bell rang at the end of the cylinder, I would write down the last sentence and put on a new cylinder and remind the narrator what he had finished saying. At night, after I'd taken my tea, I'd transcribe the cylinders. It might take two or three hours to transcribe a story. I wrote exactly as the narrator spoke, that was to present English as it was spoken in the Midlands, as it was spoken then... When I finished the box of cylinders, I'd take them to the bus station and send them back to Dublin to be shaved [recycled].[5]

Collectors were instructed to write verbatim the material they had recorded. It was taken down in octavo notebooks supplied by the Folklore Commission. Every three to six months the notebooks were bound together in leather volumes. Numbered and arranged in chronological order, there are now 1,889 volumes in the folklore archives containing more than a million and a half manuscript pages. It is thus one of the largest and richest collections in the world, and makes available folktales in both Irish and English which in many other countries have been lost. Few other countries had the opportunity or foresight to collect and record their folklore before the traditions were forgotten.

The stories in this book are somewhat unusual in that they were told in English. While there are a number of excellent collections in Irish, most of the English-language folktales in print are translations from Irish. Many publishers have found it difficult to resist the temptation to popularise collections of folktales in order to increase their marketability. This has often resulted in stories being re-written in a more readily assimilated style. The costs, in my opinion, are high for the stories invariably lose much of the artistry and colour of the narrator's own speech. The reader is left with little indication of the original language and spirit in which the tale was told. This collection differs from most previous collections in this respect. The stories are in the vernacular and represent as true and genuine a record of what the storyteller said as writing can convey.

The speech is that of the Irish Midlands in the first quarter of this century. All three storytellers spent most of their lives there, in Counties Westmeath and Longford. Most of the tales in this collection are what folklorists refer to as *Märchen*. *Märchen*, the diminutive form of the old German "mar" meaning short story, is the technical term for what are commonly called magic or fairy tales. *Märchen*, which centre on man's fascination with supernatural adventures, are ably discussed by folklorist Linda Dégh:

> They tell about ordinary human being's encounter with the suprahuman world and his becoming endowed with qualities that enable him to perform supernatural acts. The *Märchen* is, in fact, an adventure story with a single hero... The hero's (or heroine's) career starts, as everyone else's, in the dull miserable world of reality. Then, all of a sudden, the supernatural world involves him and challenges the mortal, who undertakes his long voyage to happiness. He enters the magic forest, guided by supernatural helpers, and defeats evil powers beyond the boundaries of man's universe. Crossing several borders of the Beyond, performing impossible tasks, the hero is slandered, banished, tortured, trapped, betrayed. He suffers death by extreme cruelty but is always brought to life again. Suffering turns him into a real hero: as often as he is devoured, cut up, swallowed, or turned into a beast, so does he become stronger and handsomer and more worthy of the prize he seeks. His ascent from rags to riches ends with the beautiful heroine's hand, a kingdom, and marriage. The final act of the *Märchen* brings the hero back to the human world; he metes out justice, punishes the evil, rewards the good.[6]

Märchen enjoyed great popularity throughout rural Europe and farther afield for many centuries. But by the 1930s when these tales were being collected in Ireland, they had virtually vanished from Western Europe.

Right — Collector Pádraig MacGréine's hand transcription of a recorded folktale. The transcriptions were taken down in octavo notebooks and later bound in leather volumes by the Folklore Commission. Circa 1940.

The roarin' bull of Orange.

Wance upon a time an' 'twas naythur my time nor your time, but 'twas somebody's time; there lived a king an' he had three only daughthers. An' he thought so much about them, that he had a wishin' chair an he promised a terrible death t'any o'them that 'id sit an (on) the chair, but he brought them gold an jewels an' everythin' they axed for only not to sit upon the chair. So wan day the father was away an' the three daughthers was alone. They opened the father's room an' they saw the chair. The very minnit they saw the chair wan o them sat in it for sport. So the very minnit she did, she wished for the Ramblin' Baker. So the next daughther sat in it wished for the Man of No Man's Land, an' the

On the Roadside in the 1930s

The following pages describe the lifestyle of Ireland's Travelling People at the time the stories in this collection were recorded. It is my belief that the reader cannot fully appreciate folktales without some knowledge of the culture in which the storytelling tradition existed. This reconstruction, which focuses on the daily life and subsistence patterns of the Tinkers,[7] is based on the recollections of present-day Travellers and country people, on early newspaper and journal accounts, and most importantly, on the results of a questionnaire on Tinkers which was sent to over three hundred correspondents by the Folklore Commission in 1950.[8] The account holds true until the 1950s, and later in some parts of the country. After that, modernisation brought far-reaching changes in the Irish countryside, eliminating most Travellers' traditional rural trades and forcing them to migrate into towns and cities.

Travellers lived out-of-doors, camped along quiet sideroads on the outskirts of towns and villages. In choosing a place to stay they looked for a sturdy wall or hedgerow to provide shelter from the wind, an ample supply of sticks for their fires, grass for their horses, and water from a well or pump. The fire was the centre of the camp and the gathering place for children and adults alike. Stretching out from the fire along the roadside were shelters of various types. The most valued among them was the barrel-top wagon, which for many country people has come to symbolize itinerant life. Irish Travellers, however, did not own wagons until the First World War when Gypsies fleeing conscription in England brought them into the country. By the 1930s many Travellers had learned to build their own by adding a bow-top superstructure on to an ordinary dray or flat cart. Some commissioned coachbuilders to make the conversion or build new wagons. A few families went to England to trade for them. The wagons were often decorated and brightly painted, as one observer wrote in 1934:

There is keen competition amongst the tinkers with regard to the exterior decoration of their caravans. Green and yellow appear to be the favourite colours and the panels usually contain crudely drawn pictures of horses, dogs and, of course, numerous horseshoes for luck.[9]
Inside, the roof was lined with a patterned chenille stretched over the framing. A layer of felt or blankets between the chenille and outer canvas provided insulation. Across the back wall was a bunk where the adults slept. Young children bedded down directly beneath them in a large cupboard-cum-bed on the wagon floor. The overflow slept in tents. As long as a few sticks of firewood were available the wagons were never cold or damp. A small wood burning stove on one wall gave out more than enough heat for the small volume of space inside. Even in the middle of winter it was often necessary to open the double windows at the front of the wagon to avoid overheating.

Initially only the better-off Travelling families, primarily horse dealers, could afford wagons. But by the mid-1930s approximately half the Traveller population owned them. As late as 1960, 61 per cent of Ireland's 6,591 itinerants were still living in wagons.[10] Practically the only wagons to be seen today, however, are the cheap plywood and rubber tire imitations rented to tourists. As Travellers have become motorised they have abandoned their wagons for trailers.

Families without wagons owned carts, generally light spring-carts which were converted from a means of transport during the day into a shelter at night. The cart was tipped on its "heels", shafts pointing skywards, then canvas was lashed around the wheels and another piece hung between the shafts.

But tents were the most common shelter of all. There were two types both constructed of bent hazel branches covered with oil-soaked bags or canvas. The smaller variety, no more than waist high at its peak, was known as a "wattle" or "bender" tent. The floor of the tent was covered with a deep bed of straw or hay on which the family slept wrapped in blankets and shawls. Families with older children had several tents, with boys in one and girls in another. The "shelter" tent was taller and much roomier, seating a dozen people or more. Found mainly in Connaught, it was an adaptation to a harsh, open landscape, lacking the many sheltered camping places found in Leinster. Moreover, Connaught Travellers tended to be very poor: many did not have wagons and therefore needed the larger interior living space provided by shelter tents. The tents were big enough to build a fire inside, common practise in cold weather.   The smoke rose through the ceiling. As one informant recalled:

> With light sacks the smoke would go out through and the heat of the big stick fires would keep the rain out. Them were oat sacks. The flour bags were no good. They were real close – you'd be smoked. We used the flour bags to make sheets out of. Sew them all together and they make

Top — A roadside camp on the outskirts of Galway. The close proximity of shelter tents indicates that the families are related. Fires are built in the centre of the shelter tents, in this case the smoke exits through the stove pipes poking through the middle of the tents.

Below — A roadside camp on the Dingle Peninsula in the late 1930s. The crude, homemade barrel-top wagon lacks the fine workmanship and detail of gypsy wagons of the period. It reflects the poverty of the Irish travellers. The large rear wheels were taken from a horse-drawn trap. The wattle tents provide sleeping space for the older boys and girls.

lovely white flour-bag sheets and pillow slips and aprons for little girls.[11] According to folklorist Pádraig MacGréine, tents are also a fairly recent innovation and were not used by Travellers until the late 1800s.[12] MacGréine's informants claimed tents were first introduced by a Tinker named Arthur MacDonough who learned their construction while travelling with Gypsies in England. A fair amount of Irish Travellers' material culture does appear to have been borrowed from Gypsies. Besides tents and wagons, they also acquired piebald and stewbald horses which are now the favourite type.

Before Travellers had shelter of their own they sought accommodation from the countryfolk they met along the way. They were often able to get a bed of straw on the kitchen floor or permission to sleep in an outbuilding or hay shed. In 1932 one observer wrote, "I know of two such houses where Tinkers used to lodge, if the weather was very wet and cold. They were charged sixpence a night and slept around the fireplace." [13]

The Traveller's horses, donkeys, and occasionally goats grazed along the roadside beyond the camp. Many families had several horses and donkeys; those who dealt in them for a living usually had a dozen or more. Finding enough good grass was sometimes difficult, especially in poor districts where local farmers were forced to graze their own animals on the roadside — the "long acre". Travellers sometimes slipped their horses into a farmer's field at night.

> Some Travellers would stay up all night if they had no food for the animals. They'd stay up until the farmer went to bed and then they'd go down and open up the gate and put in the horses. They wouldn't put them in a skinny field, they'd get the one with the good rye grass growin' in it. They'd be up early in the morning then to take out the horses and tie them up again. The farmer would come on lookin' and he'd be lookin' around and he'd see the track of the horses. He'd say 'Was there any of ye up around the field last night?' And we'd say, 'No, sure my horses were here the whole time.' Maybe the next night the farmer would be on the lookout, and they couldn't let them in. Well, they'd go on with their rope and steal a couple of bales of good hay or else they'd go on to a big cock of hay out of the land and they'd steal a bundle of that and put it under the horse's head. They'd look to see did they leave bits of hay behind, that way they wouldn't be tracked.[14]

Besides consuming valuable pasturage, horses could get into vegetable patches and cause considerable damage. Farmers who found them often demanded compensation, sometimes locking the animals in until it was paid. In some instances, their crops trampled once too many times, they retaliated by disfiguring or maiming the animals. Several Travellers mentioned experiences in which manes and tails were cut off.

The Travellers' day began by adding fresh kindling to the coals of the previous night's fire. A black and sooty tea pot was then suspended over the fire from a kettle iron — a rod with a hook at the end — stuck into the ground at an angle over the flames. Besides heavily sugared tea, breakfast consisted of whatever food was left over from the day before, for the day's foraging had not yet begun. Food was eaten out of vessels made by the men. The tent covers were drawn back to air the shelter, exposing their bent wattle skeletons. Damp clothing was hung on the nearby hedges and fences to dry. The woman washed the dishes, "vessels" as Travellers call them, and stacked them on a box or stump to dry. Meanwhile, the family's transport was looked after by the man. The horse was brought from his grazing place, dressed in his harness, and backed in between the shafts. Once hitched to the cart, the day's work began.

The means by which they earned their living varied considerably. In the 1930s Travellers could be divided into four categories according to their principal trade: tinsmiths, sweeps, hawkers and horse and donkey dealers.[15] But Travellers did not restrict themselves to one activity. The man who made cans would also swap or sell a donkey when the opportunity arose, peddle goods, and do a variety of odd jobs. Travellers had to be opportunists, willing to perform whatever service was required of them. Flexibility was crucial to survival on the road, since the jobs and services Travellers provided had a very limited or seasonal demand. A typical village, for example, could at most provide a few weeks' work for a tinsmith, chimney sweep, or pedlar. The limited local market for their skills was, of course, the reason some families had become itinerant in the first place.

Tinsmithing was the principal trade of the majority of Travellers. Carrying their tools on their backs in a box or bag known as the "budget", they travelled from farmhouse to farmhouse selling new tins and soliciting repair work. Seated on a stool in the farmyard or kitchen doorway, the tinsmith tightened loose handles, replaced worn-out and rusty bottoms, and plugged leaks with molten solder kept in place by a "tinker's dam" — a ring of dough or clay placed around the hole. As the Travellers passed through villages they often cried "any pots, pans, or kettles to mend". But much of the work was done at home beside the campfire where they could keep their soldering irons red hot.

From new sheets of tin or empty biscuit containers from the shops, the Tinker could fashion a wide variety of articles including cups, kettles, milk pails, lanterns, and buckets. Local hardware stores sometimes placed orders, but most items were simply hawked door-to-door. Among the specialised equipment made and repaired by Tinkers were the various parts needed for poteen stills.

Many Travellers were able to repair umbrellas and also clocks. Others could stitch broken china and earthenware together by drilling small holes

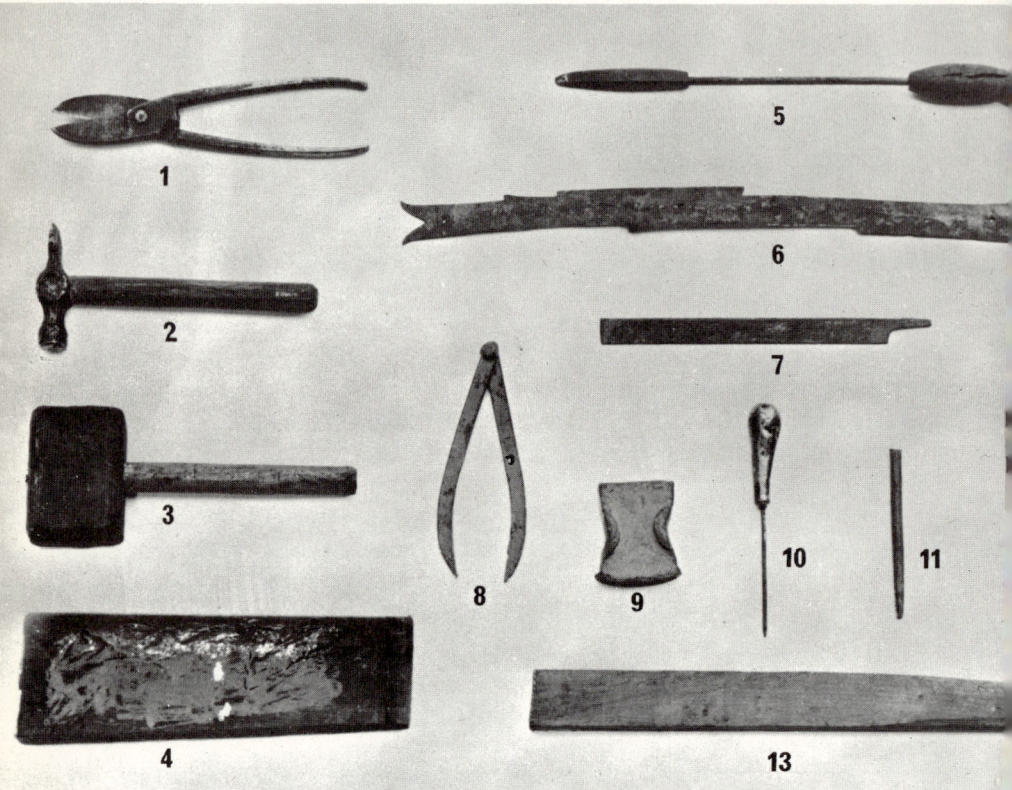

The tools of the tinsmith are as follows: (1) clips, for cutting sheets of tin; (2) hammer; (3) mallet, for flattening and shaping the tin; (4) rosin board, for coating the soldering iron; (5) soldering iron; (6) marking stick; (7) file; (8) compass; (9) hand stake, held inside the vessel as support while hammering the tin; (10) awl; (11) punch; (12) nail tool, used for making rivets; and (13) scrutcher, for flattening light tin.

in each piece and lacing them with wire. Countrypeople generally looked forward to the occasional visits of Travellers and made a mental note of repairs needed and items they might want to purchase. Before the era of the radio and the widespread circulation of newspapers, Travellers were also welcomed for the news they brought especially to remote areas. Recalling his childhood in Donegal in the 1920s, Patrick Campbell writes:

> Means of communication were limited and hard weather kept everyone near home except when one had to travel on urgent business. Consequently the tinkers were eagerly awaited, as they always had news from friends in other districts of their travels. They carried messages of good wishes, as well as dispatches of condolences. They had first-hand news of births, deaths and weddings, as this was all part of their business.[16]

Horse dealing was an important source of income for some families. At small country fairs and at individual farmhouses they swapped and sold many of the heavy workhorses and donkeys needed by farmers for ploughing and for pulling milk carts to the creamery. Large horse fairs such as Puck, Spancil Hill, and Ballinasloe, drew Travellers in great numbers from many miles around. Between fairs they bartered horses and donkeys at farms along the way or drove large herds from the West where animals were plentiful and cheap to the East where they could be sold at considerable profit. As a child, Nellie Delaney travelled with her father and mother from their home territory in Carlow to the West each year to buy and sell donkeys.

> We'd buy the donkeys in the West of Ireland, anywhere there'd be a donkey for sale. Like when you'd pitch in a place, well if you had one or two donkeys of your own that'd bring attention to the farmers that you were dealin' in donkeys. Well they'd ask our menfolk to know if they'd want to buy donkeys. The menfolk would go away with the horse and car, a light-spring car, and they'd drive an area for maybe twenty miles around. They'd pick up maybe ten or twelve donkeys that day. They'd buy them cheap, only a couple of pound a piece...

> He'd make four trips a year. The first in March to the fair in Kilrush in the County Clare and he'd have one batch of donkeys for that. And then there'd be a fair about the second of April in Ennistymon and he'd have a few more for that. Then the April fair in Limerick and then the June fair in Spancil Hill, that was the big horse fair. Well there wouldn't be a lot of profit of them but it would keep us goin' for the followin' year again.[17]

Such Travellers were knowledgeable horsemen and skilled dealers, particularly when compared to the average farmer. So shrewd in bargaining, they were sometimes asked to buy horses for countrypeople. Or, they might act as intermediaries — "tanglers" or "guinea hunters" — in the deals of others. One

Horse fair in an unknown town in the 1950s. The dealers in the foreground are showing their horses. Barrel-top wagons line the roadside beyond the town.

informant explained the role of the tangler in keeping the bargaining going.
   The seller asks the price, the fella that's buying him bids. The tangler is trying to bring the two to agreement by bringing the money right. He'll get a couple of pound out of making a deal. So he's doing his best for that fella to get as much as he can for the seller or as cheap as he can for the buyer. It's easier to deal with a middle man, he keeps it going.[18]

The Traveller's own success at dealing was sometimes aided by secretly making his animals appear younger and healthier than they actually were. By placing mustard or pepper on a horse's rectum, he could make an animal appear lively and spirited. A tack driven under an animal's hoof or into its flank or a dab or arsenic placed in its food had the same temporary effect. By the time the farmer discovered his misfortune the dealer was miles down the road. Having gotten a "tinker's deal" meant a farmer had gotten poor value for his money.

   Horse dealers were generally wealthier than the tinsmiths. Most owned barrel-top wagons a decade or more before tinsmiths did, and they dressed their horses in expensive harnesses with polished brass decorations. Although horse dealers and tinsmiths intermarried and shared a common identity as Travellers or Travelling People, country people often labelled the more prosperous horse dealers "gipsies". There were, in fact, a few English Gypsies travelling in Ireland in the 1930s, but they were clearly distinguishable from indigenous Travellers by their darker skin and exotic dress. The more astute observer would have also noticed that they spoke a different argot — Romany as opposed to Gammon — and observed many customs alien to the Irish.

   In their dealings with settled folk, Travellers often communicated with one another in an argot known as *Shelta* or *Gammon*.[19] Like all cants, its primary function is to conceal communication in the presence of outsiders. In horse dealing, they could advise one another on what or what not to say about the animal, how much to offer, when to accept a bid, and so forth without the farmer understanding. The Traveller could hide the *Gammon* he used by speaking swiftly so that the victim was not even aware of the secret language.[20] Instead he would assume that the Travellers had merely garbled their English or that he had misunderstood a word or two. The fact that so few country people knew that a Traveller's argot existed speaks for its success.

   The folklore collector Pádraig MacGréine collected and published several extensive lists of *Gammon* vocabulary in the 1930s. Interestingly, his principal informant was the seventy year old storyteller, Oney Power, whose tales appear in this book. During the course of my fieldwork in the 1970s, some forty years later, several Travellers from the Midlands mentioned that a woman had once given away much of the *Gammon* to a "buffer" or settled person. They falsely believed that the *gardai* had gotten hold of the lists and

Mother and children hawking at the farm houses. The handmade tin churn (left) and can (right) contain milk given to them by farmers. The donkey-drawn dray contains goods to be peddled and straw for warmth and to cushion the ride for the children. The goods are always placed at the back of the dray to balance and lighten the load of the donkey. The woman's wool-lined rubber boots, called "Sheila Temple" boots by some Travellers, were common footwear in the 1930s.

learned the argot themselves, making it useless in the presence of the police. One man's judgment was that, "tellin' him the *Gammon* was like bein' a traitor to her own country."

Some Travellers swept chimneys. They worked primarily in the East and Midlands where large houses were more common and housedwellers better-off. Spring and late Autumn were the best times of year. Sweeps provided their own tools — a set of detachable rods and brushes — and were paid according to the number of tins of soot they collected. Most sweeps had a regular round of homes which they visited each year, as one woman recalled:

> Me father had maybe fifty houses in different parts of Westmeath. Most houses needed sweeping twice a year, around Christmas and Easter. The country people kept the work for him every year. He'd sweep the small country cottages during the day, but he had to go early in the morning to the big houses to get the job done before the staff had to cook breakfast. They were very big houses with an awful load of chimneys. It was a very dirty job, but there was great pay in it.[21]

For some families peddling or "hawking" was the major source of income, but nearly all Travellers did it to some extent. Large items such as "waxy" or linoleum, crockery, and glassware were carried by pony and cart and sold by the men. Most were seconds or discontinued stock purchased from wholesalers in the larger provincial towns and then distributed in the countryside. Women went hawking daily to the farmhouses, carrying a basket containing a variety of small household wares such as scissors, needles and thread, camphor balls, and religious pictures. Many of the items were hand-made. These included paper and wood flowers, reed baskets used for hauling and storing potatoes, straw brooms, horsehair brushes, wooden clothes pegs, and, of course, tinware. These items were more often bartered for food — eggs, potatoes, cabbage — than sold for cash.

Peddling was often associated with begging, and in some instances the former was just a pretext for seeking alms. Feigning great humility, eyes held downcast, and speaking in a soft, servile voice, the Travelling woman might ask: "God bless you, ma'am. Have you e'er a bit of bread or a little sup of milk to colour our tea? Holy Mary, Mother of God. I don't care about meself, ma'am. It's the poor childer I'm afeard for. They've nothin' to eat this two days." Once the first plea was met, requests for more often followed: "I suppose you wouldn't have an ole pair of shoes you might have cast off? Me feet do be terrible cramped in these wrecks."

Pleas for alms typically appealed to the religious values of rural Irish. Such a strategy was often successful as one countryman noted: "It was held to be an unlucky thing to turn a travelling person away, especially if they asked for help in the name of God." In some instances, people gave simply to avoid an unpleasant encounter, to be rid of the beggar, for Travellers could be very persistent.

> When refused help they sometimes adopt an aggressive attitude. And if they come to a house where there is only one woman it is very difficult to put them off.[22]

Some gave out of fear a curse would be placed upon them. If a farmwife refused to give, the Traveller might inform her that she was going to curse the crops or the cattle, and if she would not give milk, she might say "that you may never have a calf again." But many country people gave out of a genuine liking or concern for individual Travellers and also because they believed it was a Christian obligation to give alms to the less fortunate. Upon receiving food or clothing, Travellers generally blessed the housedweller — "God spare you" or "The Lord keep sickness and trouble from you."

Hawking could also be an entrée or cover for fortune telling. While describing her wares or haggling over prices, the Travelling woman would size up the housewife and the prospects of interesting her in having her future told. A deck of playing cards discreetly displayed in the corner of her basket was often enough to interest some farmwives. But "tossing cups", that is, divining the future from the shapes made by tea leaves adhering to the bottom and sides of an emptied tea cup, was the favourite method.

> If I was short of money and maybe I'd have nothin' to sell, I'd go along and ask did they want their fortune told. Well I'd read the cups and tell them all I could. I'd nearly know what to tell them. If it was a young person, I'd tell them they were going to be married or they were goin' to get money from friends across the water, or they were fallin' into a bit of luck. Anything just to get a livin'. Other Travellers would get a bit of glass and pretend it was a crystal ball. We'd be lookin' through that and and we'd tell them to look through it too. Sure, they'd see nothin', and we wouldn't either. We'd only tell them a pack of lies out of it. We didn't care once we got the price of food for our kids. In some houses, with what we'd call a foolish class of people in them, a Traveller would make good money at it.[23]

At fairs, fortune tellers attempting to benefit from the powers of divination ascribed to the more exotic Gypsy placed signs on their wagons such as "Genuine Gypsy, Fortunes told here".

Some Travellers devised elaborate schemes for making money. Some sold "cure-alls" which consisted of nothing more than squares of ordinary bark rolled in lavender and packaged in cellophane. They claimed the wood was from Lourdes and had been blessed by a curing priest, thus making it more powerful than holy water. But the most ingenious of their tricks was the "gladar box" — a small book-like wooden box which appeared to be a mold for minting coins. Pádraig MacGréine describes how the gladar box was used:

A Traveller advertises her fortune-telling, "cards and crystal", at Puck Fair, circa 1950.

The operator usually approaches a countryman whom he knows to be fond of money, and not averse to getting it easily. After a lot of beating about the bush he insinuates that it is quite an easy thing to turn a little money into a lot... if one knows how. Provided he is convinced that he has succeeded in creating the proper atmosphere he produces the 'gladar box'. He then proceeds to give a demonstration. He produces a ladle and a quantity of solder. The solder is melted, the 'gladar box' placed on the table, and everything is ready. Lifting the ladle, he prepares to pour the solder into the mold, but — "Get me water to cool the money," he says. While the victim turns to obey, a genuine florin is slipped into the mold and the boiling metal poured into the box. The box is opened and the hot coin falls into the water. Marvelling, the countryman examines the coin. He has already made up his mind to invest some of his earnings. It is not often he gets a chance like this: twenty pounds for five. The tinker takes the money and promises to return on a certain day. He never does.[24]

A few families were so adept at this trick that they became known as "coiners". One County Mayo family was known as the "Gladar Maughams". These schemes appear to have been most common in Connaught where earning a living on the road was particularly difficult. Not only were the farms small and poor, but the population density of Travellers compared to settled folk (1 to 365) was twice that of Leinster (1 to 683). By all accounts, the exploitation of farmers from the illegal grazing of horses and donkeys to the poaching of farm produce and turf also appear to have been most common in the depressed areas of the West. Even in these areas, however, the Travellers who engaged in petty theft and fraudulent money-making schemes were probably a small minority.

Travellers were sometimes able to earn money doing farm labour, particularly in parts of the country where heavy outmigration had created a shortage of casual labourers. They helped make hay when many hands were needed to get the crop in quickly, before it could be ruined by the rains. On large farms, the entire family occasionally obtained work digging potatoes, thinning beets, and helping with the harvest of oats or rye. To Travellers farm work was boring and tiresome, most could not "stick it" for more than a few days at a time.[25] Odd jobs which could be completed in less than a day were preferred. In payment, Travellers often received a meal and hay for their horses rather than cash.

Me dad was never without a few bob. If he hadn't it in the morning, he'd go up to the farmer's house and he'd ask him had they a day's work for him. He'd clean out the out-houses, the cow's stable, the pig sty, and he'd go up and make trenches. He'd do a bit of cuttin' down hedges right around the farmer's place... He'd do his hard day's work and he'd

Gladar box for minting 'money'.

get a few bob, his smoke, and a good dinner in the farmer's house. Then he'd come down the road whistling and singing to the top of his voice, "Are you there, Maggie?" Here's the money for you now. Go on and get grub for yourself." [26]

While most of the Travellers' food was obtained from farmers, they also utilised natural plant and animal resources. Many collected wild berries and fruits, some caught fish. Rabbits and hares were frequently hunted with snares, also with ferrets — small weasel-like animals. The ferret was released from its small cage at the opening of a burrow or near a hedgerow; it then located a rabbit and killed it. With the aid of a long cord attached to its leg, the hunter retrieved the ferret and, clenched in its teeth, the dead rabbit. The rabbit was taken and the ferret released to prey again. At other times, the ferrets were muzzled and turned into the burrow to scare the rabbits to the surface where they were caught. Most rabbits were skinned and stewed in a pot suspended over the campfire. Any surplus was exchanged or sold to country shopkeepers for tobacco and foodstuffs.

Travelling People lived a hand-to-mouth existence. They consumed the fruits of their labour on the day they were earned. Their possessions were few, just the bare necessities of shelter, tools, cooking utensils, bed covers, and clothing. When they had extra cash it was spent on direct pleasures, most often drink. To a Traveller wealth was measured more in terms of how a man lived and how well he had enjoyed himself than in the things he owned. As nomads they were limited to what they could carry, possessions beyond the essentials would only get in the way.

At the end of the day, around four o'clock, family members began returning to the camp with the rewards of the day's foraging and sales. Each family prepared its own meals. Potatoes, cabbage, tea, bread, and less often, meat, were the usual fare. After supper while there was still light, the men and boys might play skittles or quaits, or pitch horseshoes. They might also take their dogs out to hunt rabbits, or break and train a young horse. At dusk they returned to the campfire. The fire took the chill out of the evening air and provided light. The constant movement and flicker of its flames drew the attention of all who sat around it, helping to pass the idle hours. It was around the fire, in the stillness and monotony of long country evenings that most storytelling sessions took place. Among Travellers, like countryfolk, storytelling was a favourite pastime. But unlike countryfolk who sat in their cabins in a semi-circle facing the fire with the narrator seated next to the fireplace, Travellers sat in a full circle on stumps, buckets, and the ground around the open fire. Adults, both men and women, with a gift for telling tales took turns: "I told my story, you told your story, and he told his story" recalls one elderly Traveller. Children of all ages were allowed to listen provided they did not interrupt or unduly make noise. Most of the stories were of personal experiences – imagined encounters with fairies, hearing the banshee, haunted cemeteries, apparitions of the dead, horses balking at a haunted bridge, and the like, *Märchen* or magic stories were less common for they tended to be told only be accomplished storytellers, such as Oney Power, who were then becoming rare. It appears that as early as the 1930s storytelling of this type had already begun its decline.

Occasionally a local farmer or labourer would join the Travellers at their fire. As one informant recalls:

> In the country, now in poor cottages the labourin' man was very poor. The pay wasn't much good. Well they'd come up and sit down by the fire with the Travellin' People. And the Travellin' People would go down to their house for a ramble at night. There was no television at that time, and there wasn't many radios either. So they used to sit around the fire and tell stories and sing a song. That's what the Travellin' People were very fond of. Fairy stories and all this carry on, and without any drink. They used to be far happier and have a better laugh. [27]

In the era before Travellers acquired their own shelter, they would have told their stories in the homes of the countryfolk they lodged with and, in turn, they would have listened to and learned the tales of their hosts. But by the 1930s when nearly all Travellers were living on their own there was little opportunity for such mixing.

Their travelling habits were closely related to their work. Travellers were unlike most of the world's nomadic peoples whose movements are determined by the seasonal variation and distribution of different wild plants and animals. Most pastoral nomads, for example, make the same trip at about the same time each year – going to the highlands to graze their herds in the summer and returning to the lowlands by the same route in the autumn. The Travellers were not dependent upon the natural environment, but on the resources of the rural farm population. They received their subsistence in return for goods and services. So once they had contacted all the local inhabitants it was necessary to dismantle the tents, pack the gear, and move to a "fresh" district. The length of time they spent in an area was determined by the amount of work and charity available. On the average they stayed about a week. The size of their travel groups was also restricted by the limited market for their goods and services. One informant explained why most itinerants travelled in groups of no more than two or three families.

> Travellin' People could live better if they weren't in bigger groups. Now when you'd be out hawkin', we'll say, there'd be too much upon the one road. Too much all lookin' for the one livin'. [28]

Travelling was more than an economic necessity, it was an entire way of life. Many families, in fact, continue to travel today long after the economic need for it has vanished. They feel a strong need for a regular change in their surroundings. As one man explained, "You'd easily get fed-up looking at the one place all the time". They welcomed a new view, also there is a certain excitement in the uncertainty of each new journey — who they might meet along the way, the latest news at their destination, and new opportunities for work. Travelling was at its best during the fine weather of summer.

> In the summer it'd be lovely. A lovely day when you were goin' along, travelling there with a pony and car and sitting up just looking at the fields and scenery. You'd just pull up when you'd get tired and make a cup of tea at the side of the road. And goin' to different places, you know, and seein' different people and speakin' to them. That was the only nice thing about travelling.

> In the winter we used to have a very hard time. We were often held up in one place for weeks on the side of the road and we'd be freezed. It was very hard to get out and get anything, the weather would be so bad. We couldn't bring the pony because he'd slip and slide with the frost and break a leg. So then you'd have to walk it, and climb in through the fields to where there'd be farmers' houses.[29]

In spring and summer many families stored their barrel-top wagons, preferring to travel in light-weight open carts and enjoy the fresh air.

> In the first of March we'd have a habit of putting them up. We'd place them in a farmyard with a farmer ye'd know, a farmer that ye'd know so well that he could call your name. The caravan was an encumbrance in the summer, you could go farther in a car (cart), and you'd be more healthier camping out because the caravans were a bit closed-up (stuffy) in the months of June and July. You know, there was too much heat. You'd come back about the latter end of August to get the caravan out. When the weather begin to get chilly.[30]

Along the way Travellers left signs to mark their route. This was done primarily when they expected friends or relations to be following them. The signs included sods of grass or pieces of cloth tied in a tree.

> You'd pull up a bit of grass and you'd leave it the way you'd be goin' on. As you were turning to the right, we'll say, you'd leave grass on the right, just a bit here and there. Look at four crossroads or three crossroads and you'd see a bit of rag in the brush marking the way.[31]

If necessary a family could travel up to forty miles in a single day, but that was seldom the case. In most areas of the country there is a fairly even distribution of villages or hamlets from seven to ten miles apart and of larger towns (population 1,000 to 5,000) from twenty to twenty-five miles apart. Informants' estimates on the average distance travelled before setting up a new camp were consistently about fifteen miles. On the road the men and boys often walked while the women and children rode. The pace was slow and the women occasionally stopped at farmhouses along the way to hawk or beg. When Travellers set out on a trip they had a definite destination in mind; they were not aimless wanderers as sometimes portrayed in popular literature. They knew the territory well and returned to the same camps each visit. As MacGréine notes:

> These camping grounds are constant and are used by all Travellers in turn. You can easily find dozens of them in a day's travel. The blackened circle by the roadside, where the fire had been, the charred sticks, the clippings of tin, the discarded rags in the bushes, all tell their story.[32]

These locations became well established in the minds of local people as places where Tinkers camped, and in some villages roads were named after them such as "Tinkers Lane".

During the winter Travellers moved less often. There was little work to be obtained on farms at this time of year, so there was little need to move. Also, travelling in the cold was unpleasant. Some families wintered in towns where they camped on vacant land or rented a "yard". Those without wagons often occupied abandoned waste houses, a few rented cheap accommodation. A government report on vagrancy in 1936 noted that the demolition of unsound and derelict buildings in many towns made it impossible for Travellers to find the type of accommodation they used to inhabit, resulting in more camping out.[33]

Some Travellers came together in larger groups at their wintering places, particularly in towns. But otherwise, fairs, weddings, and funerals were the only occasions when Tinkers congregated. For that very reason, they were popular social occasions for drinking, visiting, renewing friendships, and making "matches" or marriages. At the fair, disputes between rival kin groups sometimes escalated into notorious "faction fights". These skirmishes, once common among the peasantry as well, were considered a special treat by many fair-goers. A schoolteacher-correspondent for the Irish Folklore Commission wrote of one encounter he witnessed in the 1920s:

> I remember the wholesale use of sticks, stones, soldering irons and even iron bars, and the wholesale wounding of men and women whose shouts and curses made a bedlam that roused the whole neighbourhood. Some of the wounds made me shudder in disgust. The injured men boasted of their prowess during the battle and the words of encouragement from their women seemed to placate the pain of their injuries. Those who were the best fighters, always the least wounded, hobnobbed over pints of stout in one of the local pubs and spoke of the wounds they inflicted on their opponents...[34]

Over the last several decades the Travellers' rural way of life has been dramatically altered by the effects of modernization. Nearly all their traditional trades and services have become obsolete. In search of a new livelihood, they have left the countryside for Ireland's towns and cities. The new economic and social patterns which have developed in response to an urban, semi-settled existence have hastened the breakdown of the Travellers' oral traditions. Most families have substituted modern entertainment — radio, television, the cinema, and more frequent visits to public houses — for the old-fashioned storytelling sessions. Even the outdoor campfire which drew all the families in a camp to a central location is giving way to bottled gas and a retreat indoors in roomy trailers. The decline in oral traditions among Travellers is following the same pattern it has taken among the settled population; for although Travellers live on the fringes of settled society, they are not immune to its changes.

Notes — see page 182

Portrait of two Travelling families in Co. Longford in the 1930s. The three men appear to be brothers. The shawl (left) was once the traditional costume of Travelling women as well as many country women. Many Travellers wore a "Galway" shawl which was reversible: the coffee-coloured side being worn out on Sundays and the plaid side during the rest of the week.

Part 1

The Folktales of Oney Power

The stories in this chapter were collected between 1930 and 1932 from a Travelling woman named "Oney" Power. Born Nora Ward in Boyle, Co. Roscommon in 1861, Oney was seventy years old when she recited these stories. Much of her early life was spent in the West of Ireland but in her later years, as a widow living with one son, she travelled the border area between Longford and Westmeath.

In 1977 I interviewed Oney's granddaughter, Nan Donoghue, a sixty year old Travelling woman. This is what she remembers of Oney from her childhood:

> She was a very small little woman, awful tiny. She had terrible tiny feet, and very blue eyes. There was something very, very nice and gentle in her. It was hard to see her in bad humour...

> Me granny was great at the fairy stories. She was great at that, and they [country people] knew her so well around. She'd go maybe once a month around. Maybe drop in now and again to see them, and they'd love to see her comin'. They'd have a cup of tea, and she'd read the tea cups just for a laugh. Some of the young farmers, girls and boys, they'd sit there and have a cup of tea with her, and she'd be readin' hands or the tea cups. And she'd tell them stories. She often went up then at night to the houses, sit down, and tell them all the fairy stories or ghosts she'd seen. Sure, she'd never seen half the things. She wouldn't see a ghost at all but she'd only be tellin' them this.

> They'd often give her things. They were very good to her. They'd give it to her because she was an old widow woman only just left with the one son, John. And the two of them was lonely and they used to go around with their own little camp — their donkey and their car[t]. Settled

people knew them so well that they could pull in the yard and stay there till morning. And they were that lonely that they used to go to settled people's houses and sit down at night and have a talk and tell them stories. At that time there was no television in the house, and they used to love stories and a sing-song.[1]

The folklore collector, Pádraig MacGréine, described to me how he first met Oney:

I was cycling around a bye-road one day. It must have been in the mid-1920s, and I saw this poor dilapidated tent. A poor tent on the roadside and a little old woman sitting by a stick fire. I stopped for curiosity more than anything else and I started to talk to her. So I asked her who she was and she told me, "A Power". I said, "Do you know any stories?" "Ah," says she, "I could tell you stories from this day to this day week." [2]

Sometime later, upon receiving an Ediphone from the Folklore Society, Pádraig invited Mrs. Power to his home to record some of her tales. For three consecutive days she arrived on her donkey and cart and, with the Ediphone cup (microphones) pressed tightly against her lips, sat in his sitting room telling all the stories she knew. Like the collector, Oney did not receive payment for her efforts. On one occasion, however, she let it be known that she was in great need of a new tent cover, as her present one was leaking. MacGréine purchased a canvas cover for her in a second-hand shop in Dublin, a gift which over the years became wildly exaggerated among her relatives. Before I ever became interested in Traveller folktales or had heard of Oney Power, I had listened to stories about the small woman from Longford who was given a donkey, a cart, and a tent cover all for telling stories to a school teacher.

MacGréine recorded more tales the following year in Ballymahon where Oney was living in a disused stable. He travelled twenty miles on a bicycle each Saturday to record her. Unable to carry the weighty Ediphone on his bike, MacGréine stored it in a pub near Oney's home. During one recording session Oney remarked, "Do you know, sir, that we Travellers can speak in our own language?" This was the first time Pádraig MacGréine had heard about *Shelta*. Having taken down a few dozen words, he informed Séamus Ó Duilearga, the director of the Folklore Commission, of his discovery. Ó Duilearga asked him to collect all the cant he could. The resultant texts, collected principally from Oney Power and published in two issues of *Béaloideas* in 1932 and 1934, remain to this day an important contribution to the study of *Shelta*.

As a storyteller, Oney Power was at the end of her career when these stories were recorded in the early 1930s – a settled, widowed Tinker woman she had no one to tell her stories to; she had lost her far flung audience.

Although it might have been several years since she had told her tales, she told them with the skill and force of a practised *seanchai*. The collector recalls, "Her stories flowed like water, she never missed a word." Oney was reputed to be able to repeat them over and over again without changing a word.

Oney Power died in 1937 in Ballymahon and was given an enormous funeral. Travellers from all the surrounding counties attended. Her relatives bought an expensive coffin and they hired a hearse, but they carried the coffin behind the empty hearse two miles to the little graveyard of Cloncallow on the banks of the River Inney. Oney had good company on her last journey.

NOTES
1. Recorded by G. Gmelch in Dublin, July 1977.
2. Recorded by G. Gmelch in Dublin, August 1972.

Johnnie and Tommie

THERE WAS WANCE an' wance an' very good times it was. There was a poor labourin' man, an' he was only a herd. An' he had two sons and wan daughter. An' the poor woman used to be workin' in the big house every day for her day's wages, for to help to rear the family. Whin poor Johnnie an' Tommie used to come home from school, they used to have to go to the wood to gether a lock of sticks; an' the little girl used to do the housework at home.

So this day, after school time, the two of them — the two *gossoons* — they wint to the wood for sticks. Well, Tommie sat down behind a three and never looked for a stick. "Oh, Johnnie," he says, "look at the grand bird!" And the two of them spint their evenin', tell night-fell, follying the bird, an' had no sticks gethered. "Come an home," says Johnnie, "we'll get sticks at ould Peggie's." Ould Peggie was an ould woman that lived wit' hersel' an the roadside.

So, they wint and pult' a few sticks out o' an ould house. And whin they wint home, the mother said she'd tell their father they gethered no sticks but whin the father came home, she said nothin'. (A bad mother always hides the faults of the child) So, begorras, she never said a word, only struggled with the fire she had.

So, the next mornin', off she sint the pair o' thim for two big bundles o' sticks, to bake a bit of bread for dinner. "Let ye not be long away," she says. "All right," says they, and off they wint.

So, they weren't long out, whin they saw the bird. "Oh God, look at the bird!" says Tommie. "I'll tell me father," says Johnnie, "if ye don't gether the sticks." "Oh, then not a wan stick will I gether, if all the fathers in Ireland was here," says he. So, Johnnie was lyin' there two hours while Tommie follied the bird. An' whin evenin' came, not wan stick had they gethered.

So, they came home. "Musha," says the mother "an' is it ne'era stick at all yez have?" "We couldn't, mother, Johnnie follied the bird." "Aye, an' so did Tommie too," says Johnnie. "An' now," says she, "as sure as God is me judge, I'll get ye flogged in the mornin'." "We'll go down down an' get the other two ould sticks belongin' to Peggie; she'll never miss thim, they're in th' ind o' the house." "All right," says the mother.

So, the next day was a Saturday, an' there was no school. "Now," says she, "let ye be sure an' get the fire; an' let ye not be 'ithout it. For, if ye do, yer father'll flog ye."

So, the very min'it ever they wint inta the wood, Tommie gathered his bundle a sticks; an' afther the bird wit' Tommie. So, the sorra stick had Johnnie. An', in th' evenin' didn't the bird fly over leck that, and Johnnie caught him. "Now, Tommie," says he, "I have the bird and you have the sticks."

So, whin he got home, he got an ould can; an' he bored an ould hole in it, an' put the bird in it, an' put an ould rag or somethin' on the top o' it.

So, in the mornin', whin the father got up, he looked at the bird and said he never seen the lieck. All the colours o' the sky was in it. An' whin he looked, wasn't there an egg in the cage. He took it out an' put it in an ould saucepan to bile it. An', sure, if he was at it since, it wouldn't boil.

So, he wint to town wit' th' egg; an' wint to a goldsmith or a jeweller. An' he says: "I'll gi'e ye £5 for that egg an' for every egg lieck it you bring me."

So, he gave him th' egg; an' he didn't go to work that day. He didn't go to work for a long time. An', this day, the King came. "What do ye maen by neglectin' me cattle and place," says he. So, he tould him about the bird. "I'll gi'e ye a hundred pounds for the bird," says the King. But he wouldn't sell. The King looked at the bird. An' undher her wing was a bit o' paper. An' twas wrote an the paper that whoever et the heart o' the bird would be the masther o' a purse o' goold every mornin', an' whoever would ate the liver would be crowned King o' the World. "I'll tell ye what," says the King. "I'll gi'e ye two milch cows an' a farm o' ground; an' I'll marry your daughter." "All right," says the man.

So, they got ready for the weddin'. An' the day o' the weddin', they were all above at the King's house, an' Tommie and Johnnie was left mindin' the house. "Now, isn't it quaer," says Tommie. "What?" Says Johnnie. "Twas huz caught the bird, an' they have all the fun. Come an up, an m'be we'd get a beef bone we could pick." So, up they wint. An' whin th'ould cook seen them, "Oh," says she, "yez are the two *gossoons* I want. Come an an' bring me in a few buckets o' wather."

So, they brought in the wather. An' whin they came into the kitchen, there was the heart and liver of the bird roastin' in front o' the fire, skivered to a turkey. An' the cook tould them that if she hadn't them two articles for the King before twelve o'clock, her head would go on the block.

So, while the cook was workin', Tommie wint over an' took the liver an' swallet it. "I may's well have somethin' for mesel'," says he, raechin' for the heart. "Ye were always maen. Sure, I often see ye staelin' the maet o' me father's plate," says Johnnie. "I'll have this," puttin' over his hand an' swallyin' the heart. So, the cook came over to look an' says she: "Did ye see the two little bits o' maet was there?" "No, ma'am," says they, "m'be they fell down inta the fire?" "Oh Lord, bless us!" says she. "I'll be kilt be twelve o'clock. Me head is goin' to go an the block." "Wait tell we bring in a couple o' gallons o' wather," says he, "an' we'll look in the ashes for it." Whin they got out: "Take care," says she. "Did ye aet it?" "Ah, no ma'am," says Tommie. "I seen it fall inta th' ashes." Whin they get outside the gate, they laid down the buckets; an' away grey wit' them. "B' God, we'll be kilt!" says they. "We'll go 'way wit' oursels'. We'll go now and seek our fortunes, an' let thim brew as they bake. For we'll be kilt if they found out we et them," says the two *gassoons*.

So, we'll follie the *gossoons*; an' laeve the marriage, an' laeve the King, an' laeve them all there.

So, the poor *gassoons* was goin' along, goin' along; a long, long way. An' they were hungry and waery; an' none o' thim was any good for beggin'.

So, they came to a house, an' says Tommie: "Do you g'win there an' aks for lodgin'." "Ah, yer always wantin' me to do things, an' me always gettin' the blame." "Oh, all right, I'll go mesel'." So, he wint an' he tipped the door. "Come in."

So, they wint in. "Who are yez?" says the woman. "We're two poor scholars an' we're benighted. An' would ye give us a bit t'aet an' lodgin' till mornin'? An' we'd be very thankful." "I will, an' wilkim," says she.

So, they got their supper; an' she put the two o' thim in the wan bed. An' in the mornin', whin they got up, she had a basin o' wather an' a towel for thim to wash theirsels', an' gev thim their breakfast. So, they thanked her; an' the two o' thim wint out.

So, begorras, they wint out an' wint as far as the crassroads a little bit below the house. An' didn't the woman go down in the room. An' didn't she find the purse wan side o' the bed an' a piece o' paper t'other side. "Bedad, they must have forgot these," says she. So, she wint to the dure; an' the two o' thim was stayin' there the whole time. "Come here," says she, "I want ye for a min'it." "Ha, ha!" says Tommie. "Bad luck to you Jackeen. I always knew you were a bould lad. I often heard me mother sayin' before that ye used to wet the bed." "I didn't. God knows," says Jackeen. "Sure, ye must; or she wouldn't call us back."

So, the two o' thim wint back. She says: "Which o' ye lay inside?" "Ah, it was Johnnie, ma'am; he often wet the bed. I seen me mother often baetin' him." "What harm now," says she, "let ye stay today, an' ye can rest yersels'. An' I have plenty t'aet and drink for ye. Which o' ye lay inside?" "I lay inside," says Tommie. "I lay outside," says Jackeen. So, tomorra' came, an' tomorra', an' she kep' thim for a week.

So, says Tommie, "well, we'll stay no longer, ma'am," says he. "We'll go in the name o' God, for we're too much bother to ye." "Well, come an down in the room," says she, "tell I show ye what ye have." "Ye have eight purses o' gold, Johnnie," she says. "An' you have eight bill t' yer name Tommie; an' before this day twelve month, yer to be crowned King o' the World." "All right," says they. "You have the gift," says she to Jack, "no matter what comes or goes, of appurse o' gold under yer head every mornin'." "That's the heart and liver that we et," says the two o' them, "that belonged to the bird." "Didn't I tell ye that we'd be lucky an' that we wouldn't know our fortune yet."

So, they parted at the crassroads. "Well, good bye now, Tommie," says Johnnie. "I'm goin' to seek me fortune; an' if I'm alive this day twelve month, I'll meet you here." "Good bye, Johnnie," says Tommie, "an' if I'm alive, I'll meet you here. An' we'll know the place b' the house o' the woman that gev us lodgin'."

So, we'll follie Johnnie an' laeve Tommie go his own way.

So, poor Johnnie came along. An' he had his purse o' goold in his pocket, an' he gev another to Tommie. (He left all the rest to the woman because she was so good to thim.)

So, he came along tell he came to where there was a big mill and a shop beside it. So, he was very hungry and he wint in. An' whin he did, there was all sorts of aetin' an' drinkin'; beer an' whiskey, an' everythin'. He walked over an' he asked the woman would she give him his dinner. An' she said: "Why not?"

So, he ordhered it, an' jist-an' he aetin' it didn't a knock come behind him, an' whin he turned 'round didn't he see a girl an' she playin' cards wit' hersel', an' no wan wit' her. She says, "Would ye have any objection," says she, "to have a game?" she says to Jack. "Not the slightest," he says, "whin I have me dinner et." So, afther the dinner, into it to the cards wit' them, an' sure, 'twasn't long till she had the purse o'goold won from Jack. So, there was Jackeen, an' his money gone. So, she aksed him to stay the night; an' the next day he had another purse o' goold an' she won that from him.

So, begorras, Jack stopped for a week an' she won the purse o' goold every day, an' whin he wanted to go she wouldn't let him. "Sure," she says, "y' ought to marry me." "How could I," says he, "an' I havin' no house or place o' me own to bring ye." "Sure, I have this shop an' place, an' you'll never want for anythin'."

So, they got marrit, an' 'twas a privit marriage, for they sint for the ministher an' got marrit in the house.

So, the next mornin', Jackeen had his purse o' goold, but she didn't aks to win it from him that day, on account of they being marrit, but she wanted to find out how he got it. She aksed him. "Well," he says, "as I'm yer husband, I suppose I'll have to tell ye. 'Twas be a bird we caught, an' I et the heart, an' that's how I got the purse every day."

So, she said nothin' for three or four days, an' this day afther they were walkin' down be the lake — "Oh, dear! Oh, dear! Yer lookin' very bad!" she says. "Oh, yer dyin' me love!" "Oh, yer lookin' terrible bad!" "There's nothin' wrong wit' me any more then there was a month ago." "Oh, ye look terrible bad. Come, an' I'll gi'e ye a hot dhrink."

So, she got the dhrink an' what did she give Johnnie but a vomit an' didn't he vomit up the little heart. The minnit he did, she dipped it in a bowl o' claen wather an' swallied it down. She took a rod she had behind the door, an' she turned

Johnnie into an ould grey ass. So, poor Johnnie was the ass now, an' she had the little heart down in her stomach. So, she called a man: "Drive that old ass down to the miller, maybe he'd find some use for him."

So, th'ould ass was down there three or four months. An', this night, it came teemin' heaven an' earth an' th'ould ass stuck his head in the dure. "Musha, God help ye," says the miller. "Come in out o' that rain." "It's near time for ye spaek to me," says Jack. "God bless us," says the man. "Who are ye?" "Oh," says he, "don't ye remember the man that marrit that daisy-picker here above, three weeks, or a month ago?" "I do," says he. "Well, I had a gift an' she took the gift o' me an' turned me into an ass." "Now," says he, "come here. Stay there for a few minnits. I'll have ye in yer own shape and uniform inside two hours." "Well, if ye do," says he, "dead or alive I'll never forget it to ye." "Now," says he, "the house where she lies is t'atched, an' the publichouse side is slated. Well, I'll g'up an' set fire to the t'atched ind, an' when the fire starts I'll stael the three rods she has behind the dure."

So, up he goes an' sets fire to the house; just a little bit, don't ye know. "Oh, dear! Oh, dear! The house is afire! The house is afire! What did yez light in there to set the house afire?" "Are ye asleep, or what ails ye at all?" "Oh Lord!" says she, jumpin' out, "what is it?" whin she saw all the smoke in the room. She ran out. "Go an' call the min," says she, "to quinch it."

So, he wint an' got gallons an' watherin' cans; an' he whipped the three rods while ye'd say "boo," an' stuck them down the leg o' his throusers. An' he threw a few gallons o' wather on top o' the thing an' quinched it. "Now," he says, "let ye mind the place better. It's terrible, an' so many in the place, but thank God there's not much harm done."

So, down he came to where Jackeen was stan'in' in th' ould millhouse, whin he gev him a tip o' the green rod. An' he was changed back to his own shape an' uniform; an' twice a nicer an' a betther man nor he was before. "I turn thanks to God, an' you; an' the longest day I'm alive I'll never forget this to you." "Right," says the millman, "but we'll burn these rods, for if she found them out she'd turn us all to green stones." An' he stuck them into the fire. "Well," he says, "I'll gi'e ye a feed afore ye go."

So, he stuck his hand in his pocket an' pult out a tablecloth, an' he wished be the wish o' his tablecloth all sorts of aetin' an' dhrinkin', that ever was seen or known, to be left upon the tablecloth for Jack an' himself.

So, th' et full and plenty an' he ordhered the tablecloth to fould up ag'in an' go back into his pocket. "Well, begorras," says Jack, he says, "that's a beautiful article." "Well," says he, "I'm goin' to give it to you for a present, an' m'bbe you'd stan' to me ag'in." "Well," says Jack, "if ever I get me gift back ag'in I will."

So, he gev him the tablecloth. (An we'll laeve the miller there, an' we'll laeve the lady there.) An' away goes poor Jack afther his fortune. He was goin' along the road an' he got very hungry; an' he never thought o' the tablecloth, for he wasn't used to it; an' a bowsie man came runnin' along; a thravellin' man. "In th' honour o' God," he says, "have ye wan mouthful o' bread? They're closin' the dures all along the road, an' wouldn't give me wan mouthful. I d'know what sort o' a counthry 'tis at all." "Begor," says Jack, "I'm hungry mesel'."

So, he wint an a little bit. "Wait, come back," says Jack, findin' the tablecloth; an' he left it down upon the grass.

So, he wished be the wish o' the tablecloth all sorts of aetin' an' dhrinkin' to be left down before himself an' the thravellin' man. An' th' et full an' plenty; beer, an' every other thing in it. "Well," says the thravellin' man, "that's a great article." "'Tis," says Jack. "Well," he says, "I have as good as it." "What have ye?" says Jack. "I have a bottle o' so'diers," he says. "If I ordher" – "Well, do business wit' yours now," says he, "I'm afther doin' it wit' mine."

So, he pult the cork out o' a little bottle he had, an' says he: "I ordher two o' me so'diers to come out dhressed in regimintals leck, an' do business before this man. I ordher two more. I ordher twenty four." So, they did. "An' I ordher ye all into me bottle ag'in." "Bedad, that's great," says Jack. "It'd do me good if I had it at the mill-house th' other night." "I'll swop wit' ye," says the thravellin' man, "If ye swop wit' me." "I will," says Jack.

So, he did. An' he wint an a good bit an' he got sarry. "I had no right to part with the tablecloth the millman gev me," says he. "Me luck was in that. M'be in time to come I'd want to give it back ag'in to him." He took the cork out: "I ordher two o' my min to follie that man an' bring me back that tablecloth."

So, the two so'diers follit the man. "Me masther sint us for his tablecloth," says wan. So, he handed it back. An' they brought it to Jack. An' he had the bottle o' so'diers an' the tablecloth now, an' away grey with Jack.

47

So, he was comin' along. "An' now," says he, "I have the tablecloth to gi'me a bit t'aet, an' I have the bottle o' so'diers to gi'me help an' save me."

So, he was comin' an, an' he didn't know the divil where he was goin', an' he seen an orchard. Oh! Big apple-threes comin' out hover the wall, the beautifullest apple-three y'ever left yer eyes down an. So, he jumped, but he couldn't get a climb to get up.

So, he got up an the top o' the wall. He pult the full o' his pocket. An' they looked so nice, before he came down he took a bite, an' the very minnit he did, didn't a bunch o' horns come out, out o' his forehead. "Now," says he, "what'll I do at all at all?" "I had no right to take that poor misfortunate divil's bottle o' so'diers; I had a right to lae' thim to him. It's what he cursed me! No matther, I'll get thim off somehow, God is good." Puttin over his hand to where there was a craftan, he took a bite out o' it an' down comes the horns. "Begorras, that's great," says he, puttin' a few in his pocket. "M'be these'd come in handy."

So, he wint an for a long time. An' this day, he came rowlin' back to the mill, for he was intindin' to put the so'diers on the wan an' get thim to wallop hell out o' her. But didn't he hear that she was gone off to live in London, an' was livin' there in a fine big hotil she bought, an' that all sorts o' fine ginthry, lords an' ladies, used to be there. "Begor, I'll give her lords and ladies if I can."

So, he got a nice small little basket; wan o' thim that does be houldin' fruit in a town, ye know; an' he put th' apples in it an' wint along wit' the lovely rosy apples. "No charge. Taste before ye pay!" So, begorras, he came along an' she had her head out o' a winda; an' the minnit he copped her, he knew her. "Oh," says she, "what's the cost o' thim big rosy apples?" "Nothin', me leedy, teeste before ye pay." "Throw me up that big red one."

So he did. An' she took a bite out o' it; an' the very minit' she did, 'twas as soft as jelly in her mouth, sure, didn't the horns spread out o' her. "I have you fixed me lady," says he, an' away wood him. So, she didn't knows who done it, nor nobody did; and ascordin' as she thried to pull in her head, the horns was growin' out tell they spread all over the front o' the house.

So, there was masons comin', an' docthers comin' an' all sorts from all over the whole wide world, seein' to get the horns off her, an' they couldn't. So, the father offered a hundhert pounds t' annyone that'd get the horns off her, an' they wor cuttin' them but ascordin' as they wor, they wor gettin' bigger an' bigger.

So, Jack dhressed himself up as a thravellin' docther, wit' a false wig, an' everythin' the grandest ever ye seen, an' he came up. "Oh," says the father, "there's no more docthers to be let in. She's too waek for any more docthers." "Well," says he, "I'll cure her if ye let me in." "There's a hundhert pounds to be gev for curin' her." "Well," says Jack, "I'll cure her first afore I aks the hundhert pounds." "Well, i' ye don't cure her," says the father, he says, "ye'll never lae' this house tell I shoot ye." "Well," he says, "I promise ye I'll cure her."

So, in he come. "Oh, me poor girl," he says, "yer very bad." "Oh," she says, "I'm dyin'." "Well, take a small little teeste o' that apple." "Oh," she says, "but t'was an' apple that done it to me." "Oh," says he, "wan can kill; but th' other can cure."

So, she did, an' the horns fell off her. ('Twas a craftan he gev' her t'aet that time.) "Now," says he, "take three dhrops o' this," takin' a small little bottle out o' his pocket, "it'll settle yer nerves." An' what had he in the bottle, but the real vomit. An' whin she took it, savin' yer presence, didn't her stomach turn an' out hops the little heart. The minnit it did, Jack picked it up an' dipped it in a basin o' wather an' swallit it. "Now," says he, "I have me heart ag'in, an' I gev you horns for you turnin' me into th' ass." Thin she thought o' hersel'. "But," says he, "I could laeve the horns an ye, only I won't. I laeve ye as y' are." So, away grey wit' him; an' we'll laeve her there.

So, off he wint, back to the crassroads where he was to meet Tommie; an' here wasn't there a big castle up in the fields. "Who lives up there?" says he to th' ould woman in the gatehouse. "Oh, me son, *avic,*" says she. "*Tomaisın salach,*" says she, "that got his fortune be a bird; an' he wouldn't gi'me a bit t'aet, only for openin' these gates." "Divil a long he'll have ye openin' gates," says he. "Had y' era 'n other son?" says he. "I had," says she, "poor Jackeen." "An' he must be dead, for he never came back." "An' had y' era daughter?" "I had wan only daughter," says she, "an' the King kilt her whin Tommie an' Johnnie et the heart and liver o' the bird. An' me poor man died an' I was thrun an the waves o' the world. An' whin I came around here, Tommie put me here; an' sorra bit, bite, or sup I'd get only to keep these gates shut." "Throth, an' ye'll not starve much longer while I have his masther here in me pocket," says Jack. (The bottle o' so'diers, don't ye know.)

So, the next day they left the gates open. "Had y' era mark an

Jackeen," says he. "I had," says she, "a mowl an the back o' his neck." "Well, I'm yer son, mother. An' I'll never deny ye; an' don't you deny me; an' I'll see ye happy all the days o' yer life."

So, begorras, the King an' his lady came down to say what was the raesin that she left the gate open, an' Jack was 'ithin. "What's the raesin ye left this gate open?" "Good morra Tom," says he. "I see," says he, "that the docket came right an' left ye crowned King." "Who are you?" says he. "Musha, bad luck to ye. Don't ye know me, an' the day I parted wit' ye at the crassroads? I'm yer brother, Johnnie," says he, "that got the gift be the heart o' the bird and you got the liver." "Well, I'll soon have ye removed out o' that," says the King. "Don't go tell ye get a bit t'aet," says Johnnie; an' he took down the dure and put four stones undher it an' spread out the tablecloth. "Me mother won't be starved any longer," says he, wishin' be the wish o' his tablecloth all sorts an' sizes down an it. "Oh, it's beautiful," says the King, an' he wint an' he sint down two so'diers to take the tablecloth from Johnnie down below; the brother Tommie did; from the castle. "Go down," he says to the two right so'diers, "an bring me up that tablecloth or the head off his body." Down they came. "Oh, I'll give it to ye in a couple o' minnits," says Johnnie, takin' the cork out o' his bottle. "G' out," he says to his so'diers, "an kill wan o' thim and laeve th' other wit' only wan eye an' wan arm, an' laeve him his two legs to walk up, an' tell the King to sind down all he has above," says Johnnie.

So, he wint up an' tould the King. An' he sint down all he had, an' he had only twelve. So, Johnnie let out twelve more an' they walloped them and kilt them all. "Now," he says, "I want ye to go up an' take the crown off Tommie's head an' the crown off the lady's head an' bring me down the two crowns down here.

So, they done what he tould thim. An' he took the crown that was the lady's an' put it an his mother's head, an' Tommie's an his own; an' up they wint to the castle. "Now, Tommie," says he, "go down an' live in that gatehouse and remimber you an' yer woman'll be my humble servants all the days o' yer life. Me an' me mother is goin' to live here all the days of our lives. You'll have to be my humble servant or I'll laeve ye an example for the world to see," lettin' out about a hundhert so'diers out o' his bottle. "Johnnie," says he, "I'll be yer humble servant all the days o' me life."

So, begorras, he was above in the castle and Tommie below in the gatehouse, but he gev him plinty t'aet; he wasn't actin' as cruel to him as he was to th' mother; whin, who was knockin' about, but th' ould millman. So, he came an up to him an' Johnnie seen him happy all the days o' his life.

So, he never got marrit, an' whin the mother died, they lived happy together.

So, put down the kittle an' make tae. And, if they don't live happy, that we may.

Next page — The campfire continues to provide a focal point for the exchange of news and gossip, even among urban Travellers.

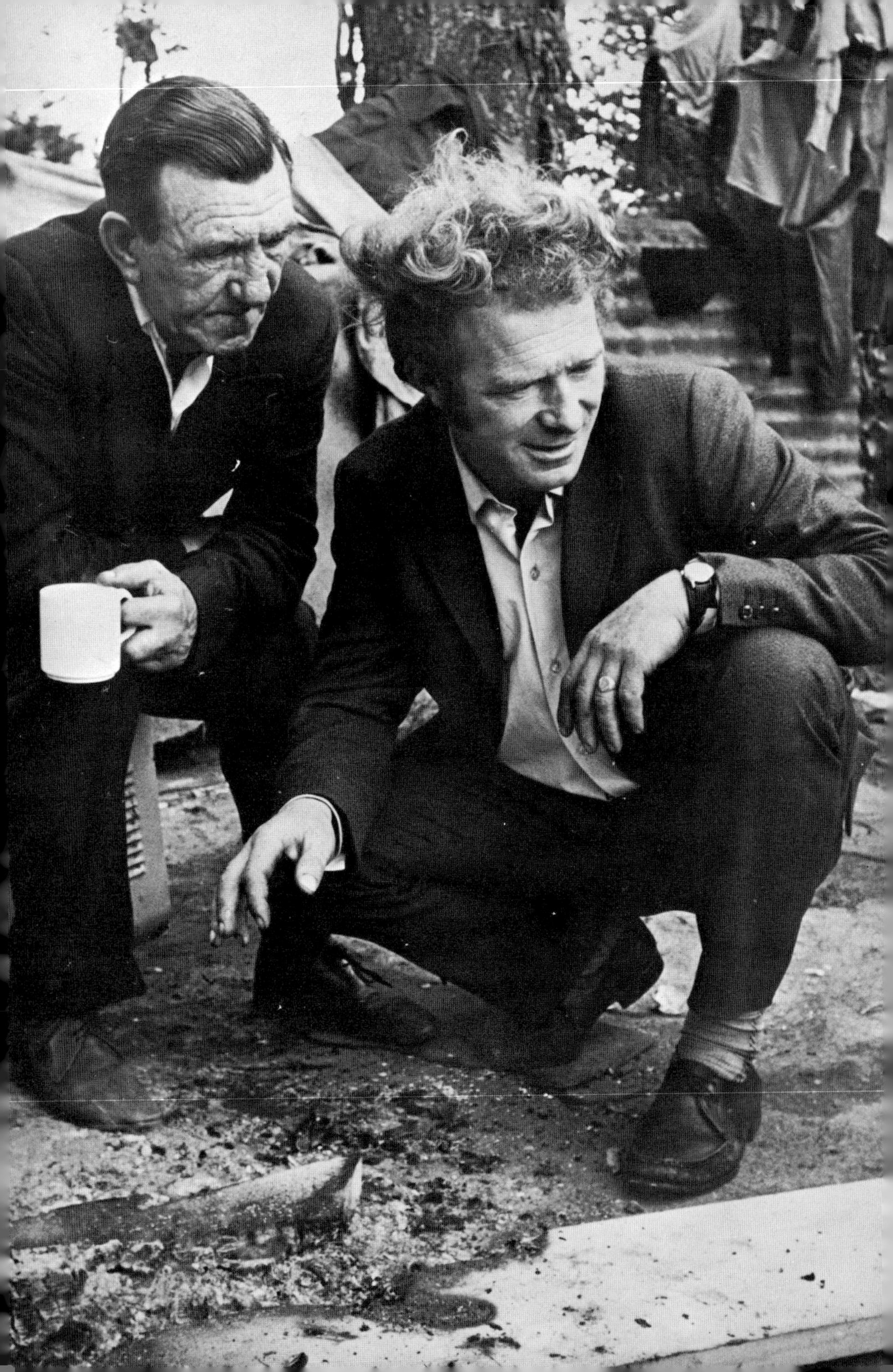

Jack the Highway Robber

WANCE UPON A TIME, there was a poor old widda woman, an' she had wan son named Jack. He was twinty-wan years o' age an' he never done nothin' for her. She was always sthrugglin' to support him the best way she could, for she was apast her age, but she couldn't support him or keep clothes an him.

"Well, Jack," she says to him wan evenin', "the king says he'll give ye work about the yard if ye g' up. Ye know I'm rint free here, but I have to work to pay the rint, so mebbe you'd be able to help." "Well, mother," he says, "I never intind to work for a farmer." "An' what d' ye intind to do Jack?" says she. "I intind," says he, to be a highway robber." "Oh, God bless us Jack; sure, that's a very bad thrade." "It is not mother," says he, "for wan night's robbery might make me up for me lifetime." "Well," says she, "I never thought I'd rear a child to be a robber." "Well, I'm goin' to be a highway robber. An' I'll never work wit' a man, only to be a robber."

So, he got up in the mornin' an' he et his breakfast, an' his mother gev him a bit to bring wit' him. An' says he, "Well, mother, if I'm alive be this day twelvemonths, I'll be back to ye; an' if I'm dead, you'll pray for me." "Well, God give ye luck," says she, "God keep ye from all harm's way."

So, he wint along, an' he was goin' about two mile o' the road, whin he met a man upon a horse. "Good morra, sir," says he. "Good morra, kindly. Where are ye goin?" "I'm in search o' a masther." "What can ye do?" "I can do nothin'," says he. "Bad enough," says the man. "Could ye milk cows? Could ye feed pigs?" "Oh, I never intind to do it." "What d'ye intind to do wit yer life?" says the man to him. "I intind," he says, "to be a highway robber." "Oh, g'wan," says the man, "I don't want ye."

So, away grey wit' him; an' he met another man, upon a horse. "Good mornin'," says he, "me boy." "Good morra, kindly, sir," says Jack. "Where are ye goin'?" "I'm goin' in search o' a masther." "What can ye do?" "I can do nothin'," says Jack. "An' where are ye goin' for a masther if ye can do nothin'?" "I can lay me mind down to nothin' but to be a highway robber." "A very bad thrade," says he. "No," says Jack, "for if ye rob wan night, ye can sit down the next." "Well," says he, "ye won't have God an yer side." "Well, if I don't, I'll have th' ould boy," says Jack.

So, he wint an an' in about two mile he met a man. "Good morra, Jack," says he. "Good morra, kindly," says Jack. "How d' you know me?" "Oh, I often seen ye," says he, "up at yer own place." "Where are ye goin'?" "I'm goin' in search o' a masther." "I'm in search o' a boy," says he. "Well, what d'ye want the boy to do?" "I want him to rob the castle up there." "You're the man I want," says Jack.

So, the robber an' himsel' wint together tell they came back to a wild forisht. An' whin he came into the forisht, they had a din in the forisht; an' there was two more min in it along wit' him. They got ready a great feed for the three o' thim. "Now, Jack," says he, "we're goin' to rob the castle tonight; an' we'll pull lots, an' whoever gets the longest sthraw'll have to go down in the chimbley." "All right," says Jack. So, whatever ways it come to poor Jack's lot that he got the long sthraw.

So, they came to the house. "Now, Jack," he says, "whin you go down in this swingless, we know where the money is; an' whin you have the money got, put it in this little boat an' sind it up to huz. An' whin ye have all jewellery an' everythin' sint up to huz, give the boat a kick, an' we'll know it's all up, an' we'll pull you up." "All right," says Jack. Poor Jack stole silver spoons, an' silver taepots, an' everythin' he could laeve his hands an. An' he stole all the money the king had, an' sint it up in the little boat. An' whin he had all sint, he kicked the little boat an' they pult it up an' left Jack there.

So, poor Jack was below, an' he didn't know what happened. "I'm in bondage now," he says, "an' I must make some rattle an' thry an' get out o' it."

So, didn't he go up the house an' down the house, an' thru' the kitchens an' everywhere. An' didn't he wind up in a sort o' a scullery where they were after killin' a bull a few days before that. An' wasn't the big hide, horns an' all, hung behind upon the back o' the dure. "Begob," he says, "if I put that an, I'd make a quare rattle." So, he got into the hide, an' the horns was stickin' out, an' didn't he begin to ring the bell, leck a divil, at the bottom o' the stairs. "Oh, dear! Oh, dear! What's that?" says the masther. An' he sint wan o' the girls to look. An' whin she came to the top o' the landin' an' seen the yoke below, didn't she fall in a dead faint. She didn't go back wit' news so he begins to break kittles an' pans below, an' rattle about. "Oh, be this an' be that," says the masther, "what's that below?" There's surely robbers in the house."

So, every girl in the house, an' there was twenty four o' them, all fainted; except the last girl, an' she was an ould woman. "Well, in the name o' God," says she, "who are ye, or what d'ye want?" "Well," he says, "I'm here for the last seven years an' this night I want me relaese." "I want," he says, "to be out o' this." He ordhered the king to come. "For," he says, "if he doesn't, I'll break an' set fire to the castle." So, the king came. "What d'ye want?" "Throw me down the kaes tell I get out," he says. So, he did. An' ascordin' as he was goin', he was lockin' behind him.

So, out he goes to the stable an' took the finest horse was in it, saddle an' all, an' thrun his leg across him. An' it wasn't long tell he was at the din where the robbers was, an' they dividin' the money; an' they makin' three parts out o' the money they wor afther robbin' out o' the castle. Jack puts an the bull's hide an' he puts in his head an' roars: "Be this an' be that, I came for ye." "Murdher!" says wan fella runnin' away. "Murdher!" says another, "I'll go too". "Well, ye won't," says Jack, tacklin' him, an' chokin' the fella that had the money in his hand. "Now," he says, "if I don't do for th' other two, they'll follie me an' take the money o' me." So, he got his gun an' goes out; an' here was the two o' thim undher a three, watchin'. So, he fires, an' knocks wan o' thim kickin'; an' he knocks t'other fella. In he comes, an' he takes a bag o' gold, an' he puts it up an the horse, an' the jewellery, an' all.

An' away he goes wit' all, tell he comes to his mother's dure; an' he wasn't a night away in all. He tipped at the dure: "Whoe's there?" she says. "Yer son, Jack," he says. "Oh, dear! Oh, dear! she says, "An' not a bit for ye in the house t'aet." "I have lots mesel'," says he. So, she opened the dure an' he takes ahoult o' the bag o' goold an' landed it in the middle o' the flure. "There now, mother," says he, "There's more for wan night's robbery than for seven years' work." "Oh, God bless us, Jack, ye'll be hung!" "No, nor thransported ayther", takin' a han'ful o' goold an' givin' it to her. "Now, mother," he says, "ye can go to the town an' bring home a good bottle o' whiskey to rouse yer ould heart, an' lots o' tae an' sugar, an' loaves, an' everythin' else too."

So, the mother wint to the town. An' she forgot to show up at the king's house that day, or the next; or for a week. So, the king came down to the gate this day. "D'ye think," he says, "what I'm med of, or what I'm keepin' the roof over ye for?" "Where's that big lazy giant iv a son o' yours?" "He's 'ithin," says she. "I want him," says he. "Oh, me son," says she, "is all right. He went away for a highway robber an' he brought back as much as'd buy 'ithin an' 'ithout." "An' he's a highway robber?" "He is." "Who owns this horse?" "Me son," she says.

So, he call't out Jack. "Are ye a good robber leck that?" says he. "Yes," says Jack. "I'll never do nothin' but robbin'." "Well," he says, "I want ye to do a robbin' now, an' if ye don't do this before twelve o'clock tonight, I'll have ye beheaded at twelve o'clock tomorra." "Very quick," says Jack. "What is it?" "Well," he says, "I want ye to stael a horse out o' my stable. An' I'll have three min wit' swords and guns guardin' the dure. An' if ye don't have out that horse an' parade him before my hall dure tomorra mornin', I'll have ye beheaded at twelve o'clock tomorra." "No throuble to me," says Jack, walkin' in.

Out he goes an' thrun his leg upon the horse, an' away to the town. An' he bought four or five quarts o' whiskey an' pints o' whiskey. Well, there was an ould lad o' a fella used to be goin' about; an' he always had a bottle o' whiskey. An' sometimes he'd be dhressed in a woman's shawl an' sometimes in a woman's jacket.

So, whin the three min was ready, an comes Jack; an' he gev a rowl, an' out falls a bottle o' whiskey out o' his pocket. "Oh, bad luck from yez, will yez look at the lad o' a fella that's always staelin' the whiskey," says wan. Over he wint an' collared the bottle o' whiskey; an' 'twasn't long tell 'twas bottomed. So, Jack came rowlin' up to the stable an' he let a quart fall; an' he pretended he was thryin' to pick it up, an' he let another wan fall. So, he lay there; an' the lads that was watchin' dhrunk all. An' 'twasn't long tell they war all dhrunk, wan snorin' here an' another there. An' the lad that was an the horse fell off the horse. So, begorras, Jack took out the horse an' had him at home at four in the mornin' tied at his own gate.

So, the king wint down at six o'clock in the mornin'. "Well," says he, "did ye do that?" "Oh, 'twas no bother," says the mother. "I had no throuble," says Jack. "Well," he says, "the next wan ye get to do'll be bother t'ye." "Now, Jack," he says, "I have a ram, an' I'll tie him to a man; an' I'll have twinty sheep afore him an' twinty afther him, an' I'll have tin min t'aech o' the sheep. An' if you don't stael that ram, I'll have yer head on the block tomorra at twelve o'clock. "Ah, that's an aesy job," says Jack walkin' in. "Now, remimber," says the king, "there's no thrick about it; no run away if ye don't do it. If ye don't do what I'll tell ye, I'll kill yer mother." "Well," says he, "me mother'll never die for me."

So, off he started to the town, an' he bought a pair o' top boots, that raeched up to his knees. I suppose he gev a pound or two for them. An' he bought two half pints o' whiskey, an' he stuck wan in aech boot. He came an an' he hid; an' he watched for the fellas wit' the sheep. An' he dhropped out wan o' the boots before the fella wit' the ram. He gev it a kick. "Bedad, that's a t'undherin' boot," he says. "Some poor fella that was dhrunk lost that. If I had the comrade o' that, wouldn't I be landed. They'd do me for years. So, he wint an about a mile, an' wasn't t'other wan lyin' before him. "God," he says, "there's t'other wan," givin' it a kick down in the dhrain. "I beg y'ur pardon min, I won't delay ye a minnit. I'll be after ye in five minnits. So, he tied the ram to a bush an' back he goes for t'other boot. The minnit he goes, out pops Jack: an' away wit' him wit' the ram. So, whin the man came back, he had no ram, only the pair o' boots an' the two half pints o' whiskey. So, what does he do, only tear his clothes; an', whin he ca'ght up wit' t'others, tould thim the ram murdhert him an' got away an him; an' Jack havin' the ram at home at his mother's house.

Now, whin the min came home, they had no ram, nor no man. So he wint down to the house. "Well, Jack, ye done that." "I did," says Jack, "an', indeed, 'twas the aesiest wan I ever got to do." "Well, ye have another wan Jack." "All right," says he, "anythin' you tell me, I'll do it." "Well, i' ye don't do this wan, I'll have yer mother kilt at twelve o'clock tomorra." "My mother," says he, 'll never die for my sake. But what is it?" says Jack. "I want you," he says, "to stael the ring off my finger an' the sheet from my bed." "Begor," says Jack, "that's a nice ordher, but I'll do it," he says.

A couple o' nights before that, there was a man; an' he died, an' he was below in the churchyard. The churchyard was just forninst the house. So, Jack goes down that night an' took up the man, an' fixed him up the best way he could, an' took him up to the castle that night. He clapped him up ag'in the winda, for he had him fixed that he'd stan' up. Here was the king, an' he lookin' out. "Be this an' be that, I have ye now, Jack," says he, firin'; an' down falls the man. "Oh," he says to the lady, "I have Jack kilt at last." Out he jumps out o' the bed! "Oh, here," he says, "mind me ring afraid an'thin' 'd happen it. I'll throw him in anyway at all in the churchyard."

So, out he goes an the hall dure, for he was nayther slow nor lazy, an' began dhraggin' the poor fella down to the churchyard. He wasn't two hundhert yards away whin in Jack pops an the winda. "Oh, dear! Oh, dear! It's terrible cold," he says. "Gi'me that sheet," he says, pullin' the sheet from undher the lady, "an' gi'me me ring." "Oh," says she, "ye wor no time away. Take care would ye lose that ring. If ye do, ye'll be talkin' about it."

So, out he goes; an' he was just goin' out an the winda, whin the masther was comin' in an the dure. "Oh, dear! Oh, dear! Yer doin' nothin' but runnin' in an' out. Yer only afther goin' out." "Gi'me me ring," says he. "Amn't I afther givin' it t' ye," says she. He knew he was done an the minnit. "Jack has me done," he says. He put his hand in the bed, an' the sheet was gone. "I'm done," says he.

So, he came down in the mornin': "Well, Jack, ye have the ring." "I have," says he, "an' the sheet too." "Well Jack," says he, "I'll give all 'ithin an' 'ithout if ye don't tell ye wor in my room." "I don't want to tell nothin'," says Jack, "but I'll play a betther thrick an you nor you did an me, with the help o' God." "Well, is all thricks over now?" "All is over now," says the king. "The place is rint free now, an' ye can do what ye leck round the place; an' I'll be yer humble servant." "Thanks," says Jack.

Away wit' Jack to the town, an' the church an' churchyard was out in front of the house leck. So, Jack wint in to the dhressmaker an' got a whole shuit med wit' wings an' all sorts, leck an angel, or leck what a ministher wear; an' he got into the church about twelve o'clock at night.

So, he began to ring all the bells an' the masther looks out an' seen the church all lit up. "What's this at all?" says he. "It must be that poor fella, I didn't bury him deep enough. It must be his ghost that's there. I must go down tell I see what it is." "All right," says the lady, "don't be long. Poor man, you'll get cold."

So, whin he wint down, here was th' angel up at the winda, an' the wings goin', an' a big book in his hand. "What ails ye?" says he. "What brought ye here?" says th' angel. "Ye brought me back from heaven to show ye example for the way ye thrun me body," says Jack. "Oh God! I'll do an'thin' y' aks me," says he. "Well, would ye leck to go to heaven?" says he, "For, I'm goin', an' I'll bring ye." "Nothin'd plaese me betther," says the king. "I'll go to heaven an' give up the world." "Well, come an in here," says he. Jack had a big coorse bag. "Now," says he, "put in yer head in there, an' no matter where I bring ye, ye needn't cry or roar, only all the words I'd have ye to say: *"Flaitheamhnas! Flaitheamhnas!"*

So, he took the man in the bag an' he brought him along an a hedge that was afther bein' cut. "That's Purgatory," he'd say. *"Flaitheamhnas!"* So, he brought him along tell the poor man was in gores o' blood. "Will I be soon in heaven?" "Ye'll be very shortly in heaven now; an', whin yer in heaven, I'll let y' out, an' ye'll be glorious wit' the wings about ye."

He brought him down to a farmer's house where the sow was in the barn goin' to have *bonamhs*. An' down he goes an' puts out the sow an' puts in the king. In about an hour's time, wan o' the girls wint out to see the pig or had she the *bonamhs* yet, an' whin she wint to the dure *"Flaitheamhnas!"* "Oh!" in she ran. "Oh, mother," she says, "the pig is spaekin' Latin!" "Ah, ye dirty ould egit. Ye wor always an egit. G' out, you Máyín, an' see what ails the pig." So, out she goes. *"Flaitheamhnas!"* "An' am I in heaven yet?" "Oh, bedad, mother," says she, "the pig is spaekin' Latin surely, about going to heaven." Out goes the father. "This is somethin' quaer," says he, whin he seen the bag in the middle o' the flure. He opened the bag. "Am I in heaven?" "Indeed y' are; surely in heaven," says the man.

So, whin he got out o' the bag, "Where am I?" "Who are ye?" says the man. "I'm sich a king," says he, "an' I thought I was in heaven, for I'm after goin' thru' Purgatory." "Someone's afther playin' a thrick an ye," says the man. "Yer naether in hell or heaven, but in sich a man's house." "Well," he says, "will ye sind me back? I was a king, an' wore the crown; but I wore a bag in th' ind. Jack is a haero; an' the greatest highway robber that ever was, or ever will be."

So, the king came home. The man had to carry him up an a car, or whatever way he had, back to the wife. He wint down to Jack. "Jack," says he, "I'll give ye the palace an' go an' live in the house, an' be yer humble servant all the days o' yer life; an' never tell the thrick ye played an me." "It's near time to make y' humble. You thried to make me humble an' kill me an' me mother, but if you don't be my boy all the days o' yer life, an' yer wife me mother's servant, I'll tell the world I slep' wit' yer wife!"

So, they put down the kittle an' med tae. An' if they don't live happy, that we may.

Opposite — Man and mare, an inseparable combination before the arrival of vans and lorries.

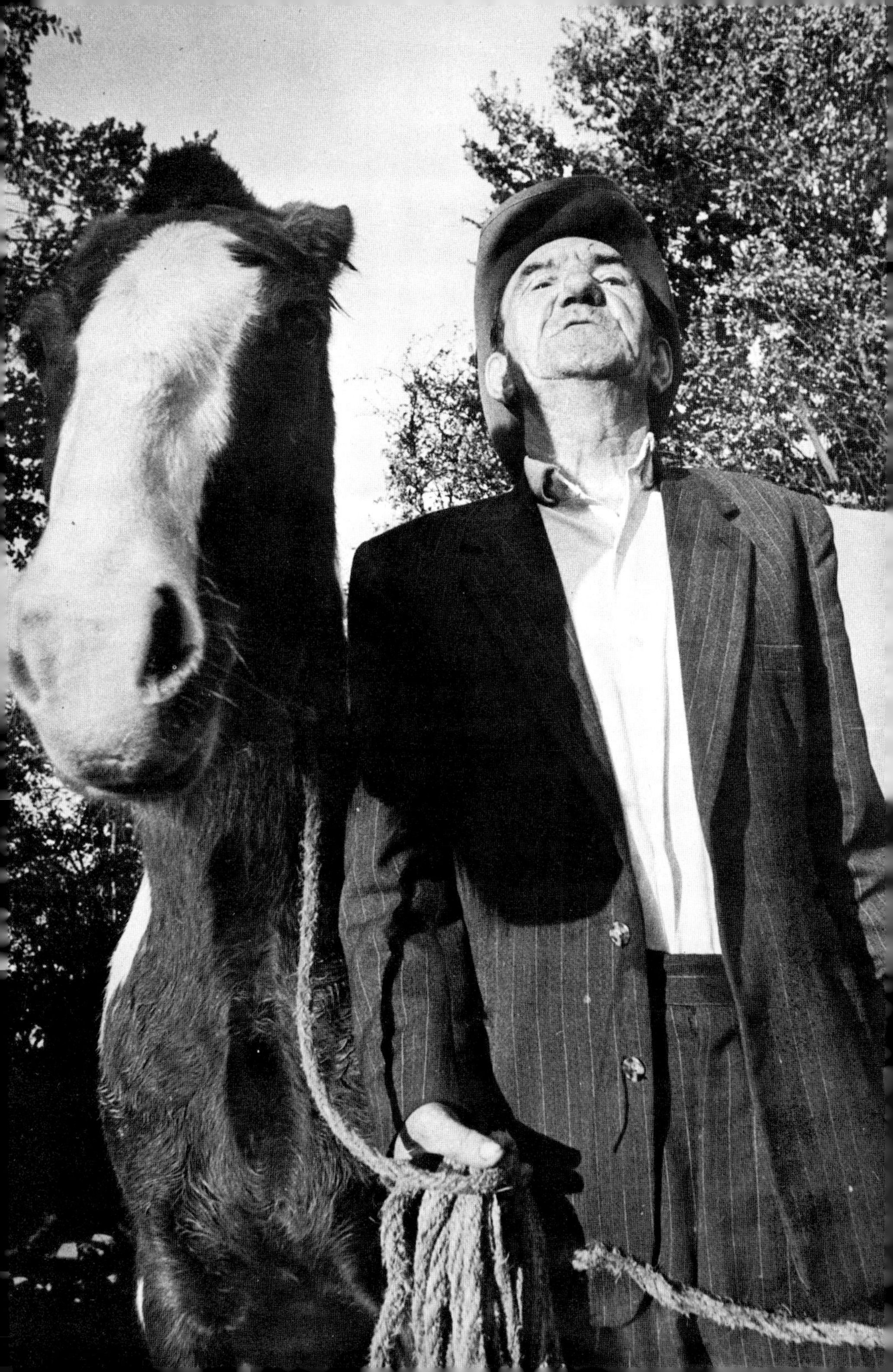

Jack from Tubberclare

THERE WAS WANCE, an' wance, an' very good times it was. 'Twas naether my time nor your time, but 'twas somebody's time. There was an old woman, a widda woman, an' she had wan son; an' he was a thick sort o' a boy. He used to do no work for her or nothin', only aet his share.

So, this day, she says: "Jack," she says, "the May rint is comin' an an' ye'll have to go to the fair wit' wan o' the cows." "All right mother," he says. "Now, be sure ye take no money but good money," she says. "All right mother," he says. So, away grey wit' him to the fair.

An', whin he was a mile this side o' the town, out steps a small little man about two foot high, wit' a red cap, an' a blue throusers, an' a green jacket. "Good morra, Jack, the widda woman's son from Tubberclare, where are ye goin'?" says he. "I'm goin' to sell the cow," says he. "Well," he says, "what d'ye want for her?" "I want twenty pound, me mother toul' me get it." "Ah, Jack," says he, "I'll gi'e ye a fiddle that'll play itsel'. Ye need only hould it in yer hand an' it'll make the whole countury dance. An' whin ye leck to stop it, twist this little wheel." "All right," says Jack, "me mother wants a step."

So, begorras, he took the fiddle an' gev the man the cow; an' away grey wit' him home to his mother. Whin he came near the house, he turned the little wheel, an' his mother took a fit o' dancin'. An' she danced until her heart was near broke. "Oh, Jack, *avourneen,* will ye stop that? If ye don't, me heart'll break. Where did ye get that?" "I got it for the cow." "Well, what matther?" says she, "It riz me ould heart in th' ind o' me days. We have two cows more left, thank God."

So, he got up in the mornin', wit' the help o' God, an' he took the second cow; an' away to the fair wit' him. He met the little man ag'in. "Good morra, Jack," says he, "Where are ye goin'?" "I'm goin' to sell the second cow," says he, "for the May rint." "Well, Jack," he says, "I'll gi'e ye a tablecloth that sich aetin' an' dhrinkin' never was seen, an' a bum'bee an' a mouse in it. An' all sort o' music the bee'll hum an' the mouse'll hop." "Begor, me mother'd leck a bit o' nice thing t'aet, an' she'd leck a nice tune too." He brought the tablecloth; an' he gev him the cow, an' back he comes. "Well, Jack, did ye sell the cow?" "I did, mother. I got plinty t'aet for the May rint." He left down the tablecloth, an' sich aetin' an' dhrinkin' never was known. An' the mouse begin to le'p an' the bee to hum, an' the mother was as well plaezed as if it was twinty pound she got. So, he rowled up the tablecloth an' left it up.

Now, the third cow wint to go for the rint. "Now, Jack, *avic*, will ye thry an' get the rint for this wan? If ye don't, we'll be thrun out the dure." "All right, mother. I will, wit' the help o' God." He started the third time, wit' the third cow, an' the little man met him. "Good morra, Jack, the widda woman's son from Tubberclare." "Good morra, most kindly," says Jack. "What d'ye want for the cow?" "I want twinty pounds," says Jack, "an' I can't take less, for me mother'll be thrun out tomorra if she hasn't the May rint." "Ah, rint be damned," says he. "I'll give ye a cord to tie her an' a stick to beat her." "All right," says Jack; an' he gev him the cow. "What'll I thry it an?" says Jack. "That three over there," says he. Jack ordhered his cord to tie him up an' his stick to baet him "tell ye make him give up me three cows an' the May rint as well."

So, he was squeezin' an' squeezin' the maneen, tell he put him into the size o' a mouse. "Oh, Jack," says he, "I'll give ye a crock o' gold if ye spare me me life." "You didn't care for me to be out. Ye gev me the three articles that'd put me out an the dure, but I want the rint now, or I'll kill ye." So, he kep' squeezin' him tell he shouts out: "Oh Jack, g'over to that three that's over there an' lift the flag that's undher it, an' ye'll get a crock o' gould undher it. An' there's yer three cows, an' bring thim." "Throth, an' I'll fix you afore I go, that ye'll never have a hoult an me ag'in. I ordher me cord to tie ye an' me stick to baet ye tell it baets the win' out o' ye." So, the cord tied him an' the stick be't him tell it be't the life out o' him.

So, he stuck the little maneen down in the hole where the crock was an' put the flag down an him. An' away he started whistlin', jolly an' gay, home to his mother, wit' his three cows, his whip an' his cord, an' his little crock o' goold undher his arm.

"Well, Jackeen, *avic,* ye have the cows back." "I have, mother, thanks be to God," says he. "Oh, why did ye take them?" says she. "Sure, that was robbery." "If ye have a word out o' ye," says he, "I'll ordher me cord to tie ye an' me stick to baet ye." So he did, an' gev her a couple o' little clouts. "That'll do," he says. He only wanted to show her the way what he got; so, he takes off the cord an' the stick. "Well, Jack," she says, "ye have the best articles ever was got." "Well, mother," says he, "I'm goin' away tomorra mornin' to seek me forkin. I'm laevin' ye the three cows. I'm laevin' ye the crock o' gold, an' I'm takin' me three articles wit' me, wherever I go. An', if I'm alive this day twelvemonth, I'll be back; an', if I'm not, pray for me."

So, away grey wit' Jack. An' we'll laeve th' oul' mother there, an' she havin' the May rint an' all. An' away he wint tell night was comin' an him. An' he came an to where there was a lord's house, a big king's house. An' he looked at the gate; an' he seen nineteen min's heads upon the gate, an' a spear for the twintieth. He had a daughther, an' no man'd get her only the man that'd knock three laughs out o' her, an' no wan ever knocked a laugh out o' her. "Begad, then, I'll knock twinty-three laughs out o' her, if I can," says Jack.

So, in he goes to the gatehouse. He says: "D'ye know where I'd get a night's lodgin' tonight ma'am?" says he. "I'll give ye lodgin'," she says. "What sort o' heads is thim out there?" says he. "Thim is nineteen gintlemin's heads, that wint up an' said they could knock a laugh out o' a lady that's up there; but, sure, divil a laugh ever was knocked out o' her, because he's killin' all the fine ginthry i' the counthry over his daughther an' the weight o' hersel' o' gold." "All right," says Jack, "If I don't do it no wan ever done it."

So, by an' by, the supper was ready, an' Jack left up the tablecloth. "I beg yer pardon ma'am, ye'll let me get the supper tonight," laevin' up the tablecloth an the table. An' he ordhered all sorts iv aetin' an' dhrinkin' that ever was seen or known. An' here goes the mouse into a glass, an' the bee up an his back an' began to sting him; an' the mouse goes runnin' round about an'... "Well, that'll knock a laugh out o' him as sure as God," says the man o' the house. "Now," he says, "I have another wan. I have a cord that'll tie, an' a stick that'll baet, an' I have a fiddle that'll dance be itsel' — or play be itsel'." "Well, you'll gain her," says the man. "Faith, an' my head'll never g' up there if I can."

So, up he goes, an' tore his ould coat, an' med himsel' rael maen lookin', a rael beggarman. The king himsel' was stan'in' at the hall dure. "What brought you here?" says the king. "To win yer daughther," says he. "Stop!" says he, "I'll shoot ye! I'll behead ye!" "Throth, an' if I gain her, I'll have to get her an' no thanks to ye," says Jack.

So, there was a lot a gentry around the place an' thim all began to jeer him an' laugh at him. So, he left down his fiddle an' it begins to play. An' there wasn't wan around the place but began to hop an' dance tell th' oul' king nearly died. "Oh, for God's sake," says he, "will ye stop the fiddle?" She took a fit o' laughin' an' she didn't stop tell she got into a faint, wit' the fit o' laughin', an' she hoppin' an' laughin'. "Bedad," says he, "I dhrew wan laugh out o' ye at anna rate."

The next thing was, he spread out the tablecloth; an' it kep' spreadin' spreadin' tell it covert the whole green field. An' here the mouse'd ran into wan glass an' the bee into another, an' she gev another laugh.

"Now," says he, "I have the hardest wan to get. I dunno what I'll do at all." So, he ordhered his cord to gether thim all, all the ladies an' gintlemin. An' here it began an' tied thim all, an' the stick began to baet, an' she gev a t'undherin' laugh. "Oh," she says, let me out. I'll marry ye."

Now, there was another lord an' he was mad wit' poor Jack. "I don't care a damn," says he, "for yer marriage. I don't want yer money, but I don't want him to be killin' every poor man." So, the marriage got ready an' Jack got a new shuit o' clothes, an' this fella came up. "Well, Jack," he says, "if ye don't spaek a word to yer wife, I'll gi'e ye a hundhert pound in the mornin'. Whin ye g'win to the room don't open a lip to her before mornin', an' I'll gi'e ye a hundhert pound," says he. "Faith, an' God knows," says he, "I'll never talk to her. If I got a hundhert pound leck that, sure, I'd play the divil wit' her."

So, that night they wint up to the room, at anna rate; an', sure, Jack turned his face to the wall an' he never turned a lip to her, an' she talkin' to him. So, in the mornin' the father came up. "I wish ye a grae'd'l o' joy —" "Joy, be damned," says she. "Sure he's worse nor a dummy. He never spoke a word all night, an' I talkin' to him. I was afeared o' me life iv him." "Ah, the poor fella is ashamed," says the father. "Oh, dada," says she, "he's terrible! I only aksed him what time it was, or to sing a little song or somethin', an' he wouldn't answer me or wouldn't spaek to me." So, the next night the same happened. He gev him another hundhert pound, an' the same: he wouldn't spaek to her. So, the third night the same happened. So, we'll make a long story short an' a short wan merry. Afther the third: "Ah, dada," says she, "we'll throw 'im into the bear." "He's only fit," says she, "to be thrown down to the bear."

So, poor Jack was taken out in the mornin' an' thrown down to where there was a bear in a tunnel; in a din leck. Jack came an down to the bear an' the bear looked at him. "I'll aet ye," says he. "Ah, no ye poor craether, sure, I'll gi'e ye lots t'aet," takin' out the tablecloth an' stuffin' loaves, an' cakes, an' all sorts into him, tell he had im' too fed leck, tell he had too much et. "Well," says he, yer the best man ever I seen." "Well," now says Jack, "whin ye have enough et, mebbe ye'd leck to dance a step." "I would," says the bear. "Well, lie down there now," says Jack, "an' I'll learn ye how to dance the Fillorum Jig." "What sort of a jig is that?" "Oh, ye have to dance it an the broad o' yer back." So, whin he got the bear lyin', he got his cord to tie 'im an' his stick to hommer him, tell he hommered the divil out o' the bear. "Oh," says the bear, "let me out Jack, an' I'll never do a ha'porth t'ye." "Ye'll stay there," says Jack, "as long as I'm here." So, the bear was there.

Now, she got marrit to th' other fella afther a couple o' days, for they thought Jack was et be the bear. "Now," says the mouse, "huz an' our masther is down here, an' we'll never get out. Can we do an'thin?" "I could g'win to his ear." "I could g' up in his nostril, an' make him vomit an' bleed; an' the princess'll get sick iv him an' get him threw down here to the bear." Out goes the mouse an' the bee unknownst to Jack an' does what they planned.

So, the next mornin', up the king came: "Wish ye a grae'd'le o' joy, an' how is the new husband?" "Oh, dada," she says, "Jack was claen. He's pukin' all night; savin' yer presence, father," says she. "Oh, throw 'im down to the bear," says she. "Jack was the claenest man I ever seen. He was grand an' claen, an' mebbe t'was only a way he had."

So they brought 'im down. "I'll aet him," says the bear. "I'll baet 'im first," says Jack. So, he loosened the cord off the bear. "I ordher me cord to tie ye an' me stick to baet ye." "I'll aet him," says the bear. "Ah, no we'll give ye a bit t'aet," says Jack. So,

Jack left down the tablecloth an' gev the two o' thim plenty t'aet. An' he tied up the fella that came down. An' the bear was as quiet as a lamb, for Jack had a bit o' the yoke round his legs, for he was afraid he'd get out.

So, the lady was out in a few days' time an' she seen Jack below in the din. "Oh, dada," she says, "look at Jack an' he below in the din." "Oh, he was too good to be et," says he. So, Jack was took out; an' whin he got up, "I ordher a coach an' four," says he, "an' all the money, for me an' me wife. An', if ye have wan word, I'll tie me cord an the castle an' take it away." "Oh, all right," says the king. So he brought out his wife, an' the coach an' four horses, an' came an the road home.

So, they came an the road home; an' he came to where there was a filly an th' edge o' the road. "Oh," she says, "let me loose," for she was tied. "An' what's the raeson yer masther wouldn't put a dacent set o' shoes an ye?" "Pull off this ould shoe," she says, "it has me lame. Oh, the villain; sure, he wouldn't let me into the field where there's a dacent bit t'aet." "Wait," says Jack, "an' I'll put a nail in that an' t'won't be so awk'a'd an ye." So, Jack got a big nail an' wint over to the filly an' dhrove it up in the quick. "Now," says he, "you might be sint afther me, an' ye won't be able to follie me."

So, Jack came an along ag'in, an' the next thing he met was a big fox. "Good morra, fox." "*Musha,* good morra, kindly, sir," says he. "Where did ye come from?" "I came up from Tubberclare," he says. "All the way?" "All the way, an' I'm afther aetin' the last goose that the widda woman had below in Tubberclare." "It's a pity," says Jack, "that ye don't get that big bushy tail cut off ye. Ye'd be able to crass the counthry twice as well. Sure, ye might get caught crassin' a big bushy hedge." "Sure, I have no wan to cut it," says he. "Throth an' I won't be long cuttin' a bit o' it for ye, poor thing," says Jack. Over he goes to a big three an' cut out a big wedge, for he had a hatchet an' all yokes. "Now," he says, "put yer tail in there an' I won't be long takin' a bit off it." So, he stuck in the tail an' Jack put in the wedge. "Now," he says, "yer afther aetin' me mother's goose, stay there tell I relaes ye." So, off he wint an' left the fox in the three.

So, away grey wit' him; an' it wasn't long, whin Jack was gone about four mile, whin the king begins to think o' himsel'. "Musha," he says, "it's that tinker. He has my poor daughther gone, that I'll never see a sight o' her ag'in," he says. "Or, what'll

I do; what'll I do?" "Ah," says he, "I'll bring the bear. An' the bear'll tear him whin he get wan sight o' 'im, an account o' what he done to him below." So, he wint down to the bear. "Will ye follie Jack an' bring back me daughther?" "I will," he says, "an' I'll aet 'im afore I bring back yer daughter."

Now, an he comes, the bear an' his masther afther Jack — Jack was gone wit' his lady — an' they came an to where the filly was. "Oh, ye poor animal," says the masther. "What ails ye that yer lyin' there an' can't get up?" "Oh," she says, "that tinker Jack, that's gone along there, he put a nail in me quick; but if I got afther him, I wouldn't be long thrampin' an him, tell I wouldn't laeve a bit o' 'im together." "Well, I'll take it out," says the masther; takin' out the nail out o' the quick.

The next thing he came to was the fox. "Oh, me purty little animal, what has ye there?" "Oh, that vill'in Jack. He tould me me tail was too long. An' whin he got it in here to cut it, didn't he put in the wedge. But, if I got out, I wouldn't be long bringin' back the lady." So, he let out the fox; an' away grey now wit' the fox, the bear, an' the filly.

Whin Jack seen thim comin': "God help me now," he says, "I haven't much help now, only the stick; an' I won't be able to keep every wan o' thim away." Over he goes an' takes out the horse, an' begins takin' out the nails, an' sharpenin' nails. "Ha, ha!" says the filly, "I'm not goin' up, he's puttin' a nail in his quick."

So, an he came an' tied the horse's feet. "Ha, ha!" says the bear, "he's makin' him dance the Fillorum Jig. I'm not goin' up, what a fool I'd be."

Thin he came an to the fox. Over he goes to a three an' gev it a big clout o' the hatchet. "Ha!" says the fox, "he's makin' a hole for my tail. I'm not goin' up." "Now," says the father, "what'll I do? I may as well go back."

So, he ordhered his cord to tie up th' ould father, coach an' all, an' he walloped him tell he wasn't able to go back.

So, Jack an' the lady came along in the coach tell they came to the poor ould mother's dure. "Are ye there mother?" "I am." "Well, I have a wife home wit' me, an' I brought her to be your humble servant all the days o' yer life." So, he brought her into the little house. "G'wan now mother," says he, "an' sit down. There's a crown an yer head all the days o' yer life. She'll have to do everythin' in this house, for I only brought her to be your maid." "Well, Jack, *avic* she's a lovely lady an' I'll work along wit' her." "Not a ha'porth ever ye'll do mother," says he. "Sit down there now upon that big stone in the corner." (They had no chairs or stools.) "An'," says he, "if yer father comes for ye, or wan belongin' to ye, I'll just do what I done to the bear."

So, they got marrit, an lived united, an' had family in basketfulls an' threw them out in shovelfulls.

So, they put down the kittle an' med tae. An' if they don't live happy, that we may.

Next page — A happy interlude on a journey to Blessington, Co. Wicklow.

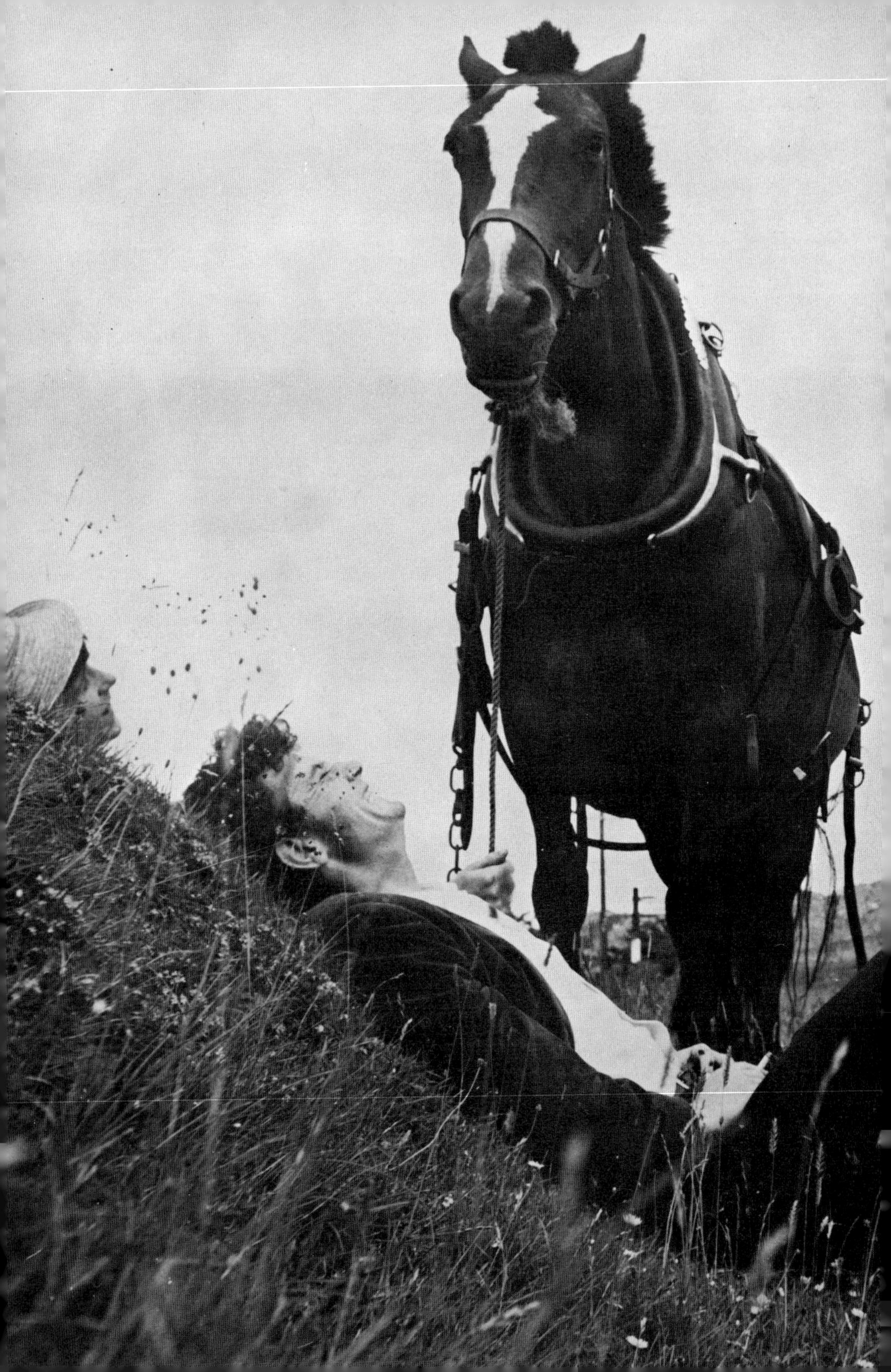

Jack the Ghost

THERE WAS WANCE, an' wance, an' very good times it was, there was a poor old woman an' she had wan only son named Jack. So, the craethur used to be goin' every day an' thryin' t'earn a bit t'aet for him; for he never knew whin he had enough et. So, this evenin', the mother came home. "What ails ye Jack?" she says. "I'm starved wit' the hunger," says he. "Well, ye won't be long hungry *asthore*. Throw a *thoséin* o' piatez an the fire." So, he took an' threw half a can o' piatez an the fire; an' 'twasn't long tell they were roasted. For there was a roarin' fire down. So, whin they were all et: "Well, have ye enough et *asthore*?" "I have," says he, "but I want somethin' to wash thim down." So, over he goes to where there was a can o' milk an the dhresser, an', sure, whin he took a mouthful, sure, he took about the half o' it. "Take a good sup *a mac.*" An', sure, he dhrank it all. So, she come over after a while; an' whin she took the gallon, it was impty. "Jackeen," she says, "did ye dhrink id all?" "Didn't ye tell me," says he. "Ah, thin be this an' be that, Jackeen, yer twinty-wan years iv age, an' it's about time ye shruck out for yersel'. Yer after aetin' a stone o' piatez an' five quarts o' butthermilk. I'm not able to feed or support ye any longer." "Well, mother," he says, "I'll go in the mornin', an' yer just sayin' the truth. I'm big enough too, to do it. So, make a little cake, an' gi'me a bottle o' milk; an' I'll go away." "God be wid ye," she says, "an' God gi' ye luck." "An' I'll come back to see ye, if I do any good, mother. An', sure, if I don't, ye'll be no worse then y'are." "God gi' ye luck," says she. "Mind the goat, an' mind Biddie, an' mind Pollie," he says. Biddie was the duck an' Pollie was the hin.

Away grey wit' him. An' he was goin', the poor fella, for miles, an' miles, an' miles, tell night fell an him, pitch-dark night. An' he came an to where there was a churchyard. An' just in the gate, wasn't there a big tall man stan'in'. "Good night," says he. No answer. "Good night," says he, "whoever y'are," goin' over to the man. An', as soon as he did, didn't the man make a box at him. "Bedad thin," says Jack, "ye won't have id all yer own way." So, the two o' thim kep' cloutin' other tell the cocks crew in the mornin'; an' wint away; an' Jack was left alone.

"Bedad, that was a maen fella; never spoke a word to me all night, but, sure, m'be the poor fella was hungry. I'm hungry too," puttin' his hand in his pocket an' takin' out the little *cáicin*. "Sure, I had a right t'offer him a bit." Says he to himsel', "Bedad, the candles isn't quinched yet. I think I'll go back to me mother."

So, back he wint. "Well, ye didn't go far Jack." "No, mother," says he. "That little cake was no good to me, I'd want a bigger wan. I never got wan to spaek to me from I left here; nor I seen no wan, only an ould man at the gate, an' he wouldn't talk to me." So, she med the cake. "Now Jack," says she, "don't come back any more." "Sure, I'll come back if I don't get an'thin' t'aet, where'd I be goin'? An' m'be ye'd have a few piatez or a little cake for me."

So, away grey wid him ag'in. An' about twelve o'clock, here he comes to the churchyard gate; an' there was the big tall man stan'in' at the gate. "Ah, sure, I knew well what vexed ye last night. Sure, ye knew well I had the little cake an' the bottle o' milk in me pocket an' wouldn't give ye a bit o' it; but, faith, then, ye'll get an even divide tonight." So, he took out the cake. "Here, now," he says, "here's the biggest half o' it." But the man up wit' his hand an' med a crack at Jack. "Faith, then, ye won't get it all yer own way," says Jack, stickin' the bit o' bread in his pocket an' givin' him a dodge. An' the pair o' thim kep' there at it tell the cocks crew in the mornin' an' the lad disappeared from Jack.

"Ah," says Jack, he's a quaer fella. Never said 'Good mornin!' or a ha'porth. I'll sit down now an' aet me cake, an' I'll go back to me mother an' get her to make two cakes. Sure, m'be he wanted a whole cake for himsel' an' didn't leck to take the half o' me little *caicin*."

So, he came back to his mother. "So, ye came back," she says. "I did," says he. "This is the last time I'm goin' to throuble ye mother. I want two cakes med: a big wan an' a little wan. An' I want two bottles o' milk: a big wan an' a small wan." "All right," says she, "but never show yer face back here ag'in, tell ye have somethin' to bring back to give me for all I'm after makin' for ye." "Well, I promise ye I won't come back," says he, "no matter what happens me, tell I have somethin' to show ye."

So, off he started, tell he came to the churchyard gate ag'in, just at twelve o'clock at night. An', here, didn't he see the big tall fella stan'in' at the gate. He walks over to him. "Ha, Ha!" says he. "Good night. I have a whole cake for yersel' tonight." An' what does the fella do, but make a clout at him. "Ha! but yer the maen fella," says Jack. An' into the two o' them. An' they kep' cloutin' wan another, an' nayther o' thim was hurted, tell the cocks crew an' daylight came, an' he disappeared.

"Well, nor wan foot will I go back to me mother," says Jack. "Haven't I the two cakes an' the two bottles o' milk? Ag'in I have thim et, m'be I'd get a bit in some other place." So, he sat down an th' edge o' the road. An' he et the cakes an' the two bottles o' milk; an' he threw away the bottles.

An' away grey wit him tell he came five or six miles, or m'be more, tell he came to where there was a gatehouse; an' a big house up in the fields. He wint in. *"Musha,* missus, an' would ye gi'me a bit t'aet?" says he. "Well, me poor fella," says she, "I have nothin' to give ye except cold piatez that's after the dinner. Cold cabbage, an' bacon." *"Musha,* God bless ye! Sure, that's what I leck," says he. So, she left him over to the table. An', sure, there wasn't wan left in five min'its but he et, an' about a half stone o' cabbage, an' a couple o' pounds o' fat bacon. "Who lives up here in this big house above?" he says. "O sich a King," says she. "Do ye think would he gi'me work?" says he. "He might," says she, "for he has a lots o' cows an' things about the yard up there, but I do see a many a wan goin' up there an' never comin' down." "Throth an," says he; "He'll want to be sthronger nor me, or I'll come back," says Jack.

Just an' he goin' up th' avenue, he met the King. "Where are ye goin'?" says he. "I'm goin' lookin' for work," says he. "I can claen the houses, or milk the goats, an' feed the hins an' ducks." "Is that all? I suppose ye could claen a big barn?" "I suppose I could," says he. "Do ye want much money?" "I want nothin' but the bit I'll aet," says he. "I'm starved wit' the hunger now," says Jack, afther he aetin' a big feed below in the gatehouse. So, up he brought him. An' he brought him into the kitchen an'

73

tould them to give him all he wanted t'aet. So, they did.

An' whin he was done, the King brought him down the fields. "D'ye see that castle over there?" "I do," says Jack. "Well, if ye sleep there tonight, I'll gi'e ye a good bed, an' fire, an' lots t'aet, an' five pound in the mornin'." "Done," says Jack. So, whin six o'clock came, he wint down. An' they left him a good fire, an' a big taepot o' tae, an' lots t'aet; an' left him there.

So, begorras, t'wasn't long tell the dure opened a bit an' in walks a big, tall man. Jack was sittin' there aetin' a bit for himsel' an' he looked up. "Ha, ha!" says Jack, "ye're the very fella I met at the chapel gate. How well ye knew I was here." But he never said a word, only took a ball out o' his pocket an' began to play ball up ag'in the wall. "Right," says Jack, "I'll have a game wit' ye." So, up he got. An' they played tell the cocks crew in the mornin'; an' the fella wint an' left him.

In the mornin', down comes the King. "Oh, good mornin', Jack. Are ye alive?" "Was that the fella ye sint to kill me? He's the most harmless fella ever I met. Ye never seen sich a game o' ball as we had here all night, only he never spoke a word. For God's sake, sind me a fella that'll talk the next time. I never knew whin I'd win or whin he'd win. The next night sind me a fella that talks. I'd glory in him. But this was a quiet, harmless fella, only he wouldn't talk; but m'be the poor fella was a dummy." "All right," says he, "come an, tell ye get yer breakfast."

So, Jack wint up an' he got the finest breakfast y'ever seen. So, whin he had it et, says the King, "D'ye see that stable?" "I do." "Well, that stable wasn't claened for the last seven year; that's all I'll gi'e ye to do today." So, Jack took a fork; an' the first forkful o' dung he took, he nearly took all that was in it out. He had it claened in half an hour, for he didn't know th'ind o' his strength. "There must be somethin' good in that boy," says the King.

They gev him lots t'aet an' dhrink that day; an', says the King, "Now, Jack, if ye sleep in that house ag'in tonight, I'll gi'e ye six pound." "Bedad, I will," says Jack. "Sure, I won't know th'ind o' me money thin. Me poor ould mother can get a cow thin. But y'ought to sind down someone wit' that fella tonight. There's not a bit o' comfort in him. He won't talk or aet a bit, or dhrink a sup o' tae. Sind down more tonight in case he'd bring company."

So, the King did. He sint down a big cake, an' a big taepot o' tae, an' a big rowl o' butther; an' had a good fire for Jack.

Jack was there whin the min comes in. "Oh, good night," he

says. "*Musha,* thank God ye brought company wood ye," whin he see the two min. "Welk'm," says he, "but have a cup o' tae afore ye play the ball, or whatever ye're goin' to do." So, wan o' thim took out a ball an' th' other took out a book, an' began sthrokin' leck. "Oh well, will I play if you're markin?" says Jack. "I will so," says he, whin none o' thim spoke, or even nodded the head.

So, they played all night an', to the best o' my opinion, Jack was the best ballplayer o' the two. So, whin the cocks crew in the mornin', they wint an' left Jack there.

So, the King came in the mornin'. "Are ye alive, Jack?" "Who did ye sind to kill me? Thims the two o' the harmlessest craekers that ever was born. Poor thing, they're all dummies in your counthry. Ha, then I talked lots to thim; an' they wouldn't aet bit, bite, or sup, so I et it all mesel'." "All right, Jack," says the King. "Come an up now, there's another barn for ye to claen."

So, he wint up an' claened th' other barn. An' they gev him plinty t'aet an' dhrink.

So, the King took him out for a walk. "Now, Jack," he says, "will ye lie be yersel' tonight an' I'll gi'e ye fifteen pound?" "Be God, I will," says Jack, "or for a month 's long as ye gi'me plinty t'aet an' dhrink. I wish to God I had me mother here, an' I'd stay forever. But, sure, mebbe she'd come sometime. Mebbe you'd sind for her an' give her a good feed for the poor craeker hasn't half enough t'aet." "Oh, she'll get plinty yet," says the King.

So, off he goes this night; an' there was two big cakes sint down, an' full an' plinty; an' a big roastin' fire; an' a big bed, an' sheets, an' quilts; an' it put in the wan room wit' him.

Jack was aetin' his supper, whin the dure was opened; an' in walks two big black min, an' a coffin between thim, an' left the coffin an the flure, an' wint out. Jack didn't leck to go near it, the led was down. "Bedad," says he," m'be it's a feed that's in it: cakes, an' maet, an' everythin'."

So, they were a long time comin' back. An' Jack wint over an' lifted the led; an' here wasn't there a dead man in it. "Me poor fella, yer lookin' very could," liftin' him out an' fixin' him the grandest ever ye seen in front o' the fire, an' rubbin' him down thryin' to warm him. So, he kep' at him for an hour or more. "M'be," says he, "ye'd leck a dhrop o' somethin' hot," warmin' a dhrop o' the tae an' raechin' it to him. The m'nit he did, didn't the dead man knock it out o' his 'hand. "Oh, is that the way?" says Jack. "Well, I'll make ye nice an' comfortable," puttin'

75

him in the bed an' rowlin' him up nice an' comfortable. But the fella was moanin' an rowlin' in the bed. "Bedad," says Jack, "I know what's wrong. I'll go an' lie beside ye an' keep ye comfortable." So, in he got; an', as soon as he did, the lad, the dead fella, gev him wan elbow that sint Jack rowlin' yards out an the flure.

"Ah, I know now what's wrong wit' ye," says Jack. "The wall is too could for ye. I'll get betune ye an' the wall. Sure, the win' is comin' thru' it an' perishin' ye, ye poor thing!" So, in he got, an' the lad started squeezin' an' elbowin' Jack tell he nearly kilt him. "Name o' God, don't kill me altogether. Name o' the Father, Son, what-do-ye maen? All I want is to help to keep ye comfortable," says Jack. "Well, Jack," he says, "yer the bravest man in the world. An' I'll make y'up all the days o' yer life, an' make yer mother up, for no wan ever could relaese me, only a man that never commit sin or never done harm." "Bedad, then," says Jack, "yer as good a man now as ever ye wor; but what about yer two harmless brothers, or uncles, or whatever th'are? I'd leck to see thim too. Thim is two daecent fellas; they never done as much to me 's you, but, all the same, I'm satisfied wit' ye." "They'll come in, by an' by, Jack," says he.

So, he came down an' opened a room; an', says he, "This room is full o' money, Jack, an' it's all yours. We're here, mesel' an' me father an' gran'father, to be redeemed be a man that never had a sin in his life, a harmless man. My son lives up there in the castle. An' anyone he ever put down here, they were kilt; but you couldn't be kilt, for 'twas God that sint ye; an' this castle is yours now, for what ye done." "All right," says Jack.

So, the King came down an' aksed Jack how he got an. "The castle is mine now," says Jack, showin' him the kay. "How's that?" says he. "Didn't I deliver y'r father from the punishment was an him," says Jack. "Well Jack," says he, "I'll give ye the ch'ice iv me three daughthers in marriage." "What'd I want wit' thim?" says Jack. "Isn't me mother at home." "Oh, well, ye'll have to marry wan o' thim." "Well, anyhow; didn't y'r father gi'me the castle?" So, he was talkin' there to him for a while.

So, the three appeared; the grandfather, the father. So, they tould how they were held spirits an' couldn't get free from hell only be a man that never commit sin; an' that was Jack, a messenger from God.

So, they tould him to give him the ch'ice iv his three daughthers. "Well," he says, "before I get me ch'ice, I want to see me mother here."

So, the King sint a coach an' four for the mother, an' she came an down. "Oh, Jackeen, *avic*," she says, "I never quit frettin' for ye since, an' cryin' after ye." "Thanks be to God. Ye have plinty t'aet now, an' bigger cakes nor what you gev me. I've a fine big house for ye, an' I'm goin' t' get a lady too." So, she looked at the grand clothes." *Musha,* Jackeen, *avic,* who did ye rob, or kill, to get thim grand clothes?" "No wan," says he, "but I'm comin' for you now." "Ah, I can't go," says she." "Get up here an the coach an' we'll bring *Póilin,* an' *Biddin,* an' the goat." "We can't bring goats and ducks in the coach," says the King." But Jack wouldn't go onless they did, so he had to bring them.

So, whin they got back, the King put up a servant to pretind she was his daughther, an' marry Jack, but the daughther steps out an' says, "The man that won me gets me," an' hersel' an' Jack got marrit.

So, put down the kittle an' make tae, an' if they don't live happy, that we may.

Next page — A family prepares their Sunday meal in a pot hung from a kettle iron. A pot of potatoes and cabbage, less often meat, has long been a staple of the Traveller diet.

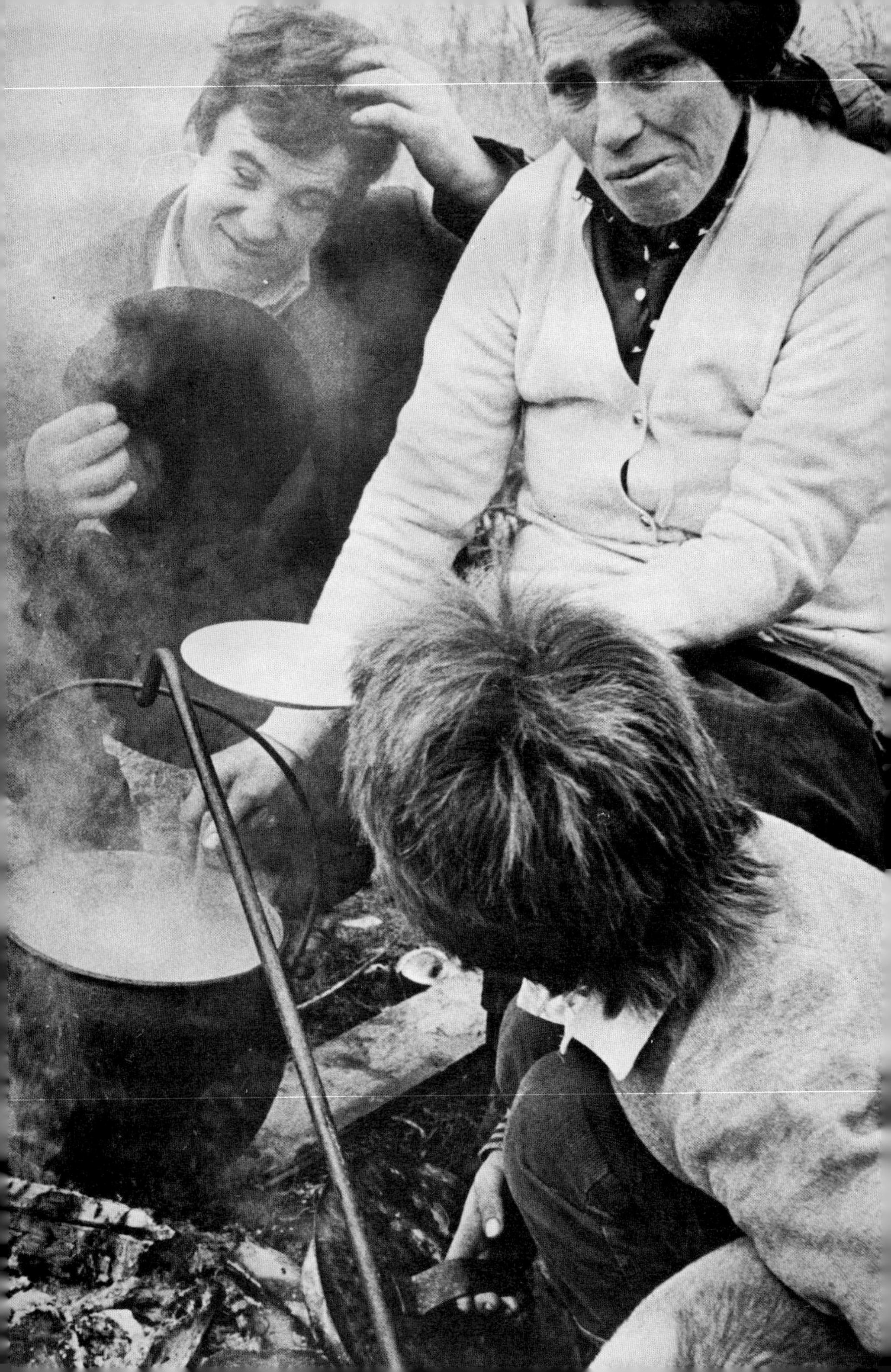

The Story of the Omadhaun Laois

ONCE, AN' ONCE, an' very good times; an' 'twas neither my time nor your time, but 'twas somebody's time; when turkeys chewed tobacco and swallows built their nests in ould men's beards, an' that's neither my time nor your time, there was a very rich man an' he had three sons: Jack, Tom, an' Bill. Jack was always called 'th' *omadhaun* laois' because he was so 'thick'.

Well, the father got sick; an' he sent for the three sons an' tould them that there was no cure for him except a bottle of the world's end wather. The three boys started out to see could they get the wather; an' they thravelled on tell they came to where there was men cuttin' timbers on th' edge o' the road. "Yez are workin' hard," says Jack, "We are," says they. "Did yez ever hear tell o' the world's end wather?" says he. "No, never," says they.

Well, there was a big swingless beside where they were working. An' Jack went over to it; an' says he to Tom an' Bill: "I'll go down here an' see what's below. An' I'll meet yez here in three days time." They laughed at him, for he was an *omadhaun,* an' said they would. So, Jack lifted the led o' the swingless an' down he went, down the big chain, an' came out at th' other end o' the world.

He thravelled about; an', when night came, he saw a light an' med for it. There was a small house there an' a little ould man in it. An' he med Jack welkim an' gev him a bit t'aet. Jack aksed him if he ever heard tell of the world's end wather; an' he said he didn't. "But," says he, "I have a brother that lives a hundhert miles away, an' m'be he knows. Anyhow, it's too late for yeh to go tonight. Wait tell mornin', an' I'll tell yeh the way."

79

Jack waited. An' when he had the breakfast et, th' ould man tould him the way, an' gev him a belt to help him along. Jack bid him goodbye an' put on the belt, an' started. When he tightened the belt, every step he gev took him an three; an' that evenin' he came to where th' other brother lived. He was an ould man too, an' he was very glad to see Jack. He gev him his supper. An' Jack aksed him if he knew an'thin' about the world's end wather; but he said he didn't. "I have another brother that lives a hundhert miles away from here," says he, "an' m'be he knows." "Anyhow," says he, "wait here tonight; an' in the mornin', I'll give yeh directions."

The next mornin', when the breakfast was et, he directed Jack an' gev him a hoop to help him along. Jack furled the hoop along, in front of him, an' t'wasn't long tell he came to where th' other brother lived. He welkimed Jack an' gev him a bit t'aet. An' Jack aksed him if he knew where he'd get the world's end wather. "I don't," says he, "but m'be I could find out. I have power over all the birds an' I'll call them an' aks them if any o' them know where it is."

He went out an' whistled; an' all the birds came. An' he aksed them, but none o' them knew an'thin'. "Bad enough," says Jack. "Wait," says th' ould man, "th' aegle wasn't there." He whistled; an' th' aegle didn't come. He whistled agin; an' he didn't come. He whistled the third time, an' an came th' aegle in a great hurry. "Why didn't yeh come when I called yeh?" says he. "I was away gettin' a dhrink o' the world's end wather," says he. "Bedad, y'r landed," says he to Jack, "he'll show yeh where it is." "Take this man," says he, "an' show him the world's end wather."

Th' aegle brought Jack away an' showed him where the well was. Jack spied a lovely princess lyin' fast asleep beside the well an' three lovely gould rings on her fingers. Over he went an' took wan o' the rings 'ithout wakenin' her. He took out his bottle an' filled it an' started back again.

Well, if the road was hard for Jack coming, 'twas aesy coming back. That evenin' he raeched the swingless an' rattled the big chain. An' the brothers were above an' shouted down: "Is that you, Jack?" "'Tis," says he. "Did yeh get the wather?" "I did," says he. "Well," says they, "send up the bottle first, in case ye'd break it, an' we'll pull y'up afther." Jack sint up the bottle. An' when they got it, they clapped down the big led; an' went off an' left him there.

Poor Jack was below an' couldn't get up. He rambled about for

Jack the Fisherman

ONCE, AN' ONCE, an' very good times; an' 'twas nayther my time nor your time; but 'twas somebody's time, when turkeys chewed tobacco an' swallows built their nests in ould men's beards; an' that was neither my time nor your time: there was a poor fisherman named Jack. There was no one but himself an' his wife; an' they were twenty-one years marrit an' had no childer. The fishin' was very bad; an' this day he was out in his little boat an' he had no luck at all. He never caught a thing. A merrymaid came up out o' the wather an' says she to him: "Yeh have bad luck." "I have," says he. "Well," says she, "I'll gi'e yeh the gift o' fish if yeh promise me wan thing." "I'll promise y' an'thin' yeh leck," says he. "Will yeh gi'me yer eldest son whin he's twenty-wan?" says she. "Bedad," says he, beginnin' to laugh, "that's aesy, for I'm marrit this twenty-wan years an' has no childer." "Never mind that," says she.

Off she went, an' he began to fish. An', sure, in a few minnits he was tired pullin' fish into the boat. He rowed his little boat to the land an' went home with his fish an' tould his wife all that passed. "Ye'd never know what'd happen," says she.

In nine months she had a son; an' they called him Jack afther his father. When he was born, he was as big as a child of three; an' when he was three, he was as big as a child of seven. He went to school, an' he wasn't long there when he knew more nor the masther.

All this time the father had great luck at the fishin'; an' he got very rich sellin' fish in all the towns about. Wan day when the boy was near twenty-wan, he was out fishin' an' the merrymaid

97

came up out o' the wather an' reminded him iv his promise. He forgot all about her, an' went home in very bad humour. He tould the woman what happened; an' she began to roar, an' cry, an' lament for her darlin' boy. Jack came in an' aksed what was up; an' the father tould him all. "Yeh have lots o' money now," says he, "so don't go near the wather any more, an' I'll go an' seek me fortune." His mother gev him a cake an' a bottle of milk, an' he started.

He thravelled a long way, an' he came to a big wood this day. He heard a terrible hullaballoo goin' an, an' he saw the Lion o' the Forest, the Hound o' the Forest, an' th' Aegle o' the Forest fightin' over the carcass iv a dead horse. "Here's a man," says the lion, "an' he'll settle the dispute for us." You know, th' animals could talk them times. Jack went over to them an' aksed them what was wrong. They tould him they couldn't agree how to divide the carcass, an' aksed him to settle the dispute for them. "That's aesy," says he. "Give th' aegle the tender bits; let the hound take the hind quarthers; an' the coorse parts is good enough for the lion, for he's well able to aet it." They were very thankful, an' thanked him; an' Jack started off for himself.

He wasn't far gone, when the lion whistled after him. "Bedad," says Jack, "I'm done now. M'be they'll start dividin' my ould carcass the way I tould them to divide the horse. He began to run, an' they ran afther him shoutin': "We won't do an'thin' to yeh, we want to gi'e yeh a gift." Jack waited tell they came up to him; an' says the lion: "I'll give yeh a gift that yeh can turn yersel' into the Lion o' the Forest; an' ye'll win over everythin', even the Lion o' the Rock." "I'll gi'e yeh a gift," says the hound, "that yeh can turn yersel' into the Hound o' the Forest; an' ye'll win over everythin', even the Hound o' the Rock." "I'll gi'e yeh a gift," says th' aegle, "that yeh can turn yersel' into th' Aegle o' the Forest; an' ye'll win over everythin', even th' Aegle o' the Rock." Jack thanked them an' went about his business.

He wasn't far gone when he heard a hunt. "What'll I do now?" says he to himsel'. "M'be the dogs'll kill me if they ketch me." "I'll turn mesel' into th' aegle." He was afraid to turn himsel' into any o' th' others, afraird they'd ketch him. He turned himsel' into th' aegle an' flew away. He wasn't used to flyin'; so, where did he light, but on the breast of a horse. There was a lovely girl on the horse an' she caught th' aegle. She called her father, for they were both in th' ind o' the hunt; an', says she, "Look at the lovely bird I caught. Come an, an' we'll go home. We have enough for one day." They went home; an' she brought the bird home along with her.

That night, when she went to bed, she brought the aegle up to her room with her. She blew out the candle an' went to bed; an' when she did, Jack says to himsel', "I think I'll turn back into mesel', an' go an' look for somethin' t'aet", for she only gave him little bits an' he was hungry. He turned back into himsel' an' didn't the girl see him. She gev a screech, but Jack tould her not to be afraird. An' he up an' tould her the whole story, about who he was an' all. She thought she never saw such a nice lookin' fella; an' she aksed him to marry her. He said how could he face her father in th' ould clothes he had on. "But if yeh gi'me the price iv a new suit o' clothes," says he, "I'll come back an' aks yer father for yeh." She went an' got him somethin' t'aet an' tould him she'd bring him out the next day an' he could go an' get the clothes.

The next day, she brought him out. An' when they got a bit away from the house, she hung a bag o' goold on his neck an' away he flew. When he flew away a bit, he turned back into himsel' an' walked into the town, an' bought a lovely suit o' clothes, an' a goold watch an' chain, an' a carriage an' four. He got into the carriage an' dhrove up to where the girl lived. "Here's a grand dhrive comin'," says she to her father. "Oh, bedad, this must be some grand prince," says he. They welkimed Jack an' got ready a grand faest. "I'd leck to marry that man," says she. "Shame on yeh," says her father. "How do yeh know but he's marrit already?" "I'll aks him," says she. She did; an' Jack said he wasn't an' that that's what brought him there. He wanted to marry her. They all agreed; an' there was a grand weddin', an' great faestin'.

Wan day, afther they gettin' marrit, they were walkin' along be the sae when up comes the merrymaid, an' pult Jack in. The poor girl ran home, roarin' an' cryin', an' tould her father. He went off to the Grand Adviser an' aksed him how they'd get Jack back. He tould him for his daughter to go down to the saeshore the next day an' jingle her three rings an' demand to see Jack's head over the wather; the day after, she was to go an' demand to see him to his hips; an', the third day, she was to demand to see him over the wather altogether.

The next day, she went down to the saeshore an' jingled her rings an' the merrymaid came up. She demanded to see her husband's head over the wather. The merrymaid showed Jack's head an' the girl went away.

The next mornin', she went down again an' jingled her rings an' demanded to see Jack to his hips. The merrymaid showed her Jack to his hips an' she went home.

The third mornin', she went down, an' said she wouldn't be satisfied if she didn't see Jack over the wather. The merrymaid showed him over the wather; an', the minnit she did, didn't he turn himsel' into th' aegle an' flew away.

The minnit he did, didn't the merrymaid grab the girl an' pull her into the sae. Jack was in a terrible way an' went off an' tould her father.

He set off an the minnit to see the Grand Adviser. The Grand Adviser tould him that the Lion o' the Forest'd have to fight the Lion o' the Rock an' kill him; that the Hound o' the Forrest'd have to fight the Hound o' the Rock an' kill him; an' that th' Aegle o' the Forest'd have to fight the Aegle o' the Rock an' kill him. An' that, when that was done, Jack'd have to take th' egg that was in th' Aegle o' the Rock an' hit the merrymaid between the two eyes with it, or he'd never get back his wife. The man went home an' tould it all to Jack.

The next mornin', Jack went down to the saeshore an' struck the big rock that was beside the sae, with a sledge, an' out hops the Lion o' the Rock. Jack turned himself into the Lion o' the Forest; an' the two o' them fought all day, an' when the sun was settin', the Lion o' the Forest tore the throat out o' the Lion o' the Rock an' left him lyin' there dead.

The next day, Jack came ag'in an' struck the rock with the sledge; an' out came the Hound o' the Rock. Jack turned himself into the Hound o' the Forest an' they began to fight. They fought all day an', in th' evenin', the Hound o' the Forest tore the neck out o' the Hound o' the Rock an' kilt him.

The next mornin', he came down early an' struck the rock with the sledge, an' out came th' Aegle o' the Rock. Jack turned himself into th' Aegle o' the Forest an' they began to fight. They fought all day an', in th' evenin', th' Aegle o' the Forest stuck his spurs into th' Aegle o' the Rock an' kilt him. Jack turned back into himself then, an' took out his knife an' opened up th' aegle; an' took out th' egg out o' him.

He went home; an' the next mornin' he went down to the sae. The merrymaid was swimmin' about, an' the girl beside her; an' she moanin' to herself an' tossin' the girl's rings from one hand to th' other. "Jack," she says, "don't throw that egg at me, an' I'll never intherfaer with yeh any more." "Yeh mightn't intherfaer with me," says Jack, "but yeh might with someone else. He up with the egg an' hit her fair between the two eyes. The minnit he did, she turned into a heap o' sand an' the girl was let free.

They went back home an' had great faestin' for days an' days afther.

Next page — An elderly couple enjoy a quiet moment at sunset.

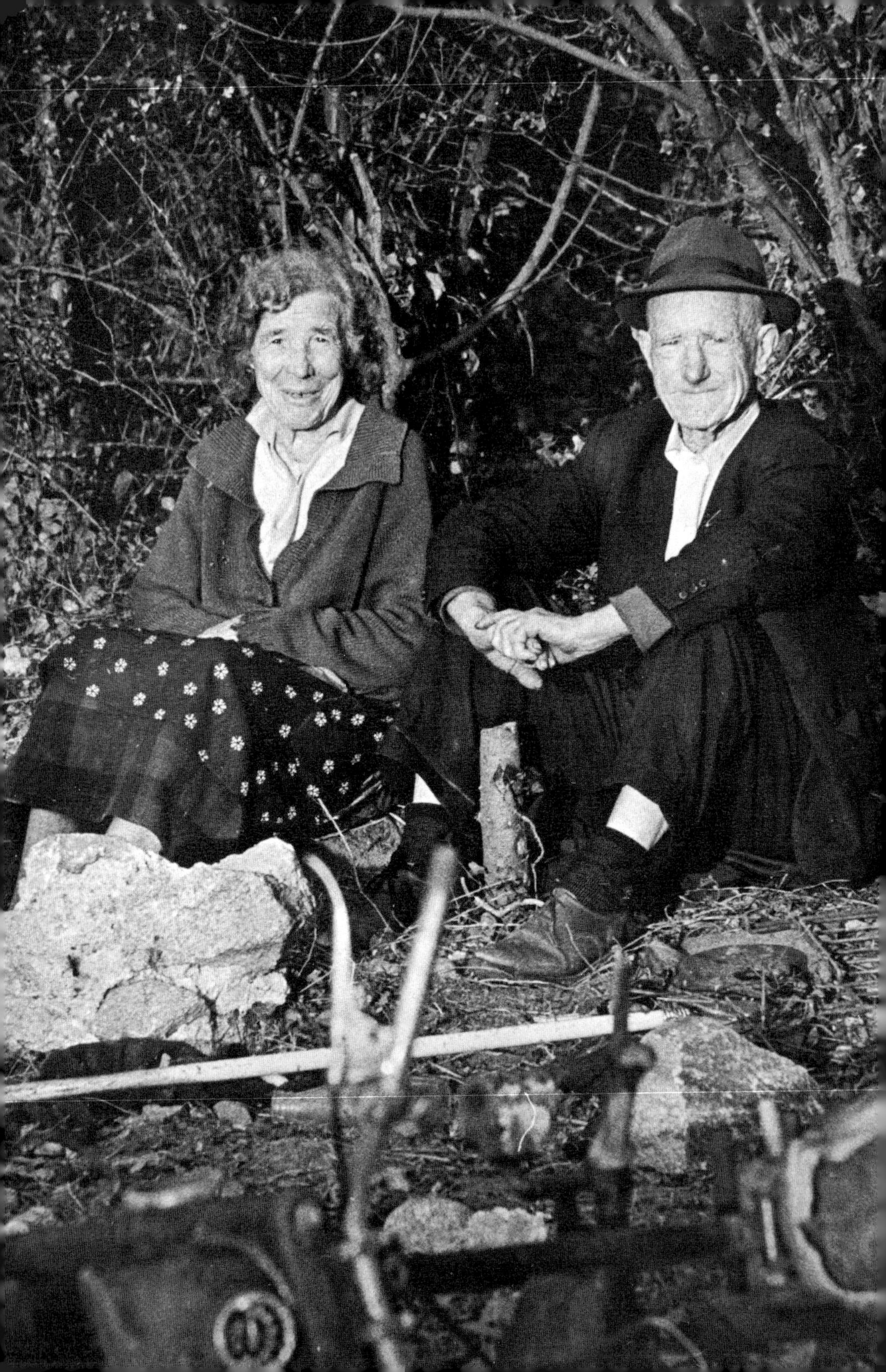

The Wild Sow
of the Forest

ONCE, AN' ONCE, an' very good times it was; there was a woman an' she had three daughthers. An' the craether had no way of livin' only accordin' as she'd go out an' do a day's work to support them. An' there was two of them very impidend an' 'd do nothin' at all for her; but the young one was a very good girl.

Well, this mornin' th' eldest girl took a notion to go to the well for a can o' wather; an' there was an enchanted lady in a bush over the well. And when she looked into the well, it was the lady's shadda she seen. "Oh, dear; oh, dear," she says, "amn't I sich a fine girl to be lost in this counthry, when I could get a fine man an' a fine place instead of livin' in this ould gatehouse."

So, she came in. "Well, mother," she says, "I'm goin' to seek me fortune." "All right," says the mother. "Bake a cake for me." "Well, is it a big one or a little one?" says the mother. "Oh, a big one," says she. "Well," she says, "which will ye have: me blessin' or me curse?" "Oh, I'll have the curse," says she. "It'll go father with me." So, out she started. "Good bye, now, to ye all," says she, "an' if I'm alive be this day twelvemonth, I'll be here; an', if I don't, the well'll be blood." "Good bye, sisther," she says to the bould one. "Good bye, sisther." "Oh, God speed ye," says she. An' says the mother:

"My curse go high, my curse go low, my curse go with ye wherever ye go."

So, she left the mother an' the two daughthers there an' away grey wit' her. An' she went, I suppose, about twenty mile afore she knew where she was goin'. She sat down to take a bit o' the cake an' a sup o' the milk she had in her pocket in a little bottle.

Ag'in she got up, it was night on her an' she found herself in the middle of a wild forisht. "Well," she says, "I d'know where to go now, an' I wisht I was at home." Well, she got up an' she wandhered around the wood; an' the night came very dark on her. An' she seen a light at the butt o' a hill; an' she med towards the light. She med towards the light. An' when she came down, she knocked at the door; an' a gintleman opened the door for her. "Oh, good night, me fair lady," says he. "Oh, I'm no lady," says she, "I'm a poor girl lookin' for a situation." "Well, if ye have no objections to come in; altho' there's min here, they're alright."

So, in she comes. An' he gev her a chair to sit down tell the supper was got ready for her. An' afther the supper was et, he gev her a book to read. An' afther that, the twelve min wint upstairs; an' th' old schoolmaster gev her a kae. "There's a room, now," he says, "an' it's for yersel'; an' no one can get into it but yersel'; an' there's the kae an' ye can lock yersel' in. An' whin ye get up in the mornin', ye know what to do: light the fire, an' put down the kittle, an' get ready the breakfast for those twelve boys; for they have to go afther breakfast." "All right," says she.

So, she got up an' she wint to bed. An' afther goin' into the room, she looked about her; an' says she, "I wish to God I was at home ag'in. This is a very lonesome place: no one to spaek to; but, as it is now, I must suffer."

So, she got up in the mornin' an' put down a fire, an' got ready the breakfast; an' the twelve boys came down. "Well, now," says the old master to her, he says, "Here is the kaes of all that's in this house, only that door there. I forbid you to open that door. If ye do, I'll punish you."

So, begorras, she was goin' an grand for about a month. An' this day she got them all away, the school masther an' the boys used to go away every mornin' an' every evenin' at seven o'clock they used to come back; an' she'd have the supper ready for them, an' they lecked her well.

So, this day when she got them away, says she to hersel': "Sure, this room; what can be in it no more nor any other wan?" So, she turned the kae in the dure an' looked in; an' whatever she seen in it, she dhrew back an' closed the dure. In five minnits, in comes the man. "Well," he says, "what did ye see in the room?" "I seen nothin'; nor I'll tell nothin', until me dyin' day." "Well, now is yer dyin' day." "I don't care," she says. So he pult a rod from behind the door an' he turned her into a millstone, an' threwn her fornint the door.

Now, we'll go back to th' other sister. All this was about a month. The other sister went out early for a can o' wather, an' here comes the lady up over her head. "Ah," she says, "I'll go as well as me sisther to seek me fortune." The same happened her now. She came an to the wood; an' it got late an her. An' she came an to the little house at duskus. An' she knocked at the door; an' the masther let her in. An' he aksed her what she wanted, an' she said a night's lodgin', or else did he want a servant? He says, "Yer the very thing I want; the very girl I want, for I have no housekeeper." So, she came in; an' he got ready a supper, an' gev her a book to read; an' he gev her the kae of a room.

So, she went to her own room. An' in the mornin', she had the fire lit an' the kittle boilin', an' the breakfast ready, for she was a very good girl.

So, begorras, he gev her the kaes of all the rooms in the house; an' he tould her not to look into this room. This day she was curious, an' she went an' turned the kae in the dure an' looked into the room, an' pult back ag'in. He came behind her an', says he, "What'd ye see in the room?" "I seen nothin', an' I'll tell nothin' until me dyin' day." "Well, this moment is yer dyin' day." So, he turned her into a millstone an' left her on top o' th' other one.

Now it happened that a year went by an' the young sister went out this day, just a year an' a day, an' looked in the well. "Ah," she says, "me two poor sisthers is dead." "I never heard ye spaekin' a word o' them since they left, mother," says she. "They worn't worth it," says she. "Well, mother," says she, "I'm goin' to find them out wherever th' are, dead or alive."

"Well," says she, "which will I make, a small or a big cake?" "Ah, *musha,* make a small cake," says she, "an' yer blessin'." She got up in the mornin'. "Now mother," says she, "if I'm alive this day twelvemonth, I'll be back; an' if I'm not, you'll see the well turned to blood." "All right," says she.

"That me blessin' go high, an' me blessin' go low;
An' me blessin' go wit' ye, wherever ye go."

"An' I'll pray for ye."

Now we'll follie the little girl along; but a bit never troubled her t' aet tell she came very near the little house. She sat down upon a stone an' she says: "This is the way me poor sisters came, so God advise me." So, she got up an' came an down to the little house, an' whin she came to the dure, there was no one 'ithin. She riz the latch of the dure; an' says a v'ice, "Come in."

So, she came in an' she sat in the chair. "Stay there, ye won't be long alone." Begor she wasn't long 'ithin when in comes a grand gintleman an' twelve young boys along with him. "Yer welkim," says he. "Thanks sir," says she, stan'in' up. "Are ye goin' far?" says he. "Well," she says, "I'm lookin' for either a missus or a masther." "Well," he says, "yer the very girl I want. I'll hire ye now for a year an' a day, an' I'll give ye so much; but wan request I'll crave o' ye: not t' open a certain room in this house; an' I'll gi'e ye the kae to open every dure in the house, but don't open that." "Very good," says she.

Bedad, she was in it up to eleven months. An' the boys loved her an' were all very good to her an' used to bring her presents an' everythin'; for she'd have their sums done, an' everythin' done, before the masther'd get up in the mornin'. They used to give her the grandest o' clothes.

Well, this mornin', whin she got them all away, says she to hersel': "Well, I'm here eleven months; twelve months all but a day; an', in the name o' God, I'll see what's in this room." She wint an' turned the kae in the dure an' peeped in, but she dhrew back ag'in. The masther came behind her. "Well, what'd ye see in the room," says he. "I seen nothin' an' I'll tell nothin', not till me dyin' day." "Well, now is yer dyin' day." "Well, no matther," says she. "Our Lord suffered more nor that." He didn't turn her into a stone or anything.

"Well now, boys," he says, "which would yez rather see, her dhrounded or burnt in a big barrel of pitch an' tar?" Well, all the boys was a sort of mismirized, for none o' thim'd leck an'thin' to happen her, she was so good an' kind to thim all.

So, says th' eldest, "Well, we wouldn't leck to see her burnt, but we'll put her in a barrel an' put her floatin' on the sae." So, the big barrel was got at anna rate an' wan fella got a big augur an' bored holes in it; an' another fella had a big bag o' corks, an' he stoppin' holes as quick as they wor med.

So, they put enough for her t'aet an' dhrink in the barrel, an' them all bid her good bye; an' they put the barrel into the wather, an' away it went, rowlin' an' tumblin'; an' where did it rowl, but up an the shore. An' there was a wild sow waitin' at the shore; waitin' for an'thin' the sae'd bring. An' whin the barrel appeared, didn't she bigin to tear at it wit' her feet. As soon as she did, she broke a stave in the barrel. The girl was sweatin' 'ithin in the barrel. "Oh, mother!" "Well," says the sow, says she, "if I'm yer mother, it's hard to say I could do an'thin' to ye." (Everything used to spaek that time.)

So, begorras, she took but the girl an' the bundles, an' all, an' the girl came, an' she took her up to a wild forisht. She brought her to a grand snug place she had in the forisht; the wild sow had. So, the girl sat down an' had nothin' to do, except aet what she had ascordin' as she wanted. An' whin that was gone, th' ould sow used to g'out every day an' bring her in a fish or a bird or somethin' for her t'aet. She was livin' very lonely, the poor girl, an' had nothin', only the books the boys gev her whin she was laevin'. An', after a year, she had hardly any clothes; but was all worn an' torn.

This day, there was a small boat comin' up the wather; an' the two min looked at her. "We'll g'over an' aks her who she is," says wan fella. "Miss, who are ye; or what are ye; or are ye shipwracked?" "Oh yis, I am," she says. "Well, if ye wish, we can bring ye away." "Oh no, I couldn't go 'ithout aksin' me mother's laeve." "An' who's yer mother, or where's yer mother?" "Oh, the Wild Sow o' the Forisht." She said she'd have a word for them the next day; so, she went home. That evenin', th' ould sow was afther bringin' in three or four birds. "Now," she says, "ye can have a good mael." "Well, mother," she says, "there was two gintlemin this evenin' an the strand, with a boat, an' th' aksed me would they bring me away." "Well," says th' ould sow, "aks them tomorrow where are they bringin' ye, or what do they want with ye."

So, the next day, says she: "Me mother wants to know where are yez bringin' me, or what do yez want with me?" "Well," says wan o' them, "I'll marry ye." "I will," says she, "if me mother lets me." She tould th' ould sow that night; an', says she, "I'll agree, if he lets me see ye three times in the week."

So, the next day, the girl tould him. An', says he, "She can see ye as often as she lecks."

So, they put the girl in the boat; an' he took her off home to his mother's house, where he was the wan only son. "Well, mother," he says, "I'm goin' to marry this girl now an' I hope "ye'll be willin'." "All right," says the mother, "she has a good countenance anyway."

So, the weddin' began an' lasted a couple o' days. An' th' ould sow came over the last day an' they gev her plenty t'aet.

So, it happened that she used to come wance a week or twice a week to see her; an', at th' end o' ten months, the lady was goin' to have her first baby. That night, when she had the baby, who appeared in the room, but th' ould masther. "What did ya see in the room?" says he. "I seen nothin', an' I'll tell nothin'; not tell me dyin' day," says she. "Now is yer dyin' day," says he. "I don't care," says she. "Our Lord suffered more nor that." So, he took the baby, an' left the girl dumb, an' went away.

Well, the next mornín', the master an' th' ould lady came down to see her an' wish her joy, an' there was no baby; the baby was gone. "Ha, ha!" says th' ould mother, "I knew there was a dhrop o' th' ould sow in her. She et the baby; an' she'll aet iz all if yez don't put her away." But they said they'd give her a chance.

The next day, th' ould sow was comin' over to see the lady; an' they shot her an' threw her into the wather, an' never let an to the lady.

Afther another year or so, there was another baby. An' the masther came in the night an' took the baby an' aksed her what she seen in the room. But she said she seen nothin' an' she'd tell nothin', not untell her dyin' day. "Well, now is yer dyin' day," an' he left her deaf an' dumb an' wint away.

So, the baby was gone. An' whin they came down in the mornin', to wish her joy o' the baby, there was no baby. "Ha, ha!" says th' ould mother, "I knew there was a dhrop o' th' ould sow in her; an' if ye don't put her away, she'll kill iz all." "We'll give her another chance, mother," says the boy.

So, they gave her another chance; an' afther a year another child was born, an' the masther came in the night an' took the child an' aksed her what she seen in the room; but, says she, "I seen nothin' an' I'll tell nothin', not tell me dyin' day." "Now is yer dyin' day," says he. "I don't care," says she. "Our Lord couldn't suffer more." So, he sthruck her deaf an' dumb, an' wint off; him an' the child.

"Well," says th' ould mother, "if yez don't do somethin' wit' her, when she's done aetin', she'll aet uz all an' everyone in the house. Yez'll have to kill her, or dhround her, or shoot her." "No, mother, I'll do naether; but I'll sind her to seek her fortune," says the son. Now, the poor girl: afther a few days, he gev her her thravellin' charges; an' she put her bundle together an' away grey for the road wit' her.

So, she thravelled a long lonesome road untell she saw a big house up from her an' she wint into the gatehouse. "Come in," says the woman. "I won't, onless ye can lodge me for the night; for I want lodgin'." "Well," says she, "there's twins, nine days ould, up at the house. An' the prince wants me to rear one, an'

I'll spaek for you to get th' other." "All right," says she.

So, the next mornin', they wint up to the big house. An' the gatehouse woman got her child an' th' other lady was gev a beautiful room in a greenhouse for hersel' an' the baby. An' naether the father or the mother was to see aether o' the children tell the nine months was up.

So, she was there wit' hersel'; an' they gev her food an' shut her up. An' there was to be a prize of a hundhert pound to whichever baby was the best at th' end o' a year. There was only a little slide for handin' in an'thin' accordin' as she wanted it.

An', the first night, who comes, but th' ould masther. "What did ye see in the room?" says he. "I seen nothin', an' I'll tell nothin'; not tell me dyin' day," says she. "Now is yer dyin' day." So, he took the baby.

Well, she stood her ground tell the nine months was up. An' whin they came to let her out, the baby was gone; an' the gatehouse woman had a lovely baby.

So, it went out how the lady et the four childher an' says the king: "We'll get out handbills an' tell the whole world to come an' see the burnin' o' the lady that et the four childher. An' we'll get a fire o' pitch an' tar ready. An' we'll put out handbills thro' the whole counthry," he says, "for she is not to be consumed tell the whole world is there to see her." So, the barrel of pitch an' tar was got ready. An' the poor lady was there, chained in an iron chair, an' the whole world was there; an' a man on top o' the castle wit' a big tilliscoop lookin' all around. "Oh, I see, I see," says he, "a big cloud comin' far away. Hold an yet." So, whin it came, who was it but her husband an' her mother-in-law an' her father-in-law. "Ha!" says the mother-in-law, didn't I tell ye there was a dhrop o' th' ould sow in her?" He said nothin' whin he saw her tied up in the chains. Thin the man wit' the tilliscoop looked up. "Hould an ," he says, "I see a cloud comin' very very far away. Houlsd an , don't set fire." So, whin it came up, who was it but the masther an' the twelve scholars; the twelve young gintlemin. So, out he got an' bursted his way in thro' everyone to where she was. "What'd ye see in the room?" says he. "I seen nothin', an' I'll tell nothin', not tell me dyin' day," says she. "Well, this is yer dyin' day," says he. "I don't care," says she. "Our Lord suffered more nor that." "Come an," he says, "loosen her." An' they did. "Well," he says, "here's a girl," he says, "an' she has me saved from all enchantments an' from the power of the divil; me an' me twelve boys," walkin' over to the coach an' takin' out her eldest

109

child, takin' out the second, an' the third, an' takin' out the king's child, an' her own two sisthers. "She has me saved," says he, "be keepin' a saecret. An' she's the best girl that ever was seen." So, whin the king seen his child, sure, it was three times as big as the gatehouse woman's. Now, the two sisthers was there, that was turned into the millstones. An' the poor ould sow, that was shot in the wather; she was the masther's wife that was undher enchantment be some bad vill'in that was in the world that time. (Thank God, there's none iv them in this now.)

So, the marriage took place ag'in: he was so glad to get his two sons an' a daughther back ag'in, an' it lasted a year an' a day. An' th' ould masther took back his wife, that was th' ould sow. An', begorras, I was knockin' about that time, an' I wint up an' I got a great dinner in it; an' they sint for th' ould mother an' the two sisthers.

So, they put down the kittle an' med tae. An' if they don't live happy, that we may.

Opposite – Young girls peer out from the family trailer.

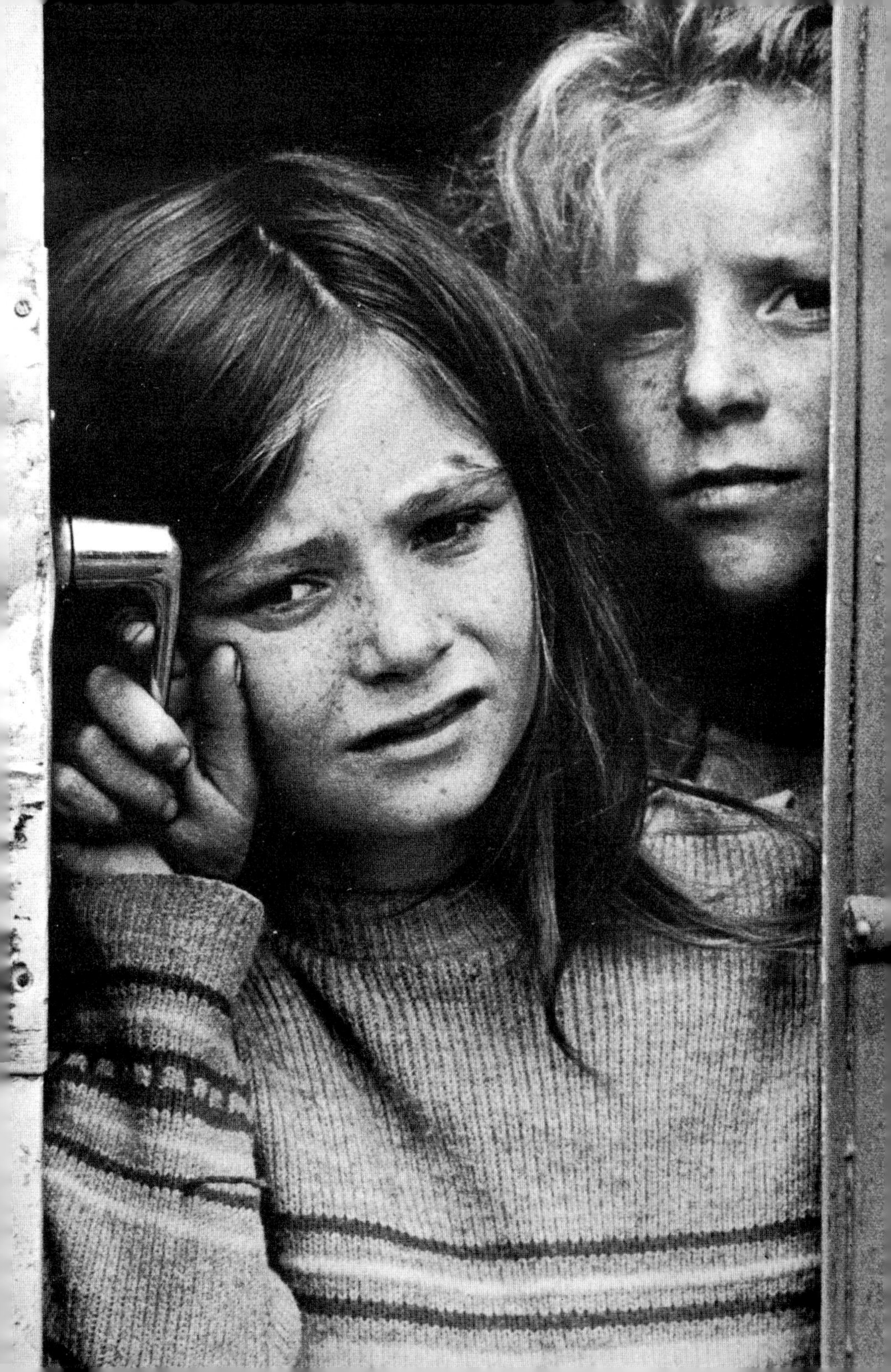

Jack the Bear

WANCE AN' WANCE an' very good times it was; an' twas nayther my time or your time, but 'twas somebody's time; there was a King an' a Queen an' they had wan son; an' his name was Jack. An' he was the greatest boy for ball playin', kickin' football, or any game that ever was. An' they'd give him to no lady, no matter who she'd be, except she'd be able to answer his mother three questions. So, he was a long time: he was up to twenty-two or twenty-three an' he could get no wife.

So, this day, they were at the hunt, an' a lady tipped him an the shoulder, an', says she, "Jack, is there any chance o' ye gettin' marrit?" "Ah," he says, "sure, I can get no wan to marry me." "Oh, yer too hard plaesed," she says. "Ah, indeed, I'm not," he says. "It's not me that's to be plaesed," he says, "but it's me mother." "Well," she says, "will ye bring me t' yer mother? An', if you marry me," she says, "I'll marry you." "Begorra," says he, "that's fair talk. An' supposin'," he says, "you're not able t'answer my mother the three questions she'll ask ye? What'll be?" "Ah, we'll marry wan an' other oursel's," she says. "There's never a man that ever I seen," she says, "took me eye wit' you, or took me heart." "Begorras," he says, "afther the hunt we'll go an' see me mother."

So, begorras, they wint an all day tell six o'clock, or whatever time the hunt was over. I don't know, nor you don't know, but 'twas over before taetime at any rate. So, she walked over to him an', "Now, Jack," she says, "Are ye ready to go?" "I am," he says. "Come on."

So, the two o' them wint an together. An' there wasn't a lady

97958

ketch him." The servant boy started off; an' he was very lame, an' couldn't ketch the hare. "I'm a bit quicker than you mesel'," says th' ould gentleman. "I'll thry an' ketch her mesel'." So, he lepped into the bog, an' follied the hare along wit' the servant boy.

Jack started to shout in the bag: "I'm goin' to heaven in a bag!" Who was passin' the way, but an ould Kerryman wit' twinty head o' cattle. He says: "Me poor man, where are ye goin'?" "I'm goin' to heaven," says Jack, "in a bag." "I'll give ye twinty head o' cattle," he says, "five pound, an' a watch an' chain, if ye let me in your place." "All right," says Jack, "only don't delay, an' loosen the sthring o' the bag." He opened the sthring. An' he put in the old Kerryman; an' he started home wit' his watch an' chain an' five pound; an' his twinty head o' cattle.

The old gintleman an' his servant boy goes an an' throws the old Kerryman into a boghole, thinkin' 'twas Jack was in it.

They came back anyways. They were satisfied when they had him dhrounded. They came back. An' when they saw all the cattle around Jack's place, an' saw him countin' a shaef o' notes, an' lookin' at his watch, they aksed him where did he get all the money an' all the cattle? "Where? Only the boghole ye threw me into. I'm very thankful," he says, shakin' the old gentleman by the hand. "Ye were th' only friend I had at last." "What boghole was it?" says he. "Oh, you know it," says he. "I don't."

They goes back to the boghole, anyways; an' the old gentleman leps in, an' an he dhounin', he started to mutther — when he was dhrounin'. "What is he sayin' now, Jack?" says the servant boy. "He's tellin' ye lep in," says Jack, "an' help him out wit' the cattle." The servant boy lepped in to help him out wit' the cattle and the both was dhrounded.

So, Jack goes back; an' he ownded the gintleman's place an' his own place. So, he got marrit.

An' they put down the kittle, an' they med tae. An' if they don't live happy, that we may.

Next page — Boy in a barrel-top wagon. The star-burst motif and absence of horse and horseshoes makes the decoration of this caravan unusual.

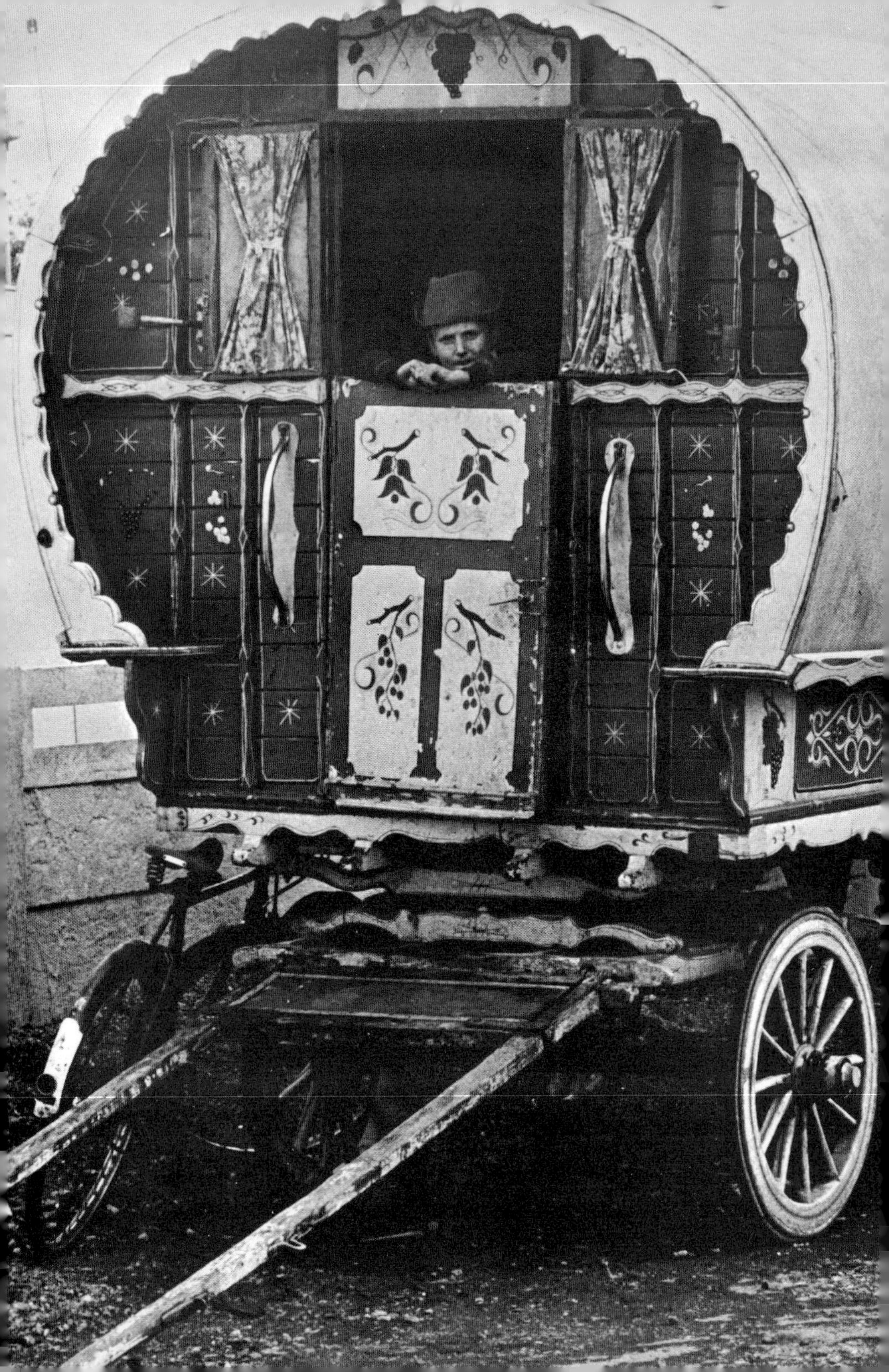

Jack the Cobbler – the Widow's Son from Ireland

THERE WAS ONCE upon a time a cobbler lived in Ireland; an' he had wan only son; an' his name was Jack. The cobbler was terrible old, an' he died. An' Jack was left with the mother, to look afther her for the rest of her life. "An' when I go," says he, "look afther your mother." "Righto," says he.

So, the ways he used to manage was, he used to go around, cobblin' boots for the neighbours around the place.

So, this night, he lay thinkin'; an' he dhraemed that he become wan o' the strongest min in the world, in time to come. So, he dhraemed that he was fit to kill two hundhert an' fifty-five lice in wan blow.

So, he got up in the mornin'. "Mother," says he, "I'm too sthrong of a man to be in this counthry." "How do ye know?" says she. "How do ye know yer sthrong?" "Oh, I dhraemed," says he, "last night that I'm a wondherful sthrong man; an' I think I'll go seek me forkin. An' if I'm alive this day twelvemonth, I'll come back. An' if not... An' if I don't return, ye'll know I'm dead; an' let ye pray for me."

So, the poor ould mother began to cry; an' she gev him a bottle o' milk an' a soda-cake goin' away.

So, he thravelled an as far as I could tell you or you could tell me, tell the night took the day an' the day took the night, an' he slep' undher the thrunk of a three that night an the side o' the road. An' the next mornin', he gets up; an' he aets his cake; an' he drunk his bottle o' milk.

An' he starts for the high road, tell he came as far as a blacksmith's forge. An' he got the blacksmith for to make a soord for him wit' a stone of iron, a stone of metal, an' also a stone of steel.

So, the blacksmith med it; an' he med it real well. An' Jack aksed him whin he had it med — he had it med in three days for him — what would he thry it an. "Thry it ag'in that millstone there," says he. Jack dhrew over the soord an' he med two halves of it. "Be this an' be that," says he, "if ye don't make me a soord that'll split me a fly off that millstone, I'll behead ye wit' it." "Righto," says he. "Spare me life, Jack," says he, "an' I'll do me best."

So, he started the next day wit' two stone iv iron, two o' mitil, an' two o' steel, for Jack. When the soord was med the follyin' day, says Jack: "What'll I thry the soord ag'in?" "Thry it ag'in that millstone there, Jack." So he did; an' as soon as he did — the very first clout ever he gev it — the soord wint in two halves. So, this time Jack floored him. "Spare me life, Jack," says he, "an' I'll make it as good as I can for ye." "Make it," says Jack, "wit' four stone of iron and four o' mitil, an' four o' steel. An' if the soord breaks, I'll take the head o' y'r body; an' that'll be th' ind o' ye." "Righto, Jack," says he.

So, he started the soord; an' Jack gev him a fortnight to make the soord. So, Jack came at th' ind of the fortnight, an' the soord was med; an', also, the poor blacksmith was afraid of his livin' life that the soord'd break. "What'll I thry it ag'in'?" says he. "Thry it ag'in' the millstone." Jack dhrew out wit' the soord an' he split it in two even halves. "Good," says he, "that's a soord." So, he ped him for the soord — I d'know what he gev him for it. So, he wint off to seek his forkin wit' the soord, that's all he had, only a few shillin's, leck, wood him.

So he came, as far as a king's castle — wan o' the largest, a wondherful castle — that was made in that counthry. An' he had that many so'diers guardin' it: as many as me or you couldn't count.

So, Jack lay across th' avenue; he fell fast asleep across th' avenue. An' he got wrote an his soord before he went: "Jack, the widdy woman's son from Ireland, that killed two hundhert an' fifty-five lice wit' wan blow." The prince was comin' down th' avenue an' he seen Jack lyin' across th' avenue; an' he looked at the wondherful man that had wrote an his soord: "Jack, the widdy woman's son from Ireland, that killed two hundhert an' fifty-five lice wit' wan blow." So, he ran back afeared of his life to his father, the King, an' tould him.

So, th' old king came up; an' he wokened up Jack. "Yer

welkim, Jack, the King's son from Ireland; the wondherful man. What are y'in search of?" "I'm in search o' work," says he. "What work can ye do?" says the King. "Any work you have for me," says he, "I'm well fit to do it."

So, the King brought him down to the house; an' he got a good dinner for him. So, he sat down; an' altho' there was seven or eight min at the table, he et all that was there: his own, as well as everyone else's. So, the King was afeared of his life of the wondherful man. So, he aksed the min would they do wit' stirabout for their supper. The min was thankful to get it. Of course, they weren't able t'aet wit' fear. So, Jack was by whin the stirabout was sint out. An' he done the same wit' that as he done wit' the dinner: he never left a plate or stirabout, but he et.

Every king in Ireland at that time — o' coorse it's years ago — every wan o' them had an adviser; a grand adviser, that'd be able to tell them where there was false witches, an' the way they'd be able to do away wit' giants. So, the King goes to the grand adviser the next mornin', an' he tell him about him. "Well," he says, "all I can tell ye, is to sind him to th' enchanted lake to plow the land, where there's an inchanted fish be some giants ages ago, that'll le'p out an' take him in; an' he's no more."

The next day, he sint down Jack wit' two horses to plough the land around this pond. An' the very minnit he wint round the pond, th' inchanted fish jumped out an' swep' wan o' the horses from undher the plough. "Good," says Jack, "but the next time ye le'p out, I'll have you, me boy." Jack wint round wit' wan horse ploughin' an' the inchanted fish lepped out, but before he was half ways back, Jack had him. An' he dhrew him out; an' he yoked him undher the plough; an' he med him plough the land in five minnits.

So, he brings him up to the giant. "Oh, put back that wondherful beast," says he. "No," says he, "I'll not put him back, put him back you." He et the two best horses that was in the land." So, Jack says he wouldn't put him back. So, the King says he'd fall out wit' him if he didn't put him back. So, Jack tould him to get a stick to put him back. So, he got the stick, an' it wouldn't put him back. So, Jack walked over an' he got a hoult iv a thrunk of a three an' he be't him back to the sea. (Of coorse, he killed him.)

So, he goes to the grand adviser's the next mornin' — the King did — an' he tould him what he done to the fish. "I d'know what ye'll do," says the grand adviser. I done all I could for ye. The best thing ye can do," says he, "is to sind him to th' inchanted

133

wood for a load o' timber, an' give him the worst horse ye have in the place. An' tell him," says he, "he's to wait in the wood tell th' owner o' the wood comes to give him laeve to cut the timber. An' he's th' inchanted giant wit' three heads that'll crush Jack to small pieces, or e'er a Jack of his name." "Righto," says the King, "thank ye very much."

So, the King sint Jack the next day to the wood for a load o' timber. An' he tould him goin', not to come, or to take no wood, tell the masther o' the wood'd come an' give him laeve. An', also, he gev Jack wan o' the worst horses upon his land that Jack couldn't dhrive away upon the black giant.

Jack came to the wood. An' he kep' waitin' an' waitin' tell he could see no one comin'. So, he started to pull the three from the roots an' pile them an the car, tell the horse fell dead undher it. An' whin the horse fell dead, he piled him an top o' the timber.

So, he wasn't very long there tell he had all this done, tell the black giant came up to him. "Fee, faw, fum, I smell the blood of an Irishman. Be him dead or be him alive, I'll have his bones for me steppin' stones," says he, "his puddin's for me garthers, an' his blood for me mornin' dhram!" "Take y'rsel' aesy," says Jack, "an' it's betther ye'll be. Remimber," says he, "I was no stableboy in me own father's place. I'm as good a man as ever ye wor." So, the giant flew at him. An' as soon as he did, Jack put him to his two shouldhers an the ground; an' he took the heads off his body, an' threw it up on top o' the load o' timber.

So, he dhragged the whole load, himsel', back to the King. The King got afraid whin he saw Jack comin' wit' the whole wood an his back: cart, horse, giant an' all. "There he is, now, for ye," says he. "He was a very impenent fella," says he, "an' I had to do away wit' him."

So, the King didn't know what to do wit' him at all. He'd give him all ever he had. So, he goes to the grand adviser the next day. Says the grand adviser: "I d'know what we'll do wit' him at all. Sind him," says he, "over to y'r uncle's house. An' let them have three hundhert so'diers at the back o' the house. An' the very minnit whin he's half-way home, let them open fire an him. An' if they don't kill him," says he, "I can't do nothin' more for ye."

So the King, next day, he sint Jack over to his uncle's house for a load of oats, an' he gev him wan o' the worst horses that was in the place. As bad as the wan the day before, he found a worse wan nor him. Of course, th' ways Jack couldn't go purty quick. Jack wint over to his uncle's house. An', of coorse, he haeped the

the car wit' all th' oats that th' uncle had. An' before he was halfways home, the so'diers opened fire an Jack. An' whin they opened fire an him, he dhropped the reins an' pulled his coat over his neck. An' he says: "That's a terrible shower o' hail!"

He goes back to the King. "Did an'thin' happen ye an the road, Jack?" says he. "Oh, nothin', sir," says he, "but we had a terrible shower o' hailstones." "O'coorse," says the King, "he thought the bullets was hailstones." "If ye don't believe me sir," he says, "there's a lot o' them here in the car yet that didn't melt."

He goes to the grand adviser the next day an' he tould the grand adviser what happened him. "In the name o' the Lord," says the grand adviser, "I d'know what ye'll do wit' him." Sind him to hell for th' ouldest divil that's in it; an' out of it, he'll never get." "An' how is he goin' to get there?" says the King. "Oh, he'll get there all right. Remember, there's some witchery in him."

So, he sint Jack the next day for th' oldest divil in hell, an' he gev him a horse goin'. However he got to hell, I can't really tell ye; but he got there. So, he went down; an' he was fightin' his way through thim in hundherts. An' he seen wan ould fella wit' a white beard that looked to be about th' ouldest fella in it. An' he took him be the beard an' he flung him to the top, tell he landed him an dhry land.

So, he took him to the King. "There he's for ye now," says he. "That's th' ouldest fella I could get for ye. So, the thrack o' the horse's hoof was in th' oul' boys' forehead. That's all o' the horse he had. He had only the horse's hoof ag'in he was done fightin' thim. "Oh," says the giant, "laeve him back, or I'll be angry wit' ye."

So, he flung him back, anyway. An' whatever way he got back, I can't tell ye. "Now," says he, "I want wan o' yer daughthers in marriage." "Oh! anyone o' thim ye leck, ye can have, if it lies in my power," says he.

So, he took the youngest daughther, an' they got marrit.

So, the King was afraid of his life. So, he goes to the grand adviser the next day; but he knew nothin'. "I can't tell ye nothin' to do," says he. "Ye'll have to laeve him there," says he. "Go back," says he, "an' tell him he'll have to go away; an' ordher him away. That's all I can do."

So, he goes back; an' he sthruck Jack. An' as soon as he did, Jack hit him. An' whether he ever fell or not, I can't tell ye. He's goin' yet, I think.

So, Jack never left wan in the house, butlers an' all, but he sent flyin'. An' he got to be marrit to his lady. An' he went for his mother; an' he brought her to his castle. An' his soord; they say his soord is in the city o' London yet: Jack the cobbler, the widdy woman's son from Ireland, that killed two hundhert and fifty-five lice wit' wan blow.

So, they put up the kittle an' med tae. An' if they don't live happy, that we may.

A boy emerges from his bed beneath a barrel-top wagon. In large families the older children sleep outside the main family shelter. Co. Wicklow.

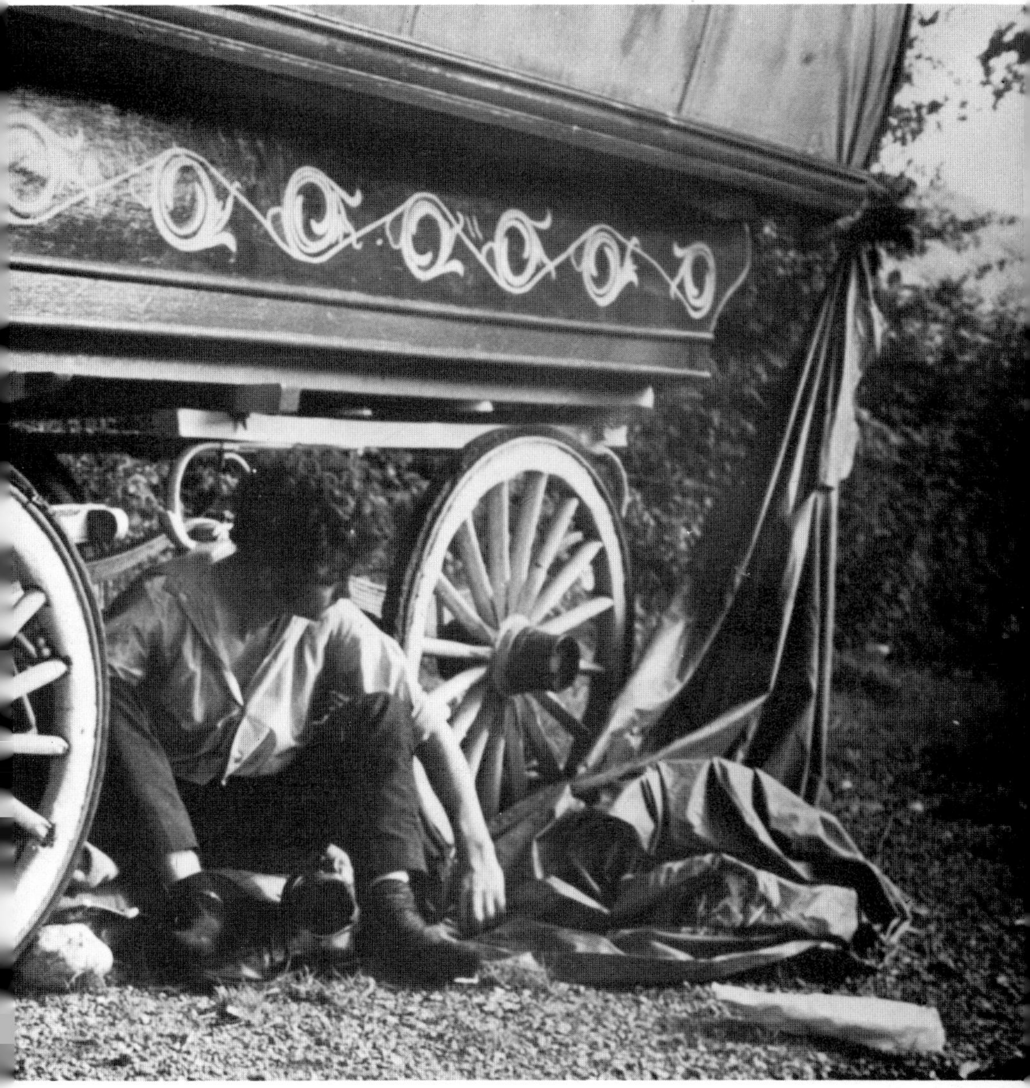

Horse, Hound and Hawk

THERE WAS A KING in Ireland, wantime, an' he had three sons: Jack, Tom, an' Bill. They were terrible wild rakes an' were always fond of huntin' in the forest.

So, the king was terrible ould, anyways, an' he died. An' when he died, he left his sons the gift of horse, hound, an' hawk. He gev them a horse, hound, an' hawk each. An' if ever they were in throuble, they could call on them; an' they'd get them out of it.

So, when the father died, wan o' them said he'd go an' seek his fortune. For three was too many to have in the house wit' the mother, an' she so old.

So, the son goes. An' before he does, he laeves a cup o' wather an the table. "If anything happens me ag'in twelve months, that cup o' wather'll turn into human blood." "Righto," says the brothers, "off ye pop."

So, he goes along, tell the night took the day an' the day took the night, tell he came to an old woman's house an the side o' the road; an' he goes in. "Yer welkim, Tom," says she, "the King's son from Ireland." "Thank you, ma'am," says he, "will ye keep me for the night?" So, she kep' him for the night; an' she also gev him a house for his horse, hound, an' hawk. So, the next day, she aksed him would he go to the wondherful hunt.

So, he goes to the hunt. An' instead o' lookin' at the wondherful hare, 'twas at the wondherful man they were lookin', wit' his horse, hound, an' hawk; as fine a man as they never saw before in their life. Jack put to wit' his horse, hound, an' hawk afther the hare. An' they wint over hills, dales, an' mountains tell they came to a fince. An' when they crossed the fince, Jack

138

seen a small, little cabin.

So, he knocked at the dure, an' a small, little woman appeared. An' he ast her if she seen e'ra hare passin'. An' she cried out: "No." At the same time, she had a hog acrass the fire, an' it roastin'. An' she aksed him would he have some dinner; and he says, "Thank ye, ma'am, I will." "Before ye have anythin' t'aet," she says, "will ye tie them wondherful animals up?" "I've nothin' to tie them wit'," says he. "Well, here's a hair from my head; an' ye can tie them," says she. "Righto, ma'am," says he. The more Jack was tyin' them, she was sayin', "Tighten, tighten," in her own mind, till she had them that tight that the' could give Jack no help if she caused him any throuble. An' when she had them well tightened, "Now, Jack," she says, "the King's son from Ireland, sorra bit o' that ye'll aet." "Well," says he, "I'll fight for it."

So, the fightin' that was in it, she took a green rod from behind the dure. But before she had it dhrew, "Help! help! horse," says he. "I can't," says the horse, "ye tightened me too much." "Help! help! hound," says he. "I can't," says the hound, "ye tightened me too much." "Help! help! hawk," says he. "I can't," says the hawk, "ye tightened me too much."

So, she turned him into a green stone; an' she left him behind the dure.

So, when th' other brether got up in the mornin', the cup o' wather that was on the table was human blood. "Oh, be this an' be that," says he, "me brether is killed; an' I'll be dead beside him b' this time tomorra night, or else I'll save him."

So, off goes Bill to seek his brether. "If anythin' happens to me, Jack," says he, "that well in the garden'll turn to human blood." "Righto," says Jack, "off ye go."

So, he goes over hill, dale, an' mountain tell he came to the same house where his brether was the night before. "Yer welkim, Bill, the King's son from Ireland," says she, "yer brether was here the night before, so ye can stop here tonight; an' I'll gi'e ye the same threatment as I gave yer brether." So, she got ready a great dinner for him. An' gev him a great house for his horse, hound, an' hawk. The next mornin', she tould him about the great hunt that was to be upon the giants' land, of all sorts of ginthry. So, he said he'd go to it. But it wasn't for the hunt he'd go, but to see his brether, in case he was in any throuble; for he knew he was.

So, he goes the next day. An' in place of the crowd lookin' at the hare, 'twas at the wondherful rider wit' his horse, hound, an' hawk. For, as fine a man as Tom was, Bill was twice as fine. So, the hare started off through the hills an' mountains. An' Jack started off; an' he left hunters of all descriptions ahind him. There was ne'er a horse in it could keep in wit' his horse, hound, an' hawk.

So, he rode over the same hills as his brother did the day before. An' they were comin' across a small fence, an' the hare an' horse was over it together. So, he knocked at the dure — he saw a small cabin — an' th' old woman came out to him, the same as she did to his brether the day before. So, he ast her did she see e'ra hare passin'. "No," she says, "but come in an' aet a bit." "So, before I give y' anythin' t'aet, will ye tie up thim wondherful animals ye have? I do be terrible afraid iv small animals leck thim." "I have nothin', ma'am," he says, "to tie them wit'." So, she gev him a rib from her head; an' he began to tie them. An' the more he tied, she was sayin' in her own mind, "Tighter, tighter, tighter," so they couldn't stir. "The sorra bit o' this food ye'll aet today," says she. "Well, I'll fight for it," says he.

So, she snatched a green rod from behind the dure. "Help! help! horse. Help! help! hound," says he. "I can't," says the horse an' the hound, "Ye tied us too tight." "Well, help! help! hawk," he says. "I can't," says the hawk, "Ye tied me too tight Jack."

So, she turned him into a green stone, the same as she turned his brother the day before.

So, the next day, the third brother went down to the well. An' before he went near it, the well was flowin' over wit' human blood. So, he went back. "Well, mother," says he, "me two poor brothers is dead. I'm goin' in search of thim tomorra. An' where they died, I'll die. An' if anythin' happens to me inside twelve months, that bush in the garden'll flow human blood." "Righto," says the mother, "God be wit' ye."

So, off he goes in search of his brothers; over hill, dale, an' hollow. Iv course he didn't know the way they went, tell he came to a small cabin b' the side o' the road; an' he knocked at the door. An old woman opened it. "Yer welkim, Jack, the King's son from Ireland." "Thank ye, ma'am," says he. "Did ye see any two sthrange min passin' here yesterday or the day before?" "I did," says she, "yer two brothers passed here yesterday an' the day before. They wint to a great hunt up there at the giant's castle. An' there's goin' to be a great day tomorra. An' you can stop here tonight; an' I'll gi'e ye lodgin' for yer horse, hound, an' hawk. An' ye can g' up in the mornin', an' mebbe ye'd find yer two brethers in it." He slep' there that night. An', the next mornin', he wint up to the giant's castle. An' there was thousands an' hundherts there; an' there was twice as many as the day before. An' they worn't lookin' at the hare, but at Jack, wit' his horse, hound, an' hawk.

So, Jack le'pt from his horse an' he ran to the king. "Be this an' be that, if ye don't tell me where me two brethers is, I'll behead ye, an' every wan that's here," says he. "Oh," says he, "I know nothin' about yer two brothers, the poor fellas. There was a horseman here yesterday, an' another the day before, but I have nothin' to do wit' them. They follit the hares; an' I don't know where they wint." So, Jack was very angry. So, he gev the giant three weeks to find his brothers; or he'd behead him. So, the king didn't know what to do wit' Jack, for he was a wondherful man; or else he had the name o' bein' a wondherful man. So, the king tould Jack to follie the hare. That 'twasn't a hare, 'twas a witch," he says. "Yer the only man I ever tould, she's undher witchery be me." "All right," says Jack, "but you'll come wit' me. Jump up behind me an this horse." "I won't," says the king. "Two min an wan horse'd be cruel." "You'll le'p up," says Jack, "an' give me no chat, tell I find out what this hare is." He le'pt up behind Jack an the horse. An' as soon as the hare started, to it wit' Jack an' his horse, hound, an' hawk.

So, whin they came an near the fince: "She'll appear here," says the king. "All right," says he, "go an, hound, an' take the hind quarther out o' the hare." So, the hound wint an; an' he took the hind quarther out o' the hare, just as she was crossin' the fince.

So, whin they le'pt the fince, there was a small cabin wit' the dure half open. An' they walked inside. An', on the floor, was an old witch, an' she bleedin' from the leg. Says Jack, says he: "Tell me where me two brothers is, or I'll behead ye in five minnits." "I will," says she, "if ye tie up thim wondherful animals." "I've nothin' to tie thim wit'," says he. "Here's a hair from me head; it'll tie thim," says she. Jack put the hair down in his pocket an' pulled wan from his own. The more he was tightenin', she was sayin': "Tighten, tighten," tell she found her mistake when she jumped up to kill him. "Help! help! horse," the horse, an' hound, an' hawk had her in a few minutes. Before they killed her, she tould him where his two brothers was. "They're two green stones behind the dure. An' here's a rod. An' tip them, an' ye'll have them back."

So, he tipped them. An' as soon as he tipped them, his two brethers was stan'in' beside him wit' their horse, hound, an' hawk.

141

"What death'll we give her?" says the king. "I don't know," says Jack. "I'll give her no death. Let me two brethers an' you thraet her, she didn't injure me." So, the brethers never done a ha'porth, only walked outside an' brought in their horse, hound, an' hawks. An' they tore her to pieces. "Ye done that," says the king, says he, "but ye'll have to do more Jack."

So, Tom an' Bill wint home to their mother wit' lots o' money that the king gev them for all their bother, but Jack had to fight for it.

So, they wint back to the castle; an' Jack aksed the king for his daughther in marriage. "Well, Jack," says he, "before ye get her, ye'll have to hide three times. An' if I'm not able to get ye the third time, ye'll have to get her." "An' thin," says he, "I'll have to hide an' you to find." "Righto," says Jack.

So, whin Jack came to the castle next mornin' — he slep' in it that night — he wint off to hide. So, Jack wint round the castle; an' he hid in what he thought was a safe place. But the king knew every inch o' the castle, an' also the black giant that lived there.

So, Jack was hidin' in it for a long time, an' the time was near up whin the little pony came over to him: "Ah, Jack," says he, "what are ye hidin' there for?" "I can't help it," says he, "I have no other place." "Pull a rib from my tail," says he, "an' hide." So, he pulled the rib; an' as soon as ever he did, he was wan instead. The black king an' the giant came an. They searched every place; went round the pony, but failed. The time was up; they gev up Jack. So, Jack stepped out o' the horse's tail. "Good luck to you, Jack; bad shoes to your advisers. Ye done that well, Jack," says he. "But ye have two more days yet to hide."

Jack wint off to hide the next day; an' he hid in a different place, but the pony came whin the time was near up. "Ah, Jack, what did ye hide here for?" "Don't ye know the king knows every nook an' corner of this place." "Pull a nail from me hoof Jack," says he, "an' ye might find a place there." He pulled a nail; an' as soon as he did, he was a nail himsel'. The king came round the horse on account of he being in it the day before, but he wasn't. The time was up, anyway, an' Jack came out o' the horse's hoof. "Well done, Jack," says he, "Good luck to you, but bad shoes to yer advisers. Ye done that well today." "Oh, I always can do it well," says Jack. "But ye have wance more," says he. "This is the last time for you to hide an' me to find." "Righto," says Jack.

Jack didn't know where to go the next day; so he started to go down to the brink o' the sea, an' to hide himsel' undher wan o' the largest shells that was in the sea.

So, the pony came down to him. "Oh, Jack," says he, "he knows yer there, he knows before ever ye hid in it at all." "Pull a tooth out o' my head an' m'be ye'd find a place there." He pulled the tooth. The black king came out an' also the giant. They searched every place. The first place they searched was the shell where Jack hid in. They had a magic tape. An' any place Jack'd hide in the line o' land, they'd find him out, 'cept he was hid by witchery.

So, they gev up the chase; an' Jack came out o' the tooth. "Good man, Jack," says he, "Good luck to you, an' bad shoes to yer advisers." "Now," says he, "it's my time to hide, an' yours to find." "Righto," says Jack, says he, "no matther where ye'll hide I'll find ye."

The king wint off hidin'. The first place ever he hid was a flag; there was a flag an wan o' the ships in the sea. Jack was searchin' all around the castle, searchin' here an' searchin' there, but the time was very near up whin the pony came out. "Ah, Jack," says he, "ye'll never find him there. There's a flag an the highest ship an the sea; an' he's the highest flag in it." "Righto," says he. Jack got a boat for sea, an' he came an' tipped the flag. "Spare me life," says he, "an' I'll give ye me daughther in marriage." The king le'pt down out o' the flag. "Good man, Jack," says he. "Good luck to you, an' bad shoes to yer advisers." "That's wan day ye found me, but ye have two more yet to find me." "Righto," says Jack, "I'll find ye."

The next day, the king went off hidin'. He hid a laef in a book: the third laef in his own book. So, Jack was searchin' every place: hill, dale, an' mountain. He searched the ship from in to out, but could not find him. So, the pony came. "Ah, Jack," says he, "he's the third laef in his own book. Ye have only five minnits to find him." Jack rushed in; an' he was goin' through rooms an' rooms tell he got to the king's room; an' he tipped the flame. "Spare me life, Jack, an' I'll give ye me daughther in marriage." "Well done," says Jack. So, the king le'pt out o' the book. "This is the last day, Jack," says he, "for me to hide an' you to find me; an' ye have me daughther in marriage." "Righto," says Jack.

The next day, he went to hide; an' Jack didn't know where to find him. He hid himsel' in a ring — gold ring — an his daughter's finger. So, he thought Jack would never stir. Jack went searchin' here an' searchin' there, an' didn't know where to search. The pony came over to him. "Oh, ye have a hard wan this time, Jack," says he. "He's a gold ring an his daughther's finger; or how are ye goin' to find him?" "I'll thry," says Jack. Jack wint in about the room, an' was goin' here an' there. An' in the latther ind, he stretched his hand to the girl. An' the girl shook hands to him. An' as soon as she did, he cotched her middle finger wit' the ring an it an' 'tacked to pull the ring off. "Spare me life, Jack," says he, "an' I'll gi'e ye me daughther in marriage." So, he gives Jack his daughther in marriage.

So, before Jack's marriage, the black king was gone wit' an army. An' they had a magic tape that no matther where Jack'd go or hide, that they'd find him, an' crucify him, an' kill him.

So, Jack had a wish. He got a wish from the pony that he could turn himsel' into anything he wished upon this earth. He came an; an' when they were very near him, he turned himsel' into the smallest grain o' sand that was in th' avenue. So, they came an wit' the magic tape; an' the tape tould them that he was the smallest grain o' sand an th' avenue. So, they turned theirselves into rakes for rakin' sand; an' they chased him to the seashore. An' he turned himsel' into the largest zeal in the sea, an' they chased him from the sea. An' he turned himsel' into the smallest bird an the land, an' they turned theirselves into twinty-five hawks an' follit him.

So, he came up th' avenue in the shape of a bird. An' he flew in about the house. An' he turned himself into a gold ring on his sweetheart's finger; so they couldn't stir him. So, they pl'ed music for three days an' three nights. An' the black king didn't know what to give them. But they aksed nothin' only the gold ring that was an his daughther's finger. "Oh, ye won't get the ring," says the daughther. "Oh, they'll have to get it," says the king.

So, she flung the ring out o' the winda. An', as soon as she did, Jack turned himsel' into the smallest grain of oats that was in the barn, where there was seven years thrashin'. So, they went in. An' they turned theirselves into twenty-five thrashers; tell they chased Jack out o' th' oats, an' chased him back to the sea ag'in.

So, he turned himsel' into a small eel; an' he wint to the bottom o' the sea. So, they turned theirselves into twinty-five divers, an' they chased him to the land ag'in. So, he knew he was finished this time. He didn't know what to do, or where to go, or what to turn himsel' into.

So, he turned himsel' into a fox; an' they turned theirselves into twinty-five geese. An' he was in a small din; an' every goose that ever put in his head, he took the head off him tell he had them all killed.

So, whin he had thim all killed, he comes back to his lady. An' they got marrit, an' he brings her back to his mother. An', in place o' the castle, they knocked down the castle, an' got a new castle built. An' his two brothers got marrit to two other king's daughters. An' they lived terrible happy in that counthry for some years.

So, they put up — they put down the kettle an' med tae. An' if they don't live happy, that we may.

Next page — A tinsmith fashions a lantern on his "stake". He has just completed a milk or water churn (foreground). Attached to his bicycle is a set of sweeping sticks for cleaning chimneys. The crude, makeshift barrel-top wagon was improvised from a flat cart.

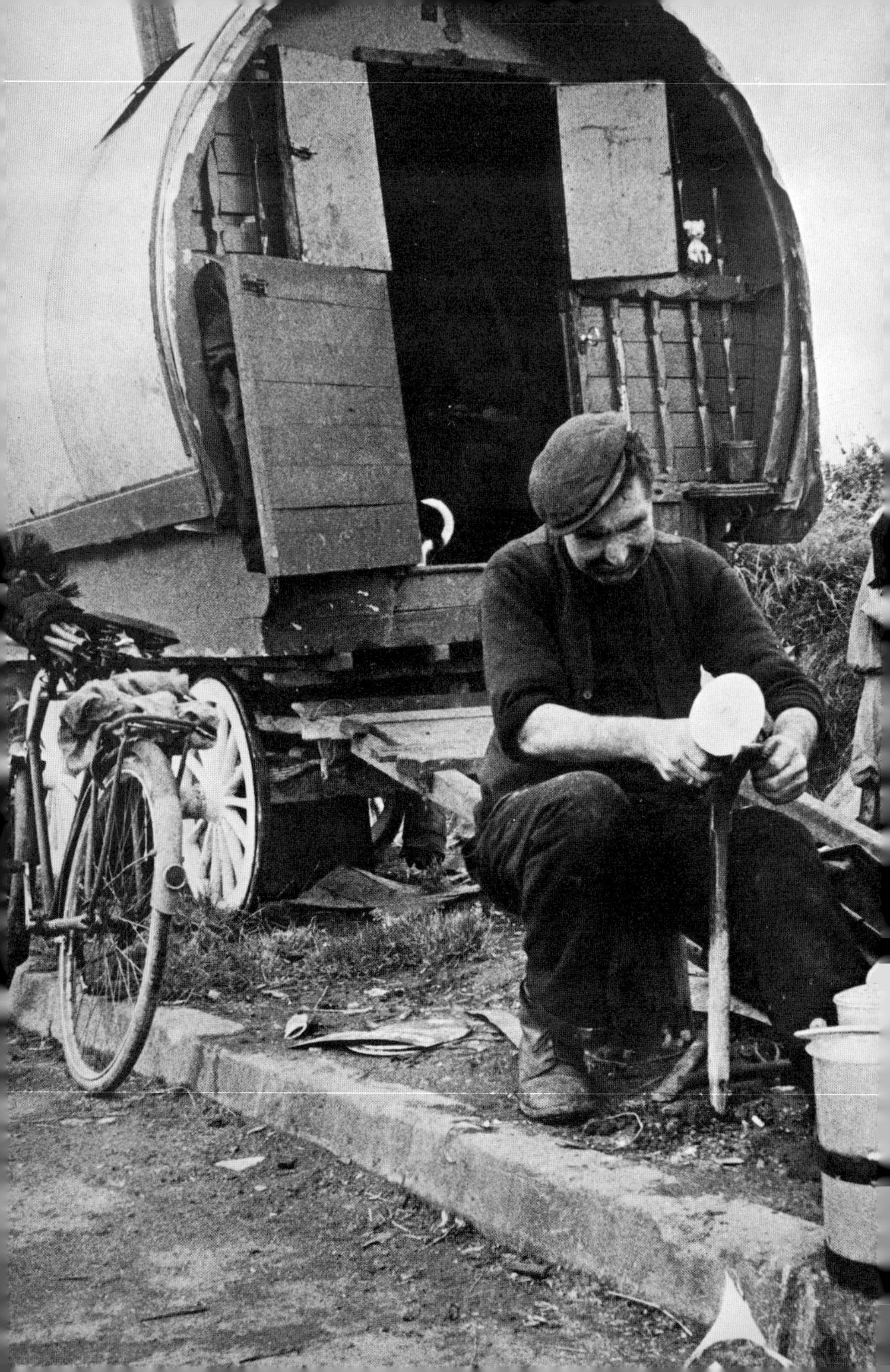

The Roarin' Bull of Orange

WANCE UPON A TIME, an' 'twas naether my time nor your time, but 'twas somebody's time, there lived a king, an' he had three only daughthers. An' he thought so much about them, that he had a wishin' chair. An' he promised a terrible death t' any o' them that'd sit an the chair, but he brought them gold an' jewels an' everythin' they aksed for; only not to sit upon the chair.

So, wan day, the father was away an' the three daughthers was alone. They opened the father's room an' they saw the chair. The very min'it they saw the chair, wan o' them sat in it for sport. So, the very min'it she did, she wished for the Ramblin' Baker. So, the next daughther sat in it wished for the Man of No Man's Land. An' the youngest daughther, she sat upon the chair afther a long time an' she wished for the Roarin' Bull of Orange.

The next mornin', an comes the Ramblin' Baker to the dure an' demanded his wife; an' she had to get her. An', the next day, an comes the Man from No Man's Land an' demanded his wife; an' he had to get her. So, the next day, the third day, the Roarin' Bull of Orange come to the dure; an' he said he'd knock down the castle if he did not get his wife. So, they sint him out a lovely servant they had.

So, he brought her an his back tell he brought her about a hundhert yards down the field, where there was a lovely golf ground. An' he asked the lady what would that be good for; an' she says, "It'd be very nice where they'd be nursin' babies." So, he brought her home an' he flung her in about the house; an' he says, "Sind me out me wife." So, they were sindin' out servants; an' ascordin' as they were sindin' them out, he was flingin' them in. At last, the daughther comes out. An' he brought her down the fields the same as he brought th' others; an' he aksed her what would that be good for. "If I had it," says she, "I'd make it for lor tennis." "You're me wife," says he.

So, he brings her away over hills, dales, an' mountains, as far as I could tell you, or you could tell me; tell he brought her to the loveliest castle that ever was seen be the sight o' man. The father was angry, to know about his daughter. He follit the Roarin' Bull of Orange; himsel' an' an army; over hills, dales, an' mountains; an' they slep' around the castle that night. So, he stole into the castle that night, an' he found the Roarin' Bull of Orange asleep, in a room wit' himsel', an' the hide beside him, of a bull. So, he stole the hide o' the bull, an' he brought it out, an' he burnt it. The next mornin', when the Roarin' Bull of Orange got up an' he missed his hide, he went up to his wife. "Oh," says he, "yer father has ruined me forever. Fare you well." An' he turned himsel' into a small bird; an' he flew out an the winda.

As soon as ever he flew out an the winda, she follit him over hills, dales, an' mountains. An' every word he'd say: "Oh, yer father ruined me." So, they wint over hills, dales, an' mountains tell they came as far as a small little house. So, he says, "G'win to that house an' get lodgin' tell mornin', an' I'll sleep in the t'atch. So, she slep' in the house; an' whin she came out in the mornin', he flew out o' the t'atch. "An'," says he, "ye needn't be follyin' me, for I have to fly all over the world; for yer father ruined me for all me lifetime." So, he brought her to a castle; an' they were in the castle for some years.

So, she had a baby. An' wan mornin', the mornin' the baby was born, a bird flew in an the winda an' took the baby out o' the room. So, the next mornin', the bird flew into the room: "Never mind," says he, "ye'll see it soon."

So, it happened to be that there was another baby in it. An' the bird flew in an' took th' other baby out. So, she was cryin' an' lamentin', when the bird flew in the next day; an' she tould him about the bird takin' the baby. "Never mind it," says he, "there's good times comin'."

So, the last baby she had, the bird flew in; but she held the baby so tight that she tore the eye out of its head. But still the bird brought it. So, she rolled the eye up in a silk hankercher in the remimbrance of the last baby.

So, the bird, she flew in the third mornin', as useval, an' she toul' him: "Well," says he, "I have to go now at last. To thravel the world," says he. "An' ye have no use in follyin' me, because ye'll never save me," says he. "For ye know yer father ruined me for the rest o' me life. So, farewell." So, "Yer not goin' 'ithout me," says she. I'll thravel wit' ye."

So, he brought her wit' him; an' they thravelled tell they came to a small house an the side o' the road. "Will ye g'win there," says he, "an' I'll sleep in the t'atch tell mornin'." "How can you," says she, "sleep in the t'atch, in undher the terrible weather an' storm?" "Oh," says he, "I have to do it. An' well ye know it." She went in anyways. An' when she went into the house there was a small baby an the floor; an' it run to her. An' she took it up in her arms.

So, she went out. An' whin she was goin' out, the woman gev her a rack. "Here's a rack," says she, "an' wherever ye go that'll be a friend to ye."

So, she went out the next mornin', an' she brought out milk an' bread. An' the bird flew out o' the t'atch; an' she gev him the milk an' bread.

So, they set out; an' they thravelled along, tell the night took the day an' the day took the night, tell they came to another little house an the side o' the road, an' they went in. An' sittin' an the table was another little baby. An' it ran over to the woman an' put its two hands round her, round the princes neck, the same as the child done in the follyin' house.

So, they came out in the mornin'; an' before she left, the woman gev her a scissors. "Here's a scissors," she says, "an' any-place ever ye go, this scissors'll prove a friend to ye."

So, she brought out a little bottle o' milk, also a bit of oaten bread to the bird that was in the t'atch. So, he flew out o' the t'atch.

So, they wint along, as far as I could tell you, or you could tell me, tell they came to another old woman's house an the side of a hill, an' she was a hundhert an' ten years of age. "Yer welkim," says she, "the princes' son from Ireland." So, she went in. An' she had a small little baby in her arms; an' it had only wan eye. (In th' old woman's arms.) "Oh, ma'am," says she, "I have an eye an' maybe it'd do." The very minnit she took the eye out o' the hankercher, it flew into the baby's eye, an' o' coorse, it was as good as ever. (She had it the whole time.)

So, the next mornin'; an' she goin' away. The bird slep' in the t'atch that night, as useval; she brought out a bottle o' milk an' a piece of oaten bread. The bird flew out o' the t'atch an' she gev him the milk as useval, an' also the bread.

So, when she was goin', the woman gev her a needle. "Here's a needle," she says, "an' wherever ye go, it'll prove a friend to ye." So, she gev her a needle.

An' as soon as ever she came out: "Fare you well, I can't stay no longer. I have to go." So, off flies the bird, an' she didn't know where to go to.

She kep' wandherin' hills, dales, an' mountains tell she came as far as the Red Sea. An' when she came as far as the sea, she sat down; an' she began to cry; an' she didn't know where to go. An' she started to take out the rack that the woman gev her, an' to rack her head. As soon as she did, the rack fell from her hand an' tipped the sea. An' as soon as it did, the grandest walk that ever was seen, be the sight o' man or woman, was acrass the sea. So she started to walk the sea, acrass the path that the rack had med; an' the far side of it there was nothin', only glassy mountains.

She didn't know how she'd get over the Glassy Mountains. So, the same as useval, she thried the scissors an the Glassy Mountains. An' as soon as ever it was, the Glassy Mountain disappeared, an' left nothin'; only an open plain for her to walk through.

She kep' over hills, dales, an' mountains, an' the last place she came to was an old mud-wall cabin an the side of a hill. As soon as ever she came, a bird flew out o' the t'atch an' flew on before her, 'cause she knew it was her own bird. So, she slep' in the house that night.

An', next mornin', she came as far until she came to the Firey Mountain. How to get over the Firey Mountain she didn't know, for between the smoke an' the fire, they were baetin' her back for yards. So, she takes the needle in her hand an' she starts to scrape round the fire; an', as soon as ever she did, the fire dies down, an' left nothin' but the loveliest walk that ever was seen, tell she got through the fire.

So, she came an to a big giant's castle upon the side of a hill; an' also a small little house convaenient to the house, where there lived an' old woman. So, she sat behind the house. An' out comes out o' the house, a young girl, an' she all raggety an' torn, for a cleeve o' turf. "Who lives in there?" says the woman. "Oh, who lives in there only an ould witch," says she. "An' she has everyone in this counthry bewitched." "Come here " says the woman, "tell I cut the thrimmin' off yer dhress." As soon as ever she put the scissors to it, she left a suit o' silk an her, walkin' into the house.

An' when she goes into the house, says th'old witch, "Where did ye get that beautiful suit," says she. "Oh," says she, "I got it from a poor woman 'ithout there at the back o' the house." "Tell that woman," says she, "what does she want for that scissors." So, out comes the servant. "Me misthress sent me out to tell her – to aks ye what'll ye take for the scissors." "Tell her," says she, "wan sight o' me husband." "Tell her that she'll get," says she.

So, she comes in. An' before she let her in, she put the girl's husband asleep. So, she left her in the room, an' she went over to him; an' she started to say over her husband:

"Oh, Green Bull of Orange, turn unto me,
Three fine babes I bore for thee.
The Firey Mountains I crossed for thee,
Roarin' Bull of Orange, return to me."
So, he was asleep an' he couldn't return.

So, the next mornin', whin she got up, she was at the loss of her scissors; an' th' oul' witch kicked her out to the same place. So, there was a worksman in the house an' he tould the princess the next day about the woman that was talkin' over him all night:

"Oh, Green Bull of Orange, turn unto me.
Three fine babes I bore to thee.
The Firey Mountains I crossed to thee,
Oh, Roarin' Bull of Orange, return to me."
"Oh," says he, "I d'know who it could be. It couldn't – y' only dreamed it," says he. "Oh, I didn't," says he. "Waken tonight an' ye'll know it."

The next day, another girl went out for a cleeve o' turf, to where the woman was sittin' at the clamp o' turf. "Come here, *agrádh*," says she, "tell I rack yer head." An' the very minnit the rack went near her, it turned into the loveliest head o' curls that ever was seen or known. "Where did ye get the lovely head o' curls, Ashy Pet?" says th'oul' woman. "I got it from a poor woman out there at the clamp o' turf," says she. "G'out an' aks her what'll she take for the rack," says she. So, she went out. "Me misthress sint me out, ma'am," says she. "What'll ye take for the rack?" "Tell her," says she, "wan sight to see o' me husband alive." So, she goes in an' tould her. "She says she'll gi'e ye the rack i' ye let her see wan sight o' her husband." "Tell her that she'll 'get," says she. So, she wint out an': "Me misthress tould ye come in ma'am," she says.

So, as the night before she had her husband dhrugged, an' also asleep. So, she stands over her husband an' she says:

"Oh, Green Bull of Orange, will ye turn unto me?
Three fine babes I bore to thee.
The Firey Mountains I crossed for thee,
Oh, Roarin' Bull of Orange, return to me."

So, the man came the next day an' he tould him. "The woman was wit' you last night, an' she's someone belongin' to ye, for she's sayin' the same words over an' over: "Roarin' Bull of Orange turn unto me." "She must be someone belongin' to ye," says the man. "Oh, no," he says, "it can be nobody belongin' to me." "You must think of yourself," says the man, "or else when she comes to you at night she drugs ye or puts you to sleep. But if she comes to you tonight an' gives ye an'thin' to dhrink, don't dhrink it. Pretind to dhrink it, but throw it wan side an' I'll take it away. For in the dhrink there'll surely be somethin' to make ye sleep, an' she'll surely be here tonight." "All right," says he, "I'll watch out."

So, the next day, another girl went out to the clamp for a cleeve o' turf; an' at the clamp was a woman, an' she cryin'. When this girl came out, she was raggedy an' torn; far worse than either of th' others. So, she goes over an' she aksed her to put a stitch in her dhress; an' the very minnit she touched her wit' the needle she had the loveliest suit that was ever seen be th' eyes of man or woman before.

So, she goes in wit' her lovely suit o' silk to th' ould witch. "Where did ye get that beautiful suit?" says she. "I got it," she says, "from a lovely lady that's out there. "Tell her," she says, "what does she want for that needle she has." So, she goes out, an' she says, "Wan sight more to see of her husband." "All right," she says. "Tell her that she'll get."

So, she went up to the room where he was an' she brought him up a dhrink. "Oh," she says, "you're very sick an' you'll have to take this dhrink." "Oh, I'm not able," says he. "But you'll have to," says she. So, he pretended he was takin' it; an' when he got her back turned, he threw it wan side. So, she thought he dhrank it, an' she brought down the mug. An' she came up in half an hour to see was he asleep. An' she burned the soles of his feet wit' a candle an' also his eyes to see would he waken; an' she reddined irons an' put them to the soles of his feet, but still he kep' still.

So, she let in the wife. "Now ye can come in to see him," says she. So, she came in; an' she stood over him; an' she said:

"Oh, Roarin' Bull of Orange, turn unto me.
Three fine babes I bore to thee.

The Firey Mountains I crossed for thee,
  Oh, Green Bull of Orange, return to me."
So, he wokened up. "Ye follit me so far," says he, "an' now there's worse goin' to happen us. This woman," says he, "has the whole counthry bewitched; an' she can turn you into any shape or form she likes. But I want," says he, "to find out where her life lies."

So, this day, he goes out into the garden; an' he aksed th' oul' witch where did her life lie. "It lies undher that three," says she. So, he went an' he planted some o' the loveliest flowers that ever was seen, undher the three.

So, when she seen him plantin' the flowers, she thought that he loved her; an' she says, "My life does not lie there, but it lies 'ithin in the hearth stone." So, he went in an' began polishin' the hearth stone, an' coverin' it wit' all sorts of ornaments.

So, when she found out that he loved her so much, she says: "My life does not lie there." She says: "My life lies in that three, at the brink of the field. An' in that three there is a nest, an' there's a bird in the nest that has to be shot. An' when that bird is shot, my life is no more." "Righto!" says he. So, he goes down to the three an' he planted flowers around it; but he brought his wife along with him. "An also," says she, "there's an egg in the nest; an' it's wit' that egg I have to be hit; hit in the forehead, before my enchantments are broke."

So, he goes down to the three the next day — himsel' an' the servant man, an' he brought a gun with him — an' started to set flowers around it. His wife was sittin' in the same place at the turf-rick. So, the very first shot he let, the bird flew out o' the three an' he dropped her on the spot. An', as he did, the man was climbin' the three. So, she was comin' down the field in a terrible rage, wit' a green rod in her hand to turn everyone that was in Ireland into serpents an' all classes of things, when he got the egg. He fired it from the three an' sthruck her in the forehead; an' she fell down in a heap o' sand upon the ground.

So, when he came back to the castle (instead of an ould hen woman's house it was a beautiful castle was in it), the three servant girls that was in it was three king's daughthers that was bewitched. An', also, they were tippin' stones; an' everyone they tipped was either a king's son or a king's daughther.

So, the three small cottages along the road where they seen the three childher, was three o' the loveliest castles goin'. An' also the three babies was in them. The Ramblin' Baker was one of the finest lords in that counthry; an' also the Man from No Man's Land, he was a king's son. They were seven years goin' about the counthry turnin' everythin' into its own shape an' form.

So, he came back an' got marrit to his wife again, they weren't marrit right. Still an' all, she follit him through the Glassy Mountains an' everytime she'd lay down to rest she was always sayin':

"Oh, Green Bull of Orange, return unto me.

Three fine babes I bore to thee.

The Firey Mountains I crossed for thee,

Oh, Roarin' Bull of Orange, return to me."

So, in place of the bird he was, he was wan o' the grandest kings in the counthry. The whole counthry was a grand counthry.

So, they put down the kittle an' med tay. An' if they don't live happy, that we may.

Opposite — Woman drinking from a "ponnie" or handmade tin mug at the fire inside a shelter tent. Roomy shelter tents can seat up to fifteen adults gathered around the central fire.

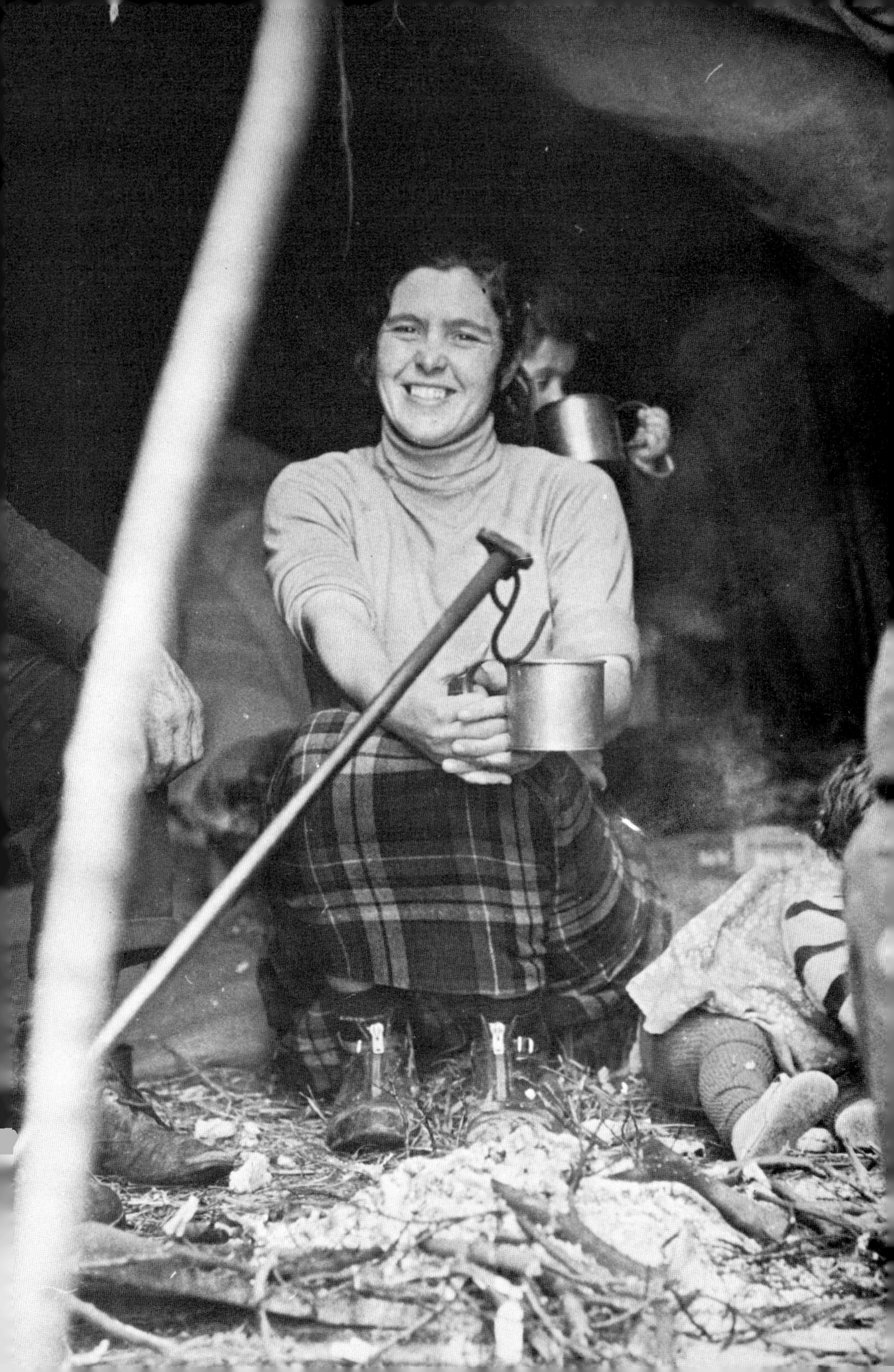

The Wonderful Sword

WANCE UPON A TIME, an' 'twas nayther my time nor your time, but 'twas somebody's time, there lived an' ould man an' woman in Ireland. They had wan only son, an' his name was Jack. All the work he used to do was fishin' an' huntin'. He could get no other work to do, for Ireland was very bad with landlords then.

So, this day, he was sittin' along wit' his father an' mother at the fireside an' he med up his mind he'd go to seek his forkin. He med up his mind, anyhow, that he'd build a house that'd do his father an' mother while he'd be away.

So, he goes to the King an' he aksed him for as much timber as'd build a house that'd do his father an' mother while he'd be away seekin' his forkin. So, the King tould him go to the wood an' take as much timber as he'd leck. So, he went to the wood an' he acted greedy. For he was such a wondherful sthrong man, that he brought every three that was nearly in the wood. So, whin the King came the next mornin' an' seen all his fine timber gone, he was terrible angry wit' Jack, the widda woman's son, for desthroyin' all his fine timber.

So, he built the house for his father an' mother. An' when he had it well built, he wint back to the King an' aksed him for as much sthraw as'd t'atch his father's house. So, the King forgot all about the day before an' the timber. So, he tould him go out to the haggard an' take as much sthraw as he wanted. An' he bein' such a wondherful sthrong man, he run a tedthers round the whole haggard an' brought it an his back.

So, whin he had his father's house t'atched, he said he'd go seek his forkin. The father had only wan shillin' in the house an' he gev it to him goin' an his journey.

So, he goes as far as I could tell you or you could tell me, an' that was a long distance; so he comes to the city o' London. (He goes to London, I meant to say.) So, he tossed up the shillin': whether he'd dhrink it or aet it. So, the tossin' was in it, the shillin' fell into a grate. So the shillin' couldn't be got.

So, he was walkin' up an' down, sobbin' an' cryin', whin an officer came over to him; an' he aksed him what he was cryin' for. He tould him that he tossed up a shillin', whether he'd dhrink it or aet it; an' that it fell into a grate; an' the shillin' couldn't be got. "Well," says th' officer. "I'll gi'e ye a shillin', if ye go with me." "Righto," says he, "I'll go." But 'twas little he knew what he gev him the shillin' for: 'twas to jine the army.

So, when he gev him the shillin', he jined the army, anyways; an' he was in the army for manys a year. So, wan day – he was in the army – says his officer to him: "We're goin' an a route march tomorra, an' this king has a great lady in pres'n, an' the first man that frees her, she has to marry him." "Righto," says he, "I'll take the job."

So, he went along wit' his army the next day an' he came as far as the giant's castle. The giant came out to him. He said he wanted to see his daughther. "Before ye get my daughther," he says, "ye'll fight for her." "Well, that I can do," he says. So, they fought, anyway. They fought with the knuckles, tell they med the hard ground soft an' the soft ground hard, tell they brought the spring-wells from undher the green grass. So, the king gev into him; an he gev him his daughther.

So, he got his daughther an' he marrit her. An' afther the marriage, he sint a terrible lot o' money home to his own father an' mother.

So, they were livin' in that counthry for a long time – they were livin' in London, an' Jack died. No, no, they had wan only son; an' the father, Jack, died, an' the son an' the mother was livin' alone in London for a long time. So, they were livin' there alone so long that the son got fed up an' said he'd go an' live in a sthrange counthry. So, they wint out to the wilds iv Indin to live.

So they wint, an' wan day they wor walkin' along the road an' the young kid found a soord. An' it was wrote upon the soord: "The man that wears me'll conquer the world." So, he was lookin' at the soord; an' the lookin' he had at it, he cut his hand wit' it. Says the mother: "I always tould ye not to be intherfaerin' wit' an'thin' that doesn't belong to ye, or an'thin' ye'd find an the road that'd do ye harm." "Never mind, mother," says he, "it'll be all right." So, he left down the soord an' he wint an further. Whin he a few yards further, he found a belt; an' what was wrote an the belt. "If the belt fits ye, go back for the soord." So, he put the belt an him, an' before he had it round him, it clinged in to his waist. So, he goes back for the soord. An' before he was tin yards from the soord, the soord flew into its scabbard.

So, they wint along, anyhow; an' they wor very lonely. An' they came to a small cottage; an' it decorated wit' all colours o' flowers. So, he riz the latch, an' he walked in. An' there was a table on the flure covered wit' all classes of aetin' an' dhrinkin' that ever ye could make mintion of. "Now, mother," says he, "afore y'aet an'thin', I'll taste everythin' that's an the table; an' if it p'izens me, you'll be safe." He tasted everythin' an' it didn't do him any harm. So, they sat down an' they had a wondherful fine dinner. So, they remained there for five or six days. An' every mornin', whin they got up, the table was always full iv all classes iv aetin' an' dhrinkin'.

So, wan day, he wint out huntin': he was very fond iv huntin' an' fishin', leck the father. An' when he was gone, a black giant appeared to his mother; so he fell in love wit' her. So, they wanted to do away wit' Jack, the two of 'em, th' way the black giant could have the mother in marriage. They didn't know how to do away wit' him so long as he held the soord o' the world; an' he was as sthrong as a thousand as long as he had the soord at his waist.

So, wan day, he came back; an' the mother tould him she was very sick, but 'twas only pertendin', the way she'd get shut of him. So, he aksed her what'd cure her. She said there was only wan thing in the world'd cure her, an' that was an apple that grew in a certain giant's garden. He didn't know where it was, but he wint in search iv it anyways. An' he thravelled as far as I could tell you, or you could tell me, tell he came an to a small cottage house an the road. So, he aksed the woman where did the Giant of No Man's Land live, an' she p'inted out a castle an top iv a hill.

So, he goes for the castle. An' when he came to the gate, there was about forty soldiers guardin' it. So, he aksed for the wondherful apple, but they tould him he'd have to fight for it. So, he dhrew his wondherful soord; an' he fought thim tell the night took the day an' the day took the night; an' he killed thim all.

So, he goes up an' he knocked at the hall dure. An' a giant came out to him wit' two heads; an' he aksed him what did he require. He said he required nothin' only an apple in the garden for his mother that was dyin'. He said he couldn't get th' apple tell he'd fight for it.

So, they fought. An' before they fought, he brought out a sheaf o' soords to Jack. "Pick any o' thim ye leck," he says. So, Jack thried thim all; an' none o' thim'd suit. He put down his hand to his belt an' he found his own soord there. "The soord I have'll do me good enough," he says. So, they fought tell the night took the day; an' Jack cut the two heads off the giant. An' they were comin' back again, whin Jack hit them wit' his lift hand an' knocked them away. "Well done, Jack," says they. "Good luck to you, but bad shoes to y'r advisers."

So, he gets the apple an' brought it back home to his mother. The next day he was out huntin'. An' the black giant came. "It's no use," says he, "ye'll have to sind him the third time to that castle before he's killed."

So, the next day, they sint him for an herb was growin' in the garden; an' if that herb was got, it'd cure the mother in three days.

So, he wint for th' herb; an' as many soldiers as was an the gate before, the day before, there was twice as many the next day. So he fought, an' he never left a guard in it, but he killed.

So, he knocked at the hall dure. An' in place of a giant wit' two heads, it was a giant wit' three heads that opened it. "Oh, y'r welcome, Jack, the widda woman's son from Ireland," says he. "What d'ye want?" "I came for an herb that's in the garden," says he. "Me mother is very sick; an' if th' apple didn't cure her, this might." "Well, ye'll fight for that herb," says he. "That I can do," says Jack. So, they fought until they med the soft ground hard an' the hard ground soft, an' tell they brought the spring-wells undher the green grass, an' Jack defeated him.

So, whin he had him be't, he got the herb. An' he goes back to his mother, an' he gev it to her.

So, he goes out huntin' the next day. An' the black giant appears to the mother; an' he says: "You'll have to sind him again, the third time," says he; "an' if he's not killed this time, he'll never be killed," says he.

So, they sint him the next day for a well that was in the King's garden — for a bottle o' the wather, it'd cure any disease that ever was in the wide world; an' there was twenty li'ns guardin' it, an' all sorts of other beasts.

So, he went to the giant's castle the next day, an' he kilt all the soldiers that was guardin' it wit' his wondherful soord. So, he wint an' he knocked at the hall dure. So, the giant came an' opened it;

an' says he: "Yer welkim, Jack, the widda woman's son from Ireland. What do ye want?" "I want a bottle o' wather from the well in the garden to cure me mother." "Will ye fight for it?" "That I can," says Jack. So, they fought; an' Jack won. He had him kilt forever, this time.

So, whin he had him well kilt he got the bottle o' wather an' put it in his pocket an' wint into the castle to see could he find an'thin' round it. So, every room he came into was full o' gold an' silver; an' other rooms was full o' nothin', only dead bodies. He came an to wan room, a small room to the back to the left hand side, an' he couldn't open it. He thried all plans, but 'twas all in vain: he couldn't open it; 'twas an iron dure. So, in the finish up, his soord tipped ag'in it, an' the dure flew in wit' a bang, an' from the ceilin' was hangin' a girl be the hair. This was the way the giants had to torture anyone that had a secret, to get the secret out o' them. So, he dhraws his soord an' cut the hair at the top an' caught her in his arms.

So, she began to cry, an' he gev her all the gold was in the castle to build an 'ospital the far side o' the sea. An' anyone that'd wave a white handkerchief on the brink of the sea, a boat'd come over an' take him over. "Thank you, Jack," she says, "an' how will I know you if I see ye ag'in?" "Well, th' only way ye'll know me is me handkerchief wit' me name an it; gi'me yours wit' your name an it. We may meet sometime."

So, he goes back to his mother wit' the bottle o' wather; an' he left the castle there to her. So, he came back an' gev her the wather. An' she said she was grand that day; she dhrank the wather. The next day, he was out an' the black giant came. "There's no way to get at him, only let you say he's to laeve off the soord, an' for you not to see it an him ag'in for it makes you sick; an' that's the way we'll get him."

So, whin he came in that night, he had the soord an; an' she got sick. "Oh, take off that soord," says she, "that's what makes me sick. I was often goin' to tell ye before, so I'm tellin' ye the truth now." "All right, mother," says he, "I'd do an'thin' in the world to plaese ye, even if I never wear the soord again." So, he took off the soord an' hung it an the wall an' wint off to bed. 'Twasn't long until the black giant came in an' took the sword; an' left poor Jack there at his mercy.

So, they wint up an' brought Jack down. Says the black giant: "What death'll we give him?" "We'll put out his eyes," says she "an' put him out in the forest for the wild bears an' other beasts t'aet him." "Hard enough, mother," says he, "afther all I done for you, still an' all, our Lord suffered more."

So, they took his eyes out an' put him out in the forest for the wild bears an' other animals t'aet him. Whin he was in the forest, in place of the wild animals aetin' him, they wor lickin' him an le'pin' an him leck a lot o' harmless dogs. So, he went through the forest for ages an' ages, an' his clothes began to get worn. He was just almost a year in the forst now but the wild beasts brought 'im everywhere. So, he tore the branches from the trees an' what weeds he could grope wit' his hands, ashamed anyone'd see 'im goin' through the forest. But no man could see 'im, for he was in the very heart of it — in the very heart of the forest — where no wan'd ever see him again. So, he was rovin' through the forest, an' lyin' behind the thrunks o' threes at night, in th'awful hard weather. An' every time he'd think iv his false-hearted mother an' the black giant, he said that they'd meet again.

So, wan day, afther two years in the forest, he came upon a plains. An' he knew it was a plains for he found wind, cold wind, blowin' upon his face. And the bears brought him to a river, as he thought himself. So, he dipped his hand in the wather an' he found the salty taste. So he knew he was near the sea.

So, he thought for a long time. An', at last, he thought of the vow he med to the girl a long time ago, whin he kilt the black giant in the castle an' gev her all the goold to build an 'ospital the far side o' the sea, an' anyone that waved a white handkerchief'd be brought over. So he had no handkerchief to wave or no clothes. So, he started to wave his hands an' waved tell they fell to his sides wit' the pure dint of wavin'. Afther a few hours, he heard terrible v'ices, an' he heard a few shots goin', so he knew they were near hand.

So, afther a long time, a boat dhruv into the shore. An' they flung him into it the same as they'd fling a dog; an' they dhrives him over. They dhruv him over to an 'ospital, he knew it was an 'ospital; an' he was in terrible pain from his eyes.

So, wan day, he was lyin' there an' a nurse came up to him. An' whin he wouldn't eat, she sthruck him across the face wit' her hand. So, he starts to cry because a woman hit him: he only wished it was a man. So, he started to rub his eyes wit' a handkerchief. (M'be I forgot he had it wit' him.)

So, puttin' the handkerchief to his eyes, he began to cry, an' the nurse, whin she seen the handkerchief, knew the handkerchief, wit' her name wrote an it. So, she threw her arms round his neck an' began to cry. An' she was terrible sarry for he was her true lover that saved her in the castle from the terrible giants.

So, she used to bring him out every day, walkin' through the groves. An' wan day, the father seen her; an' he started t'inquire could she get no man, only a blind man. "Never mind, father," says she. "He done me a good turn. 'Twas him that saved me from the black giant of the castle. 'Twas him that gave me all the gold to build a castle the far side o' the sea." But the father was terrible angry wit' her.

So, this day, they wor out walkin' through the forest; an' they wor passin' a small buryin' ground. An' undher a small whitethorn bush, there was a well, wit' a flag over it. An' a robin flew into the well wit' wan leg an' flew out wit' two. An' she up an' tells Jack the story about the robin flyin' in. "Bring me over," says he, "an' it might do somethin' for me eyes." She brings him over an' he dips his hand an' rubs it to his eyes; an' he had his eyesight as good as ever. An' as soon as ever he had his eyesight, he tould her the minnit he had it. She shouldn't b'lieve 'im, so she tied a white handkerchief round the fardest bush; an' he picked it out for her. The father put up a bird out of a three, so he shot it. The father thought he had glass eyes, but he hadn't. He had his real eyesight back again. The father tould him to come in; into the house, but he said he wouldn't: that he'd never sleep another night in a house tell he'd find the black giant an' his mother, an' also his wondherful soord an' belt.

So, he thravelled in search o' the belt (he never brought a ha'penny in his pocket) tell he came to London. An' when he came to London, his true love follit him wit' a bag o' gold. "Bring it wit' ye," she says, "ye might need it an the way." So, when he came to London, he bought a donkey an' got gold pots an' started thravellin' as a pedlar, th' ways he'd find his wondherful soord. So, he was years thravellin', anyway; he was nearly two years thravellin' London.

So, wan day, he was thravellin' an' he had three gold pots. An' a lady came out an' aksed him how much wor they. "Nothin'," says he, "tell ye see them an' fit them an the range." He knew his mother the very minnit she put her foot to the thres'ol' o' the dure; but she didn't know him, for she thought he was dead an' gone an' tore to pieces be the wild beasts o' the forest. He knew her, so he puts his arm in his breast an' pretended it was hurted an' that he couldn't carry in the pots. "Is yer husband inside?" "He's away," says she, "but he won't be five minnits."

So, the giant came back that very minnit; an' his own soord an' belt be his side. So, the black giant was very proud out o' the pots an' he said he'd buy three. So, he took the three. "Excuse me, sir," says he, "I'm not able to help ye carry in the pots, I got a hurt liftin' wan o' them off yesterday, an' I'm not able to carry them in." "Never mind, me poor fella, I'll carry them in mesel'. If ye just wait tell I laeve up me soord an' belt upstairs, I'll carry them in mesel'." "Thank you, sir," says he. An' as soon as he left up the soord an' belt, Jack met him an' threw him down the stairs. An' he was up the stairs an' had the soord an' belt an him in five minnits. So, he dhrew his sword an' cut the head o' the black giant. "Now, mother," says he, "I'm not goin' to thraet you the way you thraeted me. I lost me eyesight; but I got it ag'in, thanks be to God. But you may go an' thramp the world. An' this house, an' all that's in it, is for the poor o' London to live an. An' you go an' thravel the wide world, for ye'll never see me ag'in.

So, he goes back to his wife wit' his soord an' belt, an' th'ould father had to marry them over ag'in.

So, they put down the kittle an' med tae; an' if they don't live happy, that we may.

Part 3

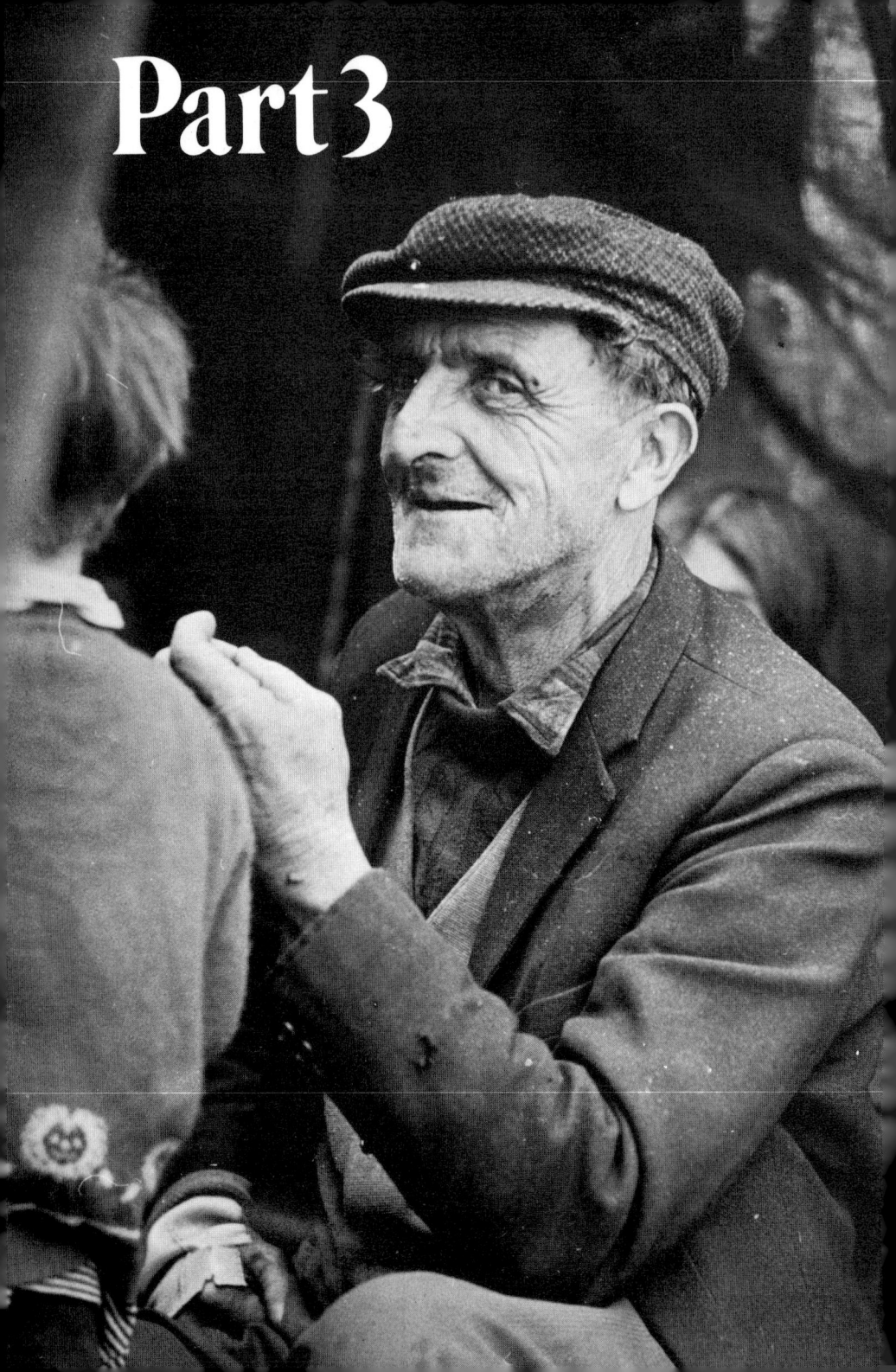

The Folktales of Mickey Greene

The following stories were told by Peter "Mickey" Green in 1972, two years before he died at the age of seventy-four. The collector, James G. Delaney, describes the storyteller in his diary and how they met.[1]

He is a man of middle height, of sturdy build, upright carriage, good features, and eyes full of merriment and good humour. He loves folktales above all things and would travel miles to hear a new one. When he was a young man there was an old woman living near him, whom he used to visit and ask to tell him a story. "I will," she'd say, "if you buy me a pint." Mickey would take the jug and off with him to the nearest pub for a pint of porter. He'd come back with it then and she would tell him a story... He has not told stories for many years and the first time he told one lately was in Mrs. Pat Redmond's house in Sarsfield Square,... Redmond's brother Colm Ó h-Iamáin was visiting there. Colm was so interested to hear a Fiannaíocht story in English that he told an t-Athair Eiric MacFhinn, who told Seán O'Sullivan, our archivist, who immediately sent me on Mickey's trail. Through the good offices of Mrs. Redmond, for whom Mickey has a great liking and respect, I was able to get into Mickey's good graces.

Mrs. Redmond on my first visit to her was very kind and affable and went off and fetched Mickey to her own house. He tried to tell a story then but was distracted by the comings and goings of children. Then I decided to bring him to my own home the next day and record there in peace and quiet. I have continued to do so every week and Mickey is now quite at home here with my wife and children.

Mickey Green was born and reared in Athlone, in Irishtown, a rough neighbourhood on the Leinster side of the Shannon. Like his father before him, Mickey was a dealer in ponies. Bought as yearlings, he trained the ponies and sold them for farmwork. He travelled the West of Ireland, particularly counties Roscommon, Mayo, and parts of Galway, trading and performing odd jobs. When the weather turned cold, he returned to Athlone and remained settled until the following Spring. During the winter months he cut firewood and sold it throughout the town. In his later years and after the demand for workhorses had declined, he worked in the bog, selling turf to townspeople. On occasion he cleaned chimneys, mended umbrellas, made bodhráns and whips from goat skin, and built an occasional cart or piece of furniture.

To more nomadic Travellers, Mickey Green was a "townie". In 1938, the Greens were housed together with a dozen other Traveller families in St. Mel's Terrace, Athlone. St. Mel's was built as part of a widespread government programme to eliminate the shacks and dilapidated dwellings then common in Irish towns. Housed together in the same terrace, none of the Traveller families in St. Mel's have lost their identity as itinerants, and St. Mel's today is looked upon as a "Tinker ghetto". Like many of the others there, Mickey locked up his house each spring and took to the roads.

A peaceful, good-humoured man, and a teetotaller, Mickey enjoyed nothing more than telling or listening to a good story. During his travels he often sought out local storytellers to hear their tales. His son, forty-five year old Larry Green, describes his father as a storyteller:[2]

> When he was telling a story you could almost picture it. You could visualize the whole thing yourself. You'd get that interested in 'em that you'd never think of anything else, just the stories. He'd bring you back, back into a generation that's gone past. Back into his time as a young man. He'd tell you a story like it happened yesterday... I often seen him, I'm not coddin' you, he'd start one story and go the whole night through. So he would!
>
> He was a very kind person. You know, if you were sick or anything, if your nerves was actin' up, if he thought you were worryin' or something, he'd tell you a story to take your mind off it. He'd bring you back to something that would make you happy. He wouldn't tell you ghost stories then, but stories that would bring you back to a happy time – thatched cottages, queens and kings, and all like that. So he would!

Shortly before Mickey Green died, he told his last story.

> He was sittin' in an old chair like this. He couldn't go upstairs because he was very badly gone and he was inclined to stay downstairs by the fire. He had this blackout, and I got word that he was gone so I went to him. The house was packed. Well, the old fella came to and he sees the house packed. He says to me, being half gone, "Larry, what's all the people here for?" I says, "They're here to hear you tell a story." "Well,"

he says to me, "Larry, there's too much talk going on and anyone who doesn't want to hear a story had better get outside the door." Now a man drawing his last, just as sure as I'm sittin' here! And 'clare to God, he was out of his mind on account of going — being ready for the bag. I says, "Stay quiet lads!" And he told the whole house a story, so he did. A story about a young fella who was too clever for his master, a real clever fella. I'm not coddin' you, the old fella told this story and how he told it being in the condition he was, I don't know. It was a great story — his last story.[3]

There was some exaggeration in Larry Green's description of his father's storytelling ability. While Mickey Green may have been an accomplished storyteller at one time, he was badly out of practice by the time his stories were recorded by James Delaney. Most noticeably, he tends to ramble and repeat himself. It should be noted, however, that Mickey Green was an excellent informant in other areas and had a tremendous knowledge of horses and horse dealing practices. Only two of Mickey Green's tales are included. Neither are of the same quality as those told by Oney or John Power. However, as one of the last Traveller storytellers his tales are valuable in their own right. They are among the last folktales recorded from Travellers by the Department of Irish Folklore and most likely represent the end of a tradition.

NOTES
1. Vol. 1795, pp. 485-486, in the archives of the Department of Irish Folklore, University College Dublin.
2. Recorded by G. Gmelch in Athlone, August 1977.
3. ibid.

The Four Kings of Ireland

WELL, THIS IS the story of the 'Fox Terrier Dog'. There was once upon a time, there was four kings in Ireland. An' those four kings was married, an' they had three daughters; three o' them had a daughter each. Well, anyway, the three girls grew up, so they did, to be sixteen or seventeen. An' didn't the giant come from the other world, part o' the world, an' took these three girls away? So, now!

Didn't... after the kings, the fathers, after their searchin' everywhere, for the daughters, they could get no account of them, didn't they call out their army, ye see, each o' them. An' they asked for any volunteers that'd go an' look for these three girls, an' get them. An' each o' them would give their daughters to whoever get them, save them, an' the weight o' theirselves o' money.

So, it happened to be, anyway, that Jack was in this Irish army an' didn't he step out, so he did. An', when he did, he had two comrades, d'ye see? An Englishman an' a Scotchman. An' didn't the two step out along with 'im, d'ye see? when they seen him steppin' out, as one out of each army.

Now! The three o' them, anyway, got together, so they did, an' they were supplied with plenty o' grub, arms; an' anything they wanted, they had it to get it. An' they could stay any time they liked, theirselves, so long as they came back with 'em.

Now! Off they started, anyway, so they did; an' after some time travellin' an' some weeks later, they landed at a Big House. An' landin' at this Big House, they went in an' had a look round, where they meant to sleep outside. An' they were havin' a great time drinkin' an' everything. So, didn't they go inside o' the house an' seen that there was no one livin' in it? They said: "Well, here's as good a place as any, to stay."

So, they st'ed here in this house; an' they used to go out wild fowlin', two o' them, each day. They used to take it on their turns for one to stay 'ithin an' cook the meals, for to have the dinner ready for th' others, when they'd come in. But, anyway, it happened to be, anyway, that the Englishman was cookin' the dinner this day, so he was. An' just as he had the dinner done, the Hairy Man o' the Forest came in. An' as he... The Hairy Man o' the Forest came in; an' himself an' the Englishman fought, so they did, over the dinner; till, finally, anyway, he put the Englishman down. He hoist' the dinner in under his arm an' off he started, an' et it.

When the other two came home, the two butties, for their dinner, d'ye see? there was no dinner for them. An' they were goin' to give th' Englishman another hidin': thought he et the dinners himself. Well, howan'ever, anyway, they got their own maels ready, the two o' them, an' went to bed that night.

An' next mornin', they got up again, an' it was the Scotchman's place, now, to stay 'ithin. So, the Englishman an' the Irishman went off, so they did, seekin' for all they could get in the line o' fowl. So, now, when they came back that evenin' again, the Little Hairy Man o' the Forest was after comin', so he was, an' baetin' the Scotchman, an' took the dinner.

So, Jack's turn, now, was the third day. So, Jack went to stay 'ithin the third day; an' he did stay 'ithin. So, Jack got ready the dinner. An' just as he had the dinner ready, he seen the Little Hairy Man o' the Forest, so he did, comin'. He never done anything, only stick a poker into the fire; an' when the Little Hairy Man o' the Forest came in, Jack had the poker ready.

He says, the Little Hairy Man o' the Forest, to Jack, he says: "Jack! Gi'me a bit o' the dinner."

"No!" says Jack, he says, "you're the boy that took'd our dinner," he says, "for the last two days; but you're not gettin' none o' this."

He says: "If ye don't give it to me, Jack," he says, "I'll half kill ye," he says, "an' I'll still aet the dinner!"

So, "No!" says Jack, he says. "Ye'll aet none o' this," he says to 'im, "as long as I'm here."

So, anyway, himself an' Jack got into the fight, the Little Hairy Man o' the Forest. An' didn't they fight for all they were worth?

But the Little Hairy Man o' the Forest was gettin' the better o' Jack, until Jack be thought of himself. Didn't he pull the poker out o' the fire? An' stickin' it in the lower part of his back, didn't he laeve the poker stuck in? An' away with the Hairy Man, so he did, account o' the iron bein' so red. He went off runnin'. An' away with Jack after the Little Hairy Man. An' he followed the Little Hairy Man till he came to a rock. An' when the Little Hairy Man came to this rock, he says:

"Open! Open! Rock! An' let the Little Hairy Man o' the Forest down!" So, the Rock opened up; an' the Little Hairy Man o' the Forest came down.

Now, Jack returned back to the buildin' again. An' when he turned back to the buildin', his two butties was 'ithin, were aetin'.

He says to the two butties: "Now!" he says, "I've found out," he says, "who gev ye the hidin'," he says, "an' who's takin' our dinners," he says. "An' it'd be about time," he says, "that we'd start after 'im," he says.

So, he up an' he told the Englishman, he says: "Well," he says, "what sort of a trade...? Are you....? Are ye any good," he says, "at makin' a rope?"

So, th' Englishman said he could make the rope. An' he got th' other, Scotchman, to make a tub. He says: "Well, I'll make the windlass," he says.

So, they made as much rope as would go for miles around, so they did. An' they brought it over; an' he made the windlass. An' they brought a bucket that he had, for to let them down; an' brought it over this rock. An' Jack says: "Now, we'll draw lots," he says, "to see who'll go down."

So, it was the Scotchman's place to go down. "Now!" says Jack, he says to 'im, "when you get tired," he says, "an' want to come up, chuck the rope," he says, "an' we'll pull you up," he says.

So, down goes the Scotchman, anyway, down in the rock. An' he went down, so he did; it would be around a couple o' mile. An' he chucked the rope; an' they pullt 'im up.

The Englishman's turn was next. He got in; an' they went down twice as far. An' he chucked the rope; an' they pullt him up. So, Jack says: "Now, when I get in," he says, "let that rope go," he says. "An', wherever it goes," he says, "let it go to the end," he says, "one way or another. But," he says, "meet me here in a year an' a day," he says, "at the mouth o' this rock," he says, "when I come back. If I'm alive," he says, "I'll return here."

So, didn't Jack land out below in another world? An' when he landed out in another world, where did he go? An' the first place he seen was a forge. An' in with it to 'im. He went into the forge. An' when he went into the forge, who was pullin' the bellows in the forge but the Little Hairy Man? An' when the Little Hairy Man seen 'im, he got afeared o' Jack, so he did. An' Jack says: "Sure, I'm not goin' to nail ye," he says to 'im. He says: "Ye needn't be afeared o' me," he says, "I'm not goin' to nail ye."

But Jack was walkin' away out o' the forge, an' the Little Hairy Man o' the Forest called 'im back. An' he says: "Jack!" he says, "take this poker," he says, "out o' my back," he says to 'im. An', he says, "If you take the poker out o' my back," he says, "I'll be your underservant 'ithin an' 'ithout," he says. "An' any time," he says, "ye want me," he says, "ye'll always have me for aksin'."

"How am I goin' to get ye?" says Jack, he says to 'im.

He says: "Here's a ring, an' all is you're to do is rub the ring," he says, "an," he says, "all is you've to shout is: 'Help! Help! Little Hairy Man o' the Forest!' an' ye'll have me beside ye," he says.

"All right!" says Jack. "Turn around!" Jack pullt the poker out of his back, anyway. An' off he started, lookin' for the girls. An' the Hairy Man gev him the ring before he went. He went on, anyway, so he did, for some time, travellin' for months, when he came across this Copper Castle. An' when he came across this Copper Castle, d'ye see! he was tolt that the girl was in it.

He went in, anyway, so he was; an' this Giant wasn't in at the time. So, he got into chat with the girl an' told (D'ye see?) her that he wanted to bring her back to her father, an' all this; that he came to save her. An' the girl was agreeable enough, so she was.

Now! Didn't the Giant come along, anyway, an' he says to Jack, he says: "Well," he says.

When Jack came in...

An' when the Giant came in, he says to Jack, he says: "What d'ye want," he says, "here? Or what brought ye here?" he says.

He says: "I came," says Jack to 'im, "for this girl," he says, "as I intend to marry 'er," he says.

"Well," says the Giant, he says, to 'im. "Ye'll have to fight me for her!" "That I'll do!" says Jack.

So, Jack an' himself fought, anyway. An', at the long run, they were fightin', so they were, for all their worth, with two swoords, till a bright spring rise up a' through the green rocks; an' that the whole place be all covered with blood. An' Jack, anyway, took the head of 'im, so he did. Now, Jack went in; an' he searched a' through the house, so he did; an' he got a pair o' shoes, that the like o' them was never seen in this world, or the world before. An' he fit them on 'imself. So, they fitted him, so he did, put them in a parcel, put them in his pocket. He says to the girl, he says: "You stay here, now!" he says. "An' I'll call for you," he says, "on me way back," he says.

So, didn't the girl tell her where the next Castle was? D'ye see? She knew it from the other Giant. He was another brother of his.

Now, when he landed at the second Giant's place... after some time travellin', didn't he land at the Giant's place? An' when he landed there, he seen the girl inside. So, the Giant was out, as usual, again, so he was; whatever he was doin'. An' Jack came along, so he did, an' he went in, so he...

When he went in, anyway, the girl gave him a feed. An' he remained there, so he did, until the Giant came. An' when the Giant came ag'in, he asked him what brought him there, how did he get there, so he did: that he wasn't goin' to go out of it alive; that he was goin' to have his life. An' this Giant had two heads on 'im.

So Jack, anyway, an' the Giant, started in to fight over the girl (D'ye see?) when he told 'im that he wanted the girl. An' the two o' them fought again, so they did, for hours. Every clout that the Giant was givin' Jack, he was drivin' him, so he was, to his knees, in the ground, with a swoord. An' every clout that Jack was givin' the Giant, he was drivin' 'im to his shoulders in the ground. But, finally, anyway, Jack managed to get off a head, so he did.

Now, after Jack gettin' off the head off o' the Giant, one o' the heads o' the Giant, the Giant begin to get fresher an' was playin' around with Jack for all he was worth with his swoord.

When Jack thought of himself, that he was too good for 'im, he says.... he rubbed the ring, an' when he rubbed the ring, he says: "I'm the Janius in that ring. What d'ye want, Jack?" he says: "Help! Help! Little Hairy Man o' the Forest!"

So, the Little Hairy Man o' the Forest came. An' between Jack an' the Little Hairy Man o' the Forest, they took th' other head off. Now, when they took th' other head off the Giant, after killin' 'im, they looked out in the field; an' they seen where cattle was goin' to their belly in aul' slush an' things, goin' across the *ceis* that was broke down. So, they dragged the carcase id the giant over, an' made a good bridge for the cattle to walk across.

When they done this, Jack came back again, so he did, an' into the girl; an' told her to stay, that he was goin' to look for the third one. So, he got ready again the next day; an' off he goes again for the third one.

An' when he came to the third one, it was a gold castle; so he did. An' he was just goin' in, so he was, the dure, when the giant came along, an', as usual, says to 'im: "You're the vinnagin little cur!" he says, "who came," he says, "here," he says, "from th' other world," he says, "to kill my two brothers. But, believe me, for it, ye won't kill me!" he says to 'im.

So, this giant had three heads on 'im. But, be hoppin' an' trottin', anyway, Jack seen that he had no change iv 'im; an' didn't he call upon the Little Hairy Man o' the Forest again? with the ring, so he did. An' when he got the Little Hairy Man o' the Forest, the two o' them was hoppin' around 'im. But, finally, they took the head of 'im; an' Jack too, another one, so he did.

Now, the giant had only one head. An', this time, Jack med a swipe at his head, so he did, an' for to take the third one off; an' he just missed 'im, when the Little Hairy Man o' the Forest cut it off with the swoord; an' it went up in th' air. An', as it went up in th' air, 'twas comin' right down upon the shoulders again. But the Little Hairy Man o' the Forest put up his swoord, an' caught it on the top o' the swoord. An' the head he held said to the Little Hairy Man o' the Forest: "Well done!" he says, "Little Hairy Man o' the Forest," he says. "If that head had to get upon them shoulders again," he says, "neither you nor Jack'd take it off," he says to 'im.

So, Jack, anyway, went off, so he did. An' he got the girl; an' he start' collectin' the girls, an' left 'em all the money that they wanted, an' brought them back to the mouth o' the hole. Now, himself an' the Little Hairy Man o' the Forest was at the mouth o' the Hole. An' he was afraid to put up the Little Hairy Man o' the Forest in the bucket, to put 'im up to th' other world, in case that he wouldn't take the girls up, or go off with 'em, d'ye see? An' he was afraid to leave them behind, to laeve 'im behind an' put up the three girls.

So finally, anyway, he med up his mind, that he'd put the Little Hairy Man o' the Forest up (D'ye see?) first, to receive the girls.

Now, he put 'im up first, so he did, to receive the girls. An'

Jack put up the girls, one after another, so he did, up in the bucket. Now, when they put the bucket last up — the last girl up in the bucket — didn't the bucket forget to come back for Jack? An' Jack lay asleep, so he did, at the mouth o' the hole till the crows o' the country had nearly every bit o' flesh that was on 'im, tore off 'im.

But, after a time, anyway, the two butties came back lookin' for 'im, d'ye see? An' when the two butties came back lookin' for Jack, they didn't know he was there, but he tolt 'em, d'ye see? So, bedad, anyway, didn't they let down the bucket? An' didn't Jack come up? An' when Jack came up, anyway, d'ye see? out o' the hole, he wanted to know from his two butties where was the girls. An' they didn't see them.

So, the Little Hairy Man o' the Forest had them, anyway, an' gev' 'em to three more fellows, so he did, to bring back, an' say that they were after fightin' for them; d'ye see? An' that they won them.

Now, it went on all right, anyway, till Jack went back, an his butties. An' when Jack went back an' his butties, t'd the King, Jack claimed (D'ye see?) that he was after doin' the fightin' an' all for these three girls; an' that he brought them back; an' how he lost 'em. So, no one'd believe them.

"Well," says Jack, "I'll tell ye so," he says, "I will," he says. He says: "If it's a thing," he says, "that them is the three min," he says, "that saved these three girls," he says. He says: "Let them place," he says, "the castles that they were in, here," he says, "over ground, in the way they were in them," he says. "An' let them place the giants," he says, "that they were fightin'," he says, "at the same time," he says.

An' the aul' King stepped out, he says: "Are you able to do it?" he says. "I am," he says, "if they're able to do it," he says to 'im. So, he: "Ask thim first." So, he did ask them. They worn't able to do it! He says: "Nayther are you!" he says. "Yes," says Jack, "I'll do it."

So, Jack rubbed the ring an' he got the Little Hairy Man o' the Forest. D'ye see? An' the ring says: "I'm the Janius," he says, "o' the ring," he says. "What d'ye want?"

He says: "I want these castles," he says, "with these girls in it," he says, "as I found them. An' I also want the giants," he says, "to be comin' in," he says, "an' show," he says, "who's fightin' them," he says, "an' who saved these girls."

So: whole thing was retold over again about the fight an' all, an' about who it was.

So, the King gev' them to Jack, the three girls, to give th' other two to whoever he liked. So, he gev one each to the two butties, so he did. An' Jack got married to the girl; an' they got a castle built for theirselves in a different place.

So, the two o' them got married.

So, they put down the kittle, an' they made tae; an' if they don't live happy, that we may!

I think I drank a sup o' that tae.

Often, older children would have to help out in the nursing of a 'new arrival'.

The Little Blue Bonnet

THERE WAS ONCE upon a time, an' a very good time it was, when there was an' old king an' his wife; an' they had one daughter. An' the old Queen was dyin'. An' when she was... Before she died, she call' in the daughter; an', she says:

"Now, daughter!" she says, "in case your father'd get married again," she says, "I want to laeve a request to him," she says. "An'," she says, "He'll do it; for me."

She says: "But the whole thing," she says, "lies with you."

"An' what is it, mother?" says the daughter.

She says: "As long," she says... "I'll make a request to him," she says, "an' tell 'im: as long as I remain in the grave, an' that he doesn't see a blade o' grass growin' over my grave, that he won't get married till he does. An' here's a little penknife," she says to the daughter, "for you. An'," she says, "you'll go to the grave," she says, "an' you'll make sure every day," she says, "that ye won't laeve a blade o' grass," she says, "growin' in the grave. An' then he can't get married, as long as you do that."

So, anyway, after some time, the Queen died. An' after that ag'in, the girl start' goin', so she did, every day, t'd the grave. An' it wasn't very long after, so it wasn't, her startin' to go to the grave, when a woman seen her, an' up an' told the King about it. She says to 'im:

"How can you get married?" she says, "an' how can grass," she says, "grow over a grave," she says, "when your daughter is pluckin' it with a knife?" she says to 'im.

So, the King didn't believe it first.

"Well," she says, "Watch 'er! An' you'll see," she says, "that she's pluckin' the grass off the grave."

So, the King hid himself in a place in the graveyard behind a tombstone an' watched the daughter. An' on comes the daughter, not knowin' that the King was in it, the father was in it. An' she start pluckin' the grass. An' didn't the King walk over to 'er? He says to her, he says:

"What are you doin'?"

"She says: "I'm only claenin'," she says, "me mother's grave."

He says: "You're pluckin' the grass of it!"

"Well," she says, "isn't that claenin' it?" she says to 'im.

He says: "That won't do," he says, "G'wan!"

He says: "Laeve it alone!"

So, be hell, anyway, didn't they come home.

Now, he sent for a Grand Adviser to see what he was goin' to do with the daughter. So, the Grand Adviser came an' told him to go out an' kill the largest bullock he had into the place an' to take the maw out of it. (That'd be his stomach, we'll say, so it would.) An' to put the girl into it an' sew her up; peg her into the sea; an' let her sink or swim; go wherever she liked.

So, accordin' to the talk, didn't they kill the bullock an' took the maw out of it; put the girl into it an' sewed it up; an' put her into the sea; an' let her float, or sink or swim. So, bedad, the girl floated, anyway, so she did, along, so she did, for a time. An' she was nearly exhausted in the vael, so she was, belongin' to the bullock. An' she was afeared to cut it. She had a little knife that the mother gev her, the one for pluckin' the grass, wud 'er. An' she afeared to cut it; afeared that she might sink an' be drowned.

So, she was goin' along; an' a short time after, didn't she feel herself hittin' against something like stone an' land? But, howan'ever, anyway, she seemed to be in the one spot. Caught. An' she says:

"God direct me!" she says, "whether I'll cut this vael or not," she says. So, be hell, anyway, didn't...eh... She took courage an' she cut the top o' the vael. An' she got out her head an' looked around. An' she was just on the brink o' the land, where she couldn't float. So, she got out o' the vael. An' when she got out o' the vael, she start walkin', lookin' around, to see where was she: did she know it? But she didn't.

But, be hell, anyway, didn't she see this big aul' place; buildin's? An' she went over to it an' start' wanderin' through it, a rael condemned lookin' place, in trees. She went in through every room that was in it. There was no one in it. An' she says:

"I'll have to stay here for a time until I find out where I am." She remained here, now, so she did, for a time.

So, she was out walkin', so she was, anyway, one early bright night, an' there was a saet in the garden, so there was, outside. An' she was... start' sittin' down. An' shortly after she sittin' down, there did a rael white pigeon fly beside 'er. An' she start pettin' the pigeon an' rubbin' it down. So, finally, anyway, before the pigeon went, she up an' she told her she was her mother, so she did. An' as she was.

"Now," the mother says. "You better," she says to 'er, "stuff every little hole," she says, "that's around this house," she says. "An' don't laeve a hole in it," she says. "Because," she says to 'er, she says, "there's wolfs here," she says. "An'," she says, "they'd aet ye!"

(Here's someone comin'.)

An' the mother went with her, t'd the house, herself. An' herself an' the daughter start' pluggin' the holes, for all they were worth, around the place. So, anyway, the mother had to go away. An' she told her she'd come back the followin' day to see her; what way she got on.

But that night, anyway, late in the night, didn't the wolfs come? An' they tried to get in. An' the girl wouldn't let them in. They asked the girl to let her in.

She says: "No!" she says, "Ye can't get in here at all."

So, they says: "If ye don't let me in, I'll huff an' I'll puff an' I'll blow this house in," they says to 'er. "Well!" she says, "ye can huff an' ye can puff," she says to 'em, "but I won't let ye in!"

So they done their best, anyway, but they failed that night. The mother was baetin' them away; d'ye see?

So, the next day, anyway, when the girl went out to the saet, ag'in, the mother came. This time, she was half black, so she was, with the baetin' she got from the wolfs (D'ye see?), tryin' to save the daughter. An' now! Didn't the girl again... The girl an' the mother went ag'in to make sure that there was no place, so there wasn't, left open for them to get in, in any way.

So, bedad, he came again the second night. An' he done the same. An' fought twice as hard a battle the second night, so he did. An' the mother fought them away. Now, the third night, was the night, but wasn't the white pigeon, now, the... half black the first time, an' now she's black completely, so she is, from the two nights fightin' them away.

So, now, the third night, anyway... The mother warned 'er,

so she did, the second day, that she wouldn't see her no more. D'ye see? An' that she'd be able to fight for her that night but she wouldn't see 'er no more; an' to make sure to try an' fight an' keep 'em out; not to open the dure upon no grounds.

So, didn't they come, anyway, so they did, the wolfs, an' they said the same thing ag'in: "Let me in!"

"No!" says she, "I won't!"

So, she says: "I'll huff an' I'll puff an' I'll blow your house in."

So 'twas no use. They tried it, anyway, but it was no use. But didn't the girl get afeared o' them? so she did, an' she started to scream an' roar. An', with that, didn't she open the door a small little bit. An' when she'd open' the door a small little bit, didn't he get in, didn't one o' the wolfs get in (D'ye see?), his hand. An' when he got his hand inside the door (D'ye see?), the girl was stoopin' down. An' didn't he get the girl, so he did, be the throat? An' all is she could do (D'ye see? She had a swoord) was to draw the swoord an' cut the hand off 'im. An' the hand remained on her throat, so it did.

Now, the' remained here, so she did. An' wasn't her father an' the quality of that time havin' a hunt? not knowin' that his daughter was alive at all; d'ye see? An' where had they to have hunt, only on this ground; d'ye see? An' wasn't there a young prince, so there was, amongst them? D'ye see? An' they were goin', so they were, for all they were worth, huntin'; when this young prince came to the castle. He was a fellow who wanted to see what was in it more than the huntin'.

He looked all through the castle, anyway, an' the girl headin' on him, hidin' on 'im.

An' the next thing was, anyway, didn't he happen to see the girl? an' he caughtch her be the hand; an' he pulled her out; an' he seen the — the wolf's — hand to her neck. He cut it off it. anyway, so he did. An' when he cut it off it, he thrun it away. He brought the girl out. He aksed her who was she. He slightly knew 'er. He aksed her who was she, but she tolt 'im.

He says: "Your father is out here, now," he says, to 'er, "huntin'," he says. "An' we didn't know," he says, "that there were anything wrong with ye," he says, "an' that ye weren't at home," he says. "We thought ye were at home."

But, anyway, didn't the girl come out? He brought the girl out with 'im forninst the crowd an' kep' her out; when the huntin' was over (D'ye see?), an' when they were all ready to go back. An' he had 'er be the hand. An' the father seen 'er.

The father stepped over to 'er, anyway, so he did, an' he says: "Can I speak to me daughter for a minute?" he says.

So, the father went over; an' when he went over, talkin' to the daughter, he says: "Daughter!" he says, "don't tell anyone," he says to 'er, "what," he says, "I done to you," he says, "about," he says, "cuttin' up the bullock," he says, "an' puttin' the maw... puttin' ye into the maw," he says, "an' peggin' ye in to sink or swim, into the sea," he says. He says: "An' I'll let ye," he says, "marry anyone ye like, an' also give ye," he says, "all I have," he says, "in my possessions for ye," he says to 'er.

So, be hell, anyway, she didn't tell no one. An' she got married to this young prince that brought 'im out, so she did.

An' they had children in basketfulls; the' thrun them out in shovelfulls. The Queen of England refused to buy for a pence a piece.

They put down the kittle an' med tae; an' if they don't live happy, that we may.

Notes for The Folktales and the Collectors *pages 9 - 14.*
and On the Roadside in the 1930's *pages 17 - 36.*

1. For examples of this theme in Irish folktales see the Department of Irish Folklore Mss. 372, pp. 278-88; 1227, pp. 702-03; and 659, pp. 557-59.
2. Tom Munnelly, "The Singing Tradition of Irish Travellers". *Folk Music Journal* (1975), vol. 3, no. 1, pp. 3-30.
3. Recorded in an interview with George Gmelch at Ballinalea, Co. Longford in August 1977.
4. In a lecture delivered at the Irish Book Fair in 1942, then director of the Folklore Commission, Séamus Ó Duilearga, explained their work. "The main task of the Irish Folklore Commission is the recording of oral traditions of Ireland wherever they are to be found, in the towns as well as in the country, in English as well as in Irish. The work is carried out by a small number of part-time and full-time workers who go around from one parish to another writing down from the lips of the old people the tales, songs, and other kinds of oral literary material which the older generation are only too willing to give." J. H. Delargy, "The Study of Irish Folklore". *Dublin Magazine* (1942), vol. XVII, no. 3, pp. 19-26.
5. See note 3.
6. Linda Dégh, "Folk Narrative". In *Folklife and Folklore,* edited by R. Dorson, (Chicago, 1972), pp. 62-65.
7. For a discussion of other aspects of the traditional lifestyle of Travellers, particularly social organization and family life, see George Gmelch, *The Irish Tinkers: The Urbanization of an Itinerant People* (Menlo Park, 1977), pp. 13-41, 113-37.
8. The system of sending out detailed questionnaires to collect folklore, used by Scandinavian Folklorists, was used extensively by the Irish Folklore Commission. Questionnaires were sent out to several hundred correspondents, mainly primary teachers. In most instances, although not in the study of Travellers, this approach was supplemented by field research.
9. Sherley McEgill, "The Tinker and the Caravan". *Irish Press* (3 March 1934), p.8.
10. *Report of the Commission on Itinerancy.* (Dublin, 1963), pp. 145.
11. Recorded in an interview with Nan Donoghue, a 56 year old Travelling woman from the Midlands, in Dublin in July 1977. (All quotations unless otherwise noted were recorded in interviews by the author, George Gmelch).
12. Pádraig MacGréine, "Irish Tinkers or Travellers". *Béaloideas* (1931), vol. 3, pp. 170-86.
13. Pádraig MacGréine, "Some Notes on Tinkers and Their Cant". *Béaloideas* (1934), vol. 4, pp. 259-63.
14. Recorded from Nanny Nevin, a 50 year old Travelling Woman from Co. Mayo, in June 1972.
15. See references 12 and 13.
16. Patrick Campbell, "Growing Up in Donegal". *Béaloideas* (1977), vol. 42-44, pp.. 62-87.
17. Recorded from Nellie Delaney, age 50 approximately, in Dublin in February 1978.
18. Recorded from the late Mick Donoghue at age 60 in Dublin in 1972.
19. Early linguists, notably John Sampson (1891) and Kuno Meyer (1891), believed that *Shelta* or *Gammon* was the remnant of a secret language created before the eleventh century in the early monastic communities of Ireland. They speculated that itinerant craftsmen who once worked and resided in the monasteries acquired the argot there. Doubts about the antiquity of *Gammon* have been raised by more recent linguists however, including Macalister (1937) and Harper and Hudson

20   (1971), although they do admit that *Gammon* has a few links with the early secret languages of Ireland.
20   The following are some examples of *Gammon* taken from Sampson (1891), MacGréine (1934), and Macalister (1937); see the bibliography for complete references.
What'll I bog for the inox? (What'll I ask for the thing?)
Salk the gored. (Take the money.)
G/eg a lus from the b/or. (Beg a drink from the woman.)
The shades is toreen, crush! (The police are coming, get out!)
I suni the glox of the sark / tori with his lork. (I saw the man who owns the field coming in his car.)
21   Recorded from Nan Donoghue, age 56, in Dublin in 1972.
22   Department of Irish Folklore, "Tinker Questionnaire". Ms. 1256, p. 109.
23   See note 21.
24   See reference 13, pp. 261-62.
25   Some Traveller families, primarily from Cos. Mayo and Galway, travelled to Scotland each summer where as contract labourers they worked the entire summer picking potatoes.
26   See note 14.
27   See note 21.
28   Recorded from Luke Wall, age 60, in Dublin in Feburary 1978.
29   Recorded from Nan Donoghue, age 56, in Dublin in July 1977.
30   See note 28.
31   See note 18.
32   See reference 12, p. 172.
33   *Report of the Departmental Committee on Vagrancy* (Dublin, 1936), chapter 8.
34   Department of Irish Folklore, "Tinker Questionnaire". Ms. 1255, p. 60.

Glossary

Italicised words are in the Irish language. They appear in the spelling of the collector, as a true reflection of what the storyteller said. Where the spelling is incorrect the proper spelling appears in brackets.

Adams — Atoms
Aech — Each
Aegle — Eagle
Aesy — Easy
Aet — Eat
Afraird — Afraid
Ag'in — Again; before; by the time.
Ag'in' — Against; within.
Agrádh — Love.
Ahind — Behind
Ahoult — Ahold, hold.
Ailded — Ailed; troubled.
Aks — Ask
A mac — Son.
An — On
Anna — Any
Apast — Past; beyond.
Ascordin' — According.
As't — Asked
Asthore (a stór) — Love.
Avic (a mhic) — Son.
Avourneen (a mhuirnín) — Love.
Awkad — Awkward.
Ayther — Either.
Bábín — Diminutive of baby.
Backways — By the rear; through the back.
Bad shoes — Bad 'cess, no success.
Beannacht leat — Good-bye.
Berrit — Buried.
Betune — Between.
Bonamh — A piglet.
Bould — Bold
Bottomed — Emptied, drank up.
Brether — Brother.
Bum' bee — Bumble bee.

Butt — Bottom; tree stump.
Caicín — Diminutive of cake.
Cailín — A young woman.
Céad míle fáilte — A hundred thousand welcomes.
Ceis — A small improvised bridge made of poles or planks and covered with sods across a drain (usual in a bog).
Chimbley — Chimney.
Ch'ice — Choice
Cotched — Caught.
Claen — Clean.
Clamp — A compact heap.
Clapped — Put, placed.
Cleave — A basket.
Collar and elbow — a style of wrestling.
Compartner — Companion and partner conflated.
Coorse — Course
Coortin' — Courting.
Cop — See.
Cove — Cub.
Craeker — Creature.
Craether — Creature.
Cravin' — Craving; demanding; begging.
Cunched — Quenched; stifled, suppressed.
Daecent — Decent.
Daelin' — Dealing.
Dhram — Dram, a small draught of whiskey.
Di'n' — Did not.
Dodge — A blow.
Drau' — Draught.
Dunkle — Dunghill.
Dure — Door.
Duskus — Dusk
Egit — Idiot.

E'ra — Ever a, any.
Et — Eaten.
Fadoms — Fathoms.
Faest — Feast.
Flaitheamhnas (flaithiúnas) — heaven.
Flure — Floor.
Follit — Followed.
Follyin' — Following; preceding.
Forisht — Forest.
Forkin — Fortune.
Fornint — Fornent, opposite, against.
Forninst — Fornenst: see Fornint.
Friend or Near Friend — A relative.
Ginthry — Gentry.
Goss' — See Gossoon.
Gossoon — A young boy.
Gothered — Gathered.
Grea' d'l — Great deal.
Grum Groudie — Grim-faced.
G'wan — Go on.
G'win — Go in.
Haep — Heap.
Haero — Hero.
Han'ke'cher — Handkerchief.
Ha'p'orth — Halfpennyworth.
Harp — The obverse side of Irish coins; tails.
Headin' — Keeping ahead of.
Hommer — Hammer.
Hone — An edge; an advantage.
Hot — Hit.
Huz — Us.
Impenent — Impudent.
Impidend — Impudent.
Impident — Impudent.
Ind — End.
Intherfaere — Interfere.
Intind — Intend.
I'self — Itself.
Janius — Genius.
Justan' — Just as, as.
J'y-bells — Joy-bells.
Kae — Key.
Kilt — Killed.
Laef — Leaf; page of a book.
Laeve — Leave.
Leck — Like.
Led — Lid.
Lift — Left.
Lepped — Leapt.
Lest'nin' — Listening.

Lock — An armful, a bundle.
Lor Tennis — Lawn Tennis.
Mac — Milk.
Machree (Mo chroí) — My love.
Mael — Meal.
Maen — Mean.
Maet — Meat.
Maneen — Diminutive of man.
Marrit — Married.
Med — Made.
Merrymaid — A mermaid.
Min — Men.
Mismirized — Mesmerized.
Mitil — Metal.
'Miss — Amiss.
Musha (Muise) — Well indeed.
Near friend — A relative, a kinsman.
Omadhaun (amadán) — Fool.
Piatae — Potato.
Piatez — Potatoes.
Plaese — Please.
Poochin' — Poaching; wandering.
Puddin' — Pudding, entrails, guts.
Quaer — Queer.
Quality — Gentry, the upper class.
Rack — A comb.
Raech — Reach; hand to.
Rael — Real.
Ramblers — Visitors, social guests.
Rattle — Noise, commotion.
Rib — A length of hair.
Rish — A rush, a marsh plant.
Riz — Raised, lifted.
Sae — Sea.
Saecret — Secret.
Saet — Seat.
Scraw — A turf, a sod.
Shadda — Shadow.
Shakehandses — Handshakes.
Sich — Such.
Skivered — Skewered.
Smithereens (smidiríní) — Fragments.
So'diers — Soldiers.
Sorra — Never; don't.
Spaek — Speak.
Spalpeen (spailpín) — Roving labourer.
Stael — Steal.
St'ed — Stayed.
Stirabout — Porridge.
Stone — A measure of weight, usually equal to fourteen pounds avoirdupois.

Swall'et. Swallowed.
Swallit — Swallowed.
Swingless — Windlass
T'aech — To each.
T'd — Toward.
Te'thers — Tethers.
Teeste — Taste.
Theirsel's - Themselves.
Thick — Stupid.
Thim — Them.
Thoséin (dosaen) — Dozen.
Thraeted — Treated.
Thres'ol' — Threshold.
Thrimmin' — Trimming; frayed ends.
Throth — **In truth.**
Tilliscoop — Telescope.
Tomáisín salach — Dirty Tommy.
Tongas — Tongs.
Tundhering — Thundering.

Twinty — Twenty.
Use'n't — Used not, did not.
Useval — Usual.
Vael — Veal.
V'ice — Voice.
Waery — Weary.
Wan — One.
Wance — Once.
Wantime — Onetime.
Welkim — Welcome.
Whileen — Diminutive of while.
Whin — When.
Wid — With.
Wood — With.
Wor — Were.
Wore — Beat.
Wrastlin' — Wresting.
Yoke — A tie, a rope (also, thing).

Index of Tale Types

The type numbers refer to Antti Aarne and Stith Thompson. *The Types of the Folktale*, Second Revision, Helsinki 1961 = *FF Communications* 184. 'Cf.' has been added before the type numbers where the versions in *To Shorten the Road* deviate remarkably from the normal pattern of the stories. Some of the tales are combinations of more than one type. Such combinations are common in Irish tradition.

Type No.	Title in The Types of the Folktale	Title in this collection	Pages
Cf.124	Blowing the House In	The Little Blue Bonnet	177-181
300	The Dragon-Slayer	The Firey Dragon	88-95
301A	Quest for a Vanished Princess	The Four Kings of Ireland	168-175
303	The Twins or Blood-Brothers	Horse, Hound and Hawk	138-145
Cf.313	The Girl as Helper in the Hero's Flight	Jack the Bear	112-123
Cf.325	The Magician and his Pupil	Horse, Hound and Hawk	138-145
316	The Nix of the Mill-Pond	Jack the Fisherman	97-101
326	The Youth Who Wanted to Learn What Fear Is	Jack the Ghost	71-77
329	Hiding from the Devil	Horse, Hound and Hawk	138-145
402	The Mouse (Cat, Frog etc.) as Bride	The Fresh Loaf or The Three-legged Lamb	83-86
425A	The Monster (Animal) as Bridegroom	The Roarin' Bull of Orange	147-154
Cf.510	Cinderella and Cap o' Rushes	The Little Blue Bonnet	177-181
551	The Sons on a Quest for a Wonderful Remedy for their Father	The Story of the Omadhaun Laois	79-81
559	Dungbeetle	Jack from Tubberclare	62-69
566	The Three Magic Objects and the Wonderful Fruits (Fortunatus)	Johnnie and Tommie	41-51
567A	The Magic Bird-Heart and the Separated Brothers	Johnnie and Tommie	41-51
590	The Prince and the Arm Bands	The Wonderful Sword	156-163
650A	Strong John	Jack the Cobbler – the Widow's Son from Ireland	131-136
Cf.650A	Strong John	Jack the Bear	112-123
710	Our Lady's Child	The Wild Sow of the Forest	103-110
1525	The Master Thief	Jack the Highway Robber	53-60
1535	The Rich and the Poor Peasant	Buddy	126-129

The manuscript and page numbers of the folktales, which are deposited in the archives of the Department of Irish Folklore, UCD, are: *The Little Blue Bonnet*, Ms.1795, pp. 551-62; *The Firey Dragon*, Ms.81, pp.169-90; *The Four Kings of Ireland*, Ms.1795, pp.537-550; *Horse, Hound and Hawk*, Ms.81, pp.27-50; *Jack the Bear*, Ms.1498, pp.39-73; *Jack the Fisherman*, Ms.80, pp.183-96; *Jack the Ghost*, Ms.81, pp.223-39; *The Fresh Loaf or The Three Legged Lamb*, Ms.81, pp.282-93; *The Roarin' Bull of Orange*, Ms.81, pp.68-90; *The Story of Omadhaun Laois*, Ms.80, pp.175-82; *Jack from Tubberclare*, Ms.81, pp.260-81; *Johnnie and Tommie*, Ms.81, pp.191-222; *The Wonderful Sword*, Ms.81, pp.2-26; *Jack the Cobbler, The Widow's Son from Ireland*, Ms.81, pp.51-67; *The Wild Sow of the Forest*, Ms.81, pp.147-68; *Jack the Highway Robber*, Ms.81, pp.240-59; *Buddy*, Ms.81, pp.103-114.

Bibliography

Arnold, Frederick S. "Our Old Poets and the Tinkers". *Journal of American Folklore* II (1898): 210-20.

Barnes, Bettina. "Irish Travelling People". In *Gypsies, Tinkers and Other Travellers,* edited by Farnham, Rehfisch, pp. 231-256, London: Academic Press, 1975.

Bewley, Victor (ed.) *Travelling People.* Dublin: Veritas, 1974.

Campbell, Patrick. "Growing Up in Donegal". *Béaloideas: Journal of the Folklore of Ireland Society* 42-44 (1977): 62-87.

Commission on Itinerancy. *Report of the Commission on Itinerancy.* Dublin: The Stationery Office, 1963.

Clifford, Sigerson. *Travelling Tinkers: Ballads.* Dublin: Dolmen Press, 1951.

Crawford, M. H., and Gmelch, George. "The Human Biology of Irish Tinkers: Demography, Ethnohistory, and Genetics". *Social Biology* 21 (1974): 321-31.

Dégh, Linda. "Folk Narrative". In *Folklife and Folklore,* edited by R. Dorson, pp. 62-65. Chicago, 1972.

Delargy, James H. *The Gaelic Storyteller.* ("Rhys Memorial Lecture"). London: Proceedings of the British Academy, 1945.

Evans, E. E. *Irish Folk Ways.* London: Routledge and Kegan Paul, 1957.

Gmelch, George. "Economic Strategies and Migrant Adaptation: The Case of Irish Tinkers." *Ethnos* 42 (1977): 22-37.

―――― *The Irish Tinkers: The Urbanization of an Itinerant People.* Menlo Park, California: Cummings Publishing Company, 1977.

―――― "Settling the Irish Tinkers". *Ekistics.* (1977) 43 (257): 230-39.

―――― and Gmelch, Sharon Bohn. "Begging in Dublin: The Strategies of a Marginal Urban Occupation". *Urban Life* 6 (1978): 439-54.

―――― "The Irish Tinkers: When Wanderers Settle Down". *Human Nature,* March 1978: 66-75.

Gmelch, Sharon Bohn. *Tinkers and Travellers.* Dublin: The O'Brien Press; Montreal: McGill-Queen's University Press, 1975.

―――― "Economic and Power Relations Among Urban Tinkers: The Role of Women". *Urban Anthropology* 6 (1977) 237-47.

―――― and Gmelch, George. "The Emergence of an Ethnic Group: The Irish Tinkers". *Anthropological Quarterly* 49 (1976): 225-238.

Harper, Jared, and Hudson, Charles. "Irish Traveller Cant". *Journal of English Linguistics* 15 (1971): 78-86.

―――― "Irish Traveller Cant in its Social Setting". *Southern Folklore Quarterly* 37 (1973): 101-14.

Irish Folklore Commission. "Toradh Ceistiuchain ar na Tincéirí". ("Tinkers Questionnaire") Vols. 1255-56, (1952). Unpublished material in the archives of the Department of Irish Folklore, University College, Dublin.

Leland, Charles G. "Shelta". *Journal of the Gypsy Lore Society,* 2 (1891): 321-23.

―――― "Shelta" and "The Tinkers". *Journal of the Gypsy Lore Society* 2 (1907-08): 73-82.

Macalister, R.S.S. *The Secret Languages of Ireland.* Cambridge: Cambridge University Press, 1937. See pages 130-282.

McCarthy, Patricia. "Poverty and Itinerancy: A Study in the Subculture of Poverty". Master's Thesis, University College Dublin, 1971.

McEgill, Sherley. "The Tinker and The Caravan". *The Irish Press,* 3 March 1934, p.8.

MacGréine, Pádraig. "Irish Tinkers or 'Travellers': Some Notes on Their Manners and Customs, and Their Secret Language or 'Cant' ". *Béaloideas, Journal of the Folklore of Ireland Society* 3 (1931): 170-86.

―――― "Further Notes on Tinkers' 'Cant' together with some Travellers' Tales, Customs, Beliefs, and Prayers". *Béaloideas, Journal of the Folklore of Ireland Society* 3 (1932): 290-303.

―――― "Some Notes on Tinkers and Their 'Cant' " *Béaloideas, Journal of the Folklore of Ireland Society"* 4 (1934): 259-63.

Meyer, Kuno. "The Secret Languages of Ireland". *Journal of the Gypsy Lore Society* 2 (1909): 241-46.

Munnelly, Tom. "The Singing Tradition of Irish Travellers". *Folk Music Journal* 3 (1975): 3-30.

O'Neill, Timothy. *Life and Tradition in Rural Ireland.* London: J. M. Dent & Sons, 1977.

O'Sullivan, J. C. "The Tools and Trade of the Tinker". In *Folk and Farm,* edited by Caoimhín Ó Danachair, pp. 208-217. Dublin: The Royal Society of Antiquaries of Ireland, 1976.

O'Sullivan, Seán. *A Handbook of Irish Folklore.* Dublin: The Educational Company of Ireland, 1942.

Sampson, John. "Tinkers and Their Talk". *Journal of the Gypsy Lore Society* 2 (1891): 204-21.

Thompson, Stith. *The Folktale.* New York, 1946.

Wiedel, Janine and O'Fearadhaigh, Martina. *Irish Tinkers.* London: Lattimer, 1976.

This bibliography includes, in addition to references cited, selected works on Irish Travellers for the reader's interest. For a complete listing of works on Travellers consult G. and S. Gmelch, "Ireland's Travelling People: A Comprehensive Bibliography." Journal of the Gypsy Lore Society: 3 (1978).

All rights reserved. No part of this book may be reproduced or utilised in any form or by any means, electronic or mechanical, including photocopying, recording or by any information storage and retrieval system without permission in writing from the publisher.

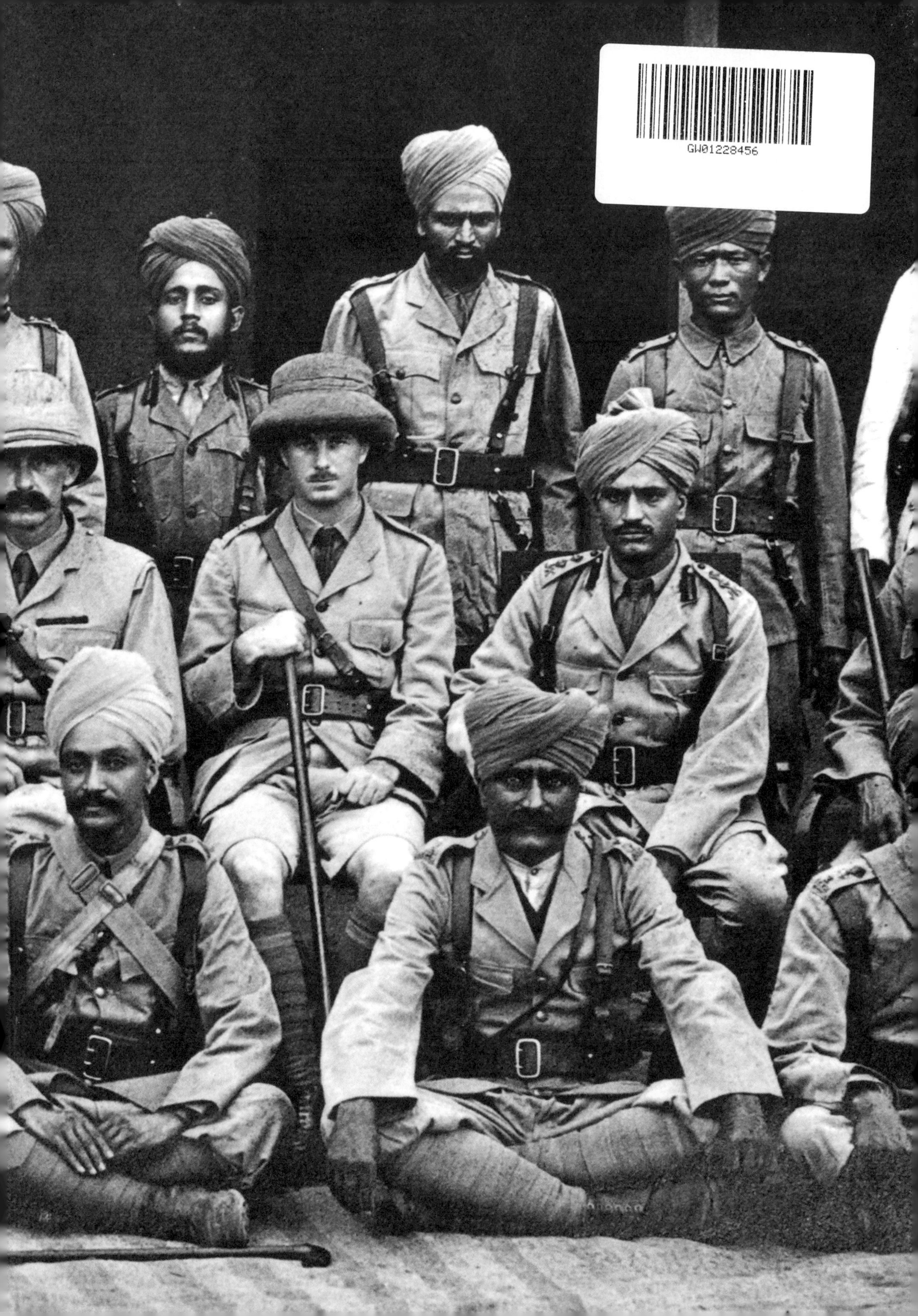

I Can Never Say Enough About the Men

A History of the Jammu and Kashmir Rifles throughout their World War One East African Campaign

'I can never say enough about the men'
Alec Kerr in his letter, commenting on the bravery and endurance of the Kashmir Rifles.

In spite of all the hardship the men of Kashmir Rifles just keep going
Left to Right: Havildar Giandar, Sepoys Hafiziullah, Mirchand and Tula.

I Can Never Say Enough About the Men

The Jammu and Kashmir Rifles

ANDREW KERR

With thanks to Jellyfish Printing Solutions Limited and John Fairweather for their assistance in bringing this publication to fruition.

Thanks to Yasin Zagar of Indus Travels for all their assistance and support.

To Major (Retd) Brahma Singh. My special thanks for reading through the early drafts of this book and for making valuable contributions to accuracy.

First published 2010 by PMC Management Consultants Limited

© Andrew Kerr, 2010

The right of Andrew Kerr to be identified as the Author of this work has been asserted in accordance with the Copyrights, Designs and Patents Act 1988.

Email the Author at andrewkerrpmc@tiscali.co.uk

All rights reserved. No part of this book may be reprinted or reproduced or utilised in any form or by any electronic, mechanical or other means, now known or hereafter invented, including photocopying and recording, or in any information storage or retrieval system, without the permission in writing from the Publishers.

Every effort was made to contact, recognise and thank all sources of material for this publication

Printed in India

Contents

Preface

Introduction

Chapter One	The Kashmir Rifles
Chapter Two	Captain Alexander Kerr and the British Officers
Chapter Three	The Battle of Tanga 2nd to 5th November 1914
Chapter Four	The Umba Valley and the Battle of Jasin January 1915
Chapter Five	Patrolling the Tsavo River Line 1915
Chapter Six	The Advance South Towards the Central Railway 1916
Chapter Seven	The Battle of Lukigura 24 June 1916
Chapter Eight	Collapse and Disintegration July 1916 to January 1917
Chapter Nine	Return to Kashmir and some Reflections on the Campaign
Appendix A	Alec's personal letter to a brother office describing the Campaign
Appendix B	Lt Cooke's letter discussing the book Marching on Tanga
Appendix C	Letter to the Inspector of Imperial Service Troops from the Brigadier
Appendix D	Malaria

"This book is dedicated to the memory of those many millions of Indians who volunteered, fought and suffered in both World Wars"

Foreword

The history that follows seeks to explain the extraordinary casualty levels that 2nd Kashmir Rifles endured.

2nd Kashmir Rifles *Casualties 1914 – 1917*	
Starting Strength - November 1914	715
Reinforcement Drafts of 909 　　　　　two thirds to 2nd Bn	+ 600
Number Standing – 8th February 1917	280
Medical Board found some 20 men fit for 　　　　　further service	-260
From 1315 to the remaining 20 is a 98% casualty rate	

'I Can Never Say Enough About the Men'

This photograph shows the Kashmir Rifles looking fit and well with uniforms and equipment in working order. It was probably taken in India, after their return from Africa in 1917.

Preface

When someone thinks of the First World War their mind is likely to be crowded with European images of mass armies taken from the trenches and mud of the Western Front. This was true for me until I started to investigate my grandfather's war. I knew he had won a Military Cross (MC) and that it was for leading an attack against the Germans in Africa. However, it was a photograph which I stumbled across in his album (on the front cover) of some very exhausted looking Indian soldiers that ignited my imagination and inspired me into the investigative actions that have led to this book. Had the story not been so remarkable I am sure it would never have been completed.

The history that follows is what I discovered and to start with was written in memory of the six generations of my family who served India but became a tribute to the uncomplaining courage and fortitude of the Kashmir Rifles. I am very keen to give back to the JAK RIFLES (The Jammu and Kashmir Rifles today's Regiment and still an all volunteer force) something of their noble history and to properly acknowledge their sacrifice and contribution to the war. It should be noted that whilst many references are made to the 2nd Battalion (Bn), the 3rd Bn was engaged throughout this account at half battalion strength and that many personnel from the other half of this battalion and from the 1st Bn were called upon as fresh drafts to a total 909 men. This is in many ways, therefore, the story of the entire Regiment.

Recently several old books on the war in East Africa and three new ones have been published, these have done their bit to raise awareness and provoke fresh thinking on this long forgotten story. This short account focusing on Alec Kerr and the 2nd Battalion 'Bodyguard' the Kashmir Rifles will I hope add a further and perhaps more personal dimension to this area of history. I have purposely made the story very visual and concentrated on battalion or company grouping – a much lower level than the theatre or divisional levels that characterise most accounts.

As the task of investigating the experiences of Alec Kerr and the Kashmir Rifles unfolded several themes and questions started to emerge and develop in my mind – some of these I have sought to answer. One train of thought surrounds motivation: what on earth made volunteers from the mountains of Kashmir perform for years on end, thousands of miles from home, in perhaps the most adverse and hostile environment of the whole war – fighting against an enemy for which they had no quarrel? Another and related topic was command: the Kashmir Rifles were used to being led by their own Kashmir Rifles officers, how did they respond to a British chain of command exercised through their attached British Officers? As the story developed I often wondered what these soldiers must have felt like propelled as it were from a rural and subsistence background into the technologies of the twentieth century with its trains, cars, ships and even aeroplanes.

Other and more traditional military themes surround logistics or more importantly the breakdown of them – why did they repeatedly march beyond their supply chain; why did they virtually all get malaria when they had quinine and were supposedly used to it in Kashmir? How were casualties evacuated over so many miles? How did other regiments cope with the conditions? What happened to the horses, oxen and mules and what about the tens of thousands of porters who were locally recruited?

The materials for this story are taken from a mix of published and unpublished sources and a bibliography of both is listed. I would particularly like to acknowledge the materials from Lt Cols Lyall and Cooke (they along with Alec were the attached British Officers to the 2nd Bn) and who between them kept and assembled records, diaries and photographs of their experiences in East Africa – these now belong to the Imperial War Museum. Also the surviving war diaries of the Kashmir Rifles held at the National Archives, Kew, London) – sadly they are very incomplete and many seem to have been lost. In piecing the story together I have tried to use first hand sources as far as possible and extracts from other historians to complement, whilst also trying to make the narrative flow – an ambitious task given so many different styles and erratic records. Please forgive this approach in the interests of trying to uncover the truth.

Writing the story and investigating has been pure joy and I am glad that my discovery in the Lyall papers of a letter written by Alec Kerr, when recovering from malaria, telling his whole story did not happen earlier as it might have prematurely quenched my thirst. Then perhaps I would not have found my way to visit the

JAK RIFLES via the Indian Military Attaché General Saush Sharma then a serving officer and from the Regiment. To him I am enormously grateful for the introduction and so it is my turn to say what a privilege it is to feel part of the JAK RIFLES family.

In June 2010 I was able to travel out to meet the 2nd Bn on UN operations in the Congo and was given the enormous honour of addressing the men and presenting this story through the photographs in a twilight outdoor evening gathering using a projector. It was an extraordinary experience under the African stars almost 100 years later and has enabled me to proudly say that I am the seventh generation of my family to have addressed Indian soldiers on operations. Colonel Lidder commands a fine battalion and I was looked after magnificently and in the finest traditions of the Indian Army.

This moment was also seized to explore the battlefields and Lt Col Dogra and I managed our own small adventure into Tanzania to view them at first hand. The greatest moment of the trip was the moving Commonwealth War Grave Cemetery beautifully kept at Tanga with the name of nearly every soldier killed carved in stone. We walked the battlefield and relived the landings and the successful attacks by our forefathers, and sort to find explanation as to why the Regiment should have performed so magnificently in contrast to many others. At Jasin we uncovered that the so-called walled fort, as described in some accounts, was at best an improvised camp built around mud huts and sisal, and totally unable to withstand artillery or machine gun fire. We drove the hundreds of miles that had been marched from Kilimanjaro south and experienced the baking heat, the lack of water and the dearth of roads. We saw the continuing evidence of malaria – and could readily understand why an army would cease to function if it was marched for months at a time without supplies.

As a result of the visit to the Regiment and the battlefield tour several changes have been made to the text and I would therefore like to make a special thank you for their help and their encouragement to complete this study and for their generous support in its publication.

In terms of producing the book a notable thank you goes to the author Ross Anderson for the introduction to sources at Kew and the Imperial War Museum —his own recently published books *The Forgotten Front* and *Tanga* are essential reading. Also to my brother, James, who took my basic photographs and prepared them for the exacting requirements of the publisher.

And of course a special and final thank you to for enabling me to meet members of today's great Regiment, and so try to understand

'I Can Never Say Enough About the Men'

what Alec Kerr meant when he said, commenting on the Kashmir Rifleman's ability to cheerfully endure hardship, 'I can never say enough about the men'.

The 2nd Battalion's return to Satwari Camp, Jammu, June 1917. There are perhaps 375 men on parade here. Lt Cooke wrote on 5 January (eleven months after their return): 'that a great number of men who returned from Africa are still unfit...'

Introduction

This introduction is written to set the scene and provide the 'big picture' context for someone who has little knowledge of the First World War in East Africa.

The fighting aspects of this story are set in what is today called Kenya and Tanzania. In the First World War this was the little-known battleground between the British and the Germans. More accurately, it started as a war between a very few Germans (initially sixty-three officers, thirty-two doctors and sixty-seven NCO's with their 2,500 native troops – the 'Askari') and a similar number from the British East African Empire, mostly the Kings African Rifles (KAR).

The relatively small-scale battles and skirmishes of 1914 and 1915 grew by early 1916 into a multidivisional theatre of operations and, when with the appointment of General Smuts, the British East African Forces were reinforced with substantial numbers of troops from South Africa and Rhodesia. At the outset there was only one regular battalion of the British Army, the 2nd Bn The Loyal North Lancashire Regiment.

The German Protectorate acted by mobilising their entire colony and by 1916 a very sizable force could be fielded and maintained the exact scale is unclear with 2,700 Europeans, 11,367 Askari, 2,531 Irregulars and 10,000+ porters often quoted. However in Edward Paice's book *Tip and Run*, the most recent study, he states '20,000 troops with 66 machine guns and sixty field guns' (p.131). At this same point of 1916 when the British, under General Smuts' leadership, attacked south into German East Africa they fielded two large divisions totalling over 44,000 men supported by a further 24,000 porters and followers, additionally there were over, 20,000 horses, 12,000 bullocks, and nearly 6,000 mules and donkeys. This scale of operation was to be exceeded by further deployments in 1917 and 1918, by which time the Kashmir Rifles – along with virtually all Indian, British, Rhodesian and South African troops – had been

The Lancer Squadron of the Kashmir State Forces.

The Journey to East Africa. The Kashmir Rifles assembled in Jammu from the 14th September (many had to first travel 100's of miles on foot – a detachment of 144 men were at Khundru, on the Indus West of Skardu) and then entrain for Bombay on the 28th September – the rail journey took five days and included stops at Lahore, Agra, Harder and then Deolali Camp - where they arrived on the 1st October for a week of 'work up' training under Brigadier Tighe - before completing the final 12 hours of the train journey to Mumbai (Bombay) 9th October. The indicative rail journey is shown ……… and it must have amounted to 1000 miles.

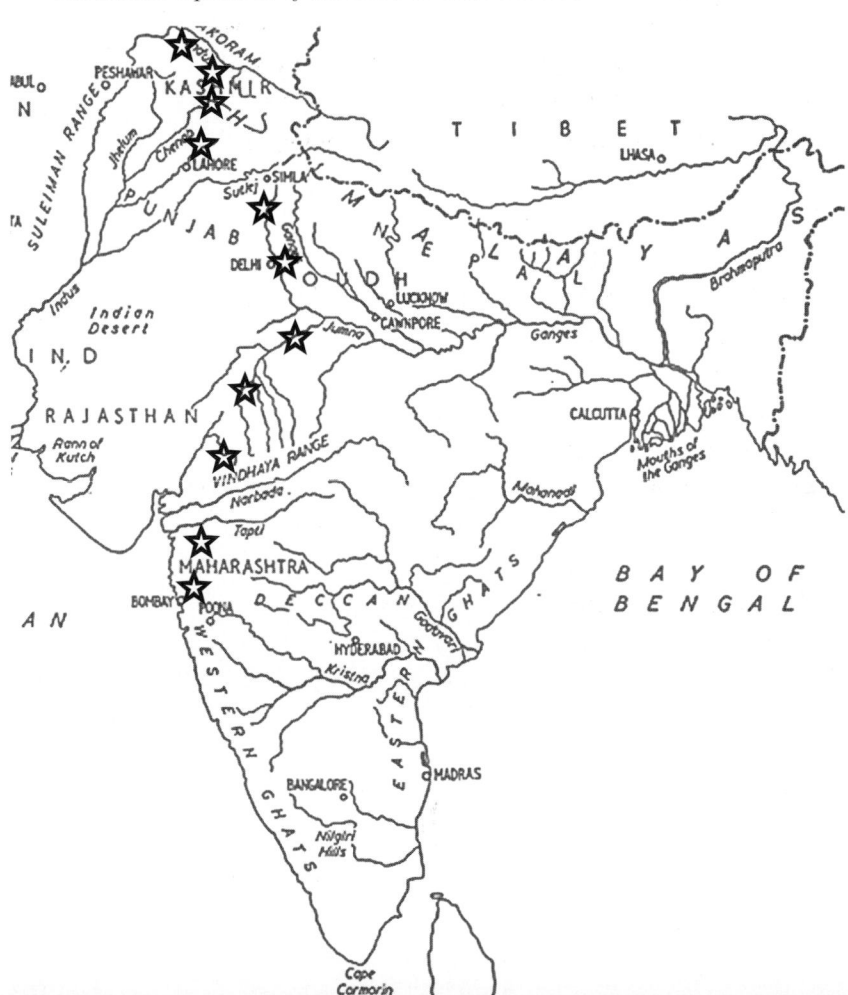

withdrawn from the theatre of operations following their complete breakdown and were replaced by the expanded Kings African Rifles (30,000 men) and troops from the Gold Coast and Nigeria.

However, before looking closely at the campaign in East Africa it is valuable to understand the strategic situation that faced Britain and her Empire in the years before the First World War. Defence policy for many decades had directed resources towards its primary maritime objective, believing that through command of the seas Britain could both secure the Empire and successfully defend the homeland. The execution of this policy was often called the 'two power standard', whereby the Royal Navy aimed to have a 10 per cent superiority over the combined strength of the next two largest fleets. To maintain this two power standard in the 'age of the Dreadnought', led to the naval arms race with Germany and the staggering British industrial and economic achievement of building, in just 12 years, forty-eight battleships and battlecruisers. The 1914 Royal Navy new construction estimate was more than twice that of Germany's. The Royal Navy total budget for 1914 was some £52 million of a total defence budget of some £75 million.*

The consequence for the British Army of this maritime emphasis was to be kept very small by comparison with the vast conscript armies of the European powers and for it to be directed towards a policing and colonial role. Its largest deployment was in India where since the Mutiny (often now called the First War of Independence) it provided a British component of 75,000 men to help the Indian Army maintain the frontiers and internal order. When the BEF (British Expeditionary Force – a combined Regular and Territorial Army) set off for France in 1914 it managed to assemble some 110,000 men and was consequently a very small and junior player on the battlefield; both Germany and France had each mobilized and equipped armies of over 3 million men.

The Indian Army was also a small all-volunteer force and it totalled some 150,000 men led by British officers who had come from similar social backgrounds, schools and military training establishments as those found throughout the British Army. However, the Indian Army had its own very distinctive culture also based on a regimental system that was tuned to meet its Indian regional, racial and religious needs – it was therefore easily misunderstood then, let alone today.

Both East African empires were young colonies founded in the 1880s with tiny European populations yet geographically dwarfing

---

* Taken from D.K. Brown, The Grand Fleet..

their supporting countries (three times the size of Germany). The British had built hers initially out of trade, whereas the German colony was blatantly based on an imperial decision, reflecting the emergence of their desire to be a great world power. To start with the financial returns were not good and the risks enormous, however in time the Germans had significant outputs of both cotton and rubber. The border in the north of German East Africa ran in a direct line from a coastal fishing village called Jasin towards Mount Kilimanjaro and then on to the middle of Lake Victoria, some 500 miles. It is in this tropical region where Alec Kerr volunteered, and also where the Kashmir Rifles were sent and where the fighting elements of this story are set. There were other war fronts in East Africa involving the Belgian Congo, Nyasaland and Portuguese East Africa. At the end of First World War German East Africa became the British Territory of Tanganyika.

Some aspects of this war have been written about and then made into films, most notably Karen Blixen's Out of Africa and C.S. Forester's African Queen. However, they do not seek to emphasize the war and the fighting there has not caught the public imagination in the same way as say Gallipoli or the countless films from the Western Front – perhaps one of the reasons being that none convey the horrifying story of disease and appalling suffering that was experienced. Casualties were proportionally on a scale to match or exceed the Somme, Passchendaele or Gallipoli but it was not the shell, bullet or bomb that was the grim reaper.

The war started in a low-key way with a Royal Navy shore barrage and the Germans seizing a few enclaves of British territory. Many on both sides in East Africa hoped the war would somehow pass them by. The local British troops, some 2,400, were organised in companies from the three Kings African Rifles' battalions. These were spread throughout the country and were far from an effective fighting force, and really only intended for local colonial control purposes. Their military capability was limited to small patrol-type operations and their weaknesses were no artillery, medical services, reserves or a staff planning capacity.

The Germans were better prepared for general war. They had bloodily suppressed the Maji-Maji in 1907 whose guerrilla actions taught them the hard way about operations and tactics in the East African tropical terrain. This had matured the Army in terms of battle drills, command and medical capability, but especially in the use of the machine gun. It had also hardened the white officers and NCO's to the rigours of the tropical climate. In particular the Germans were forced to develop

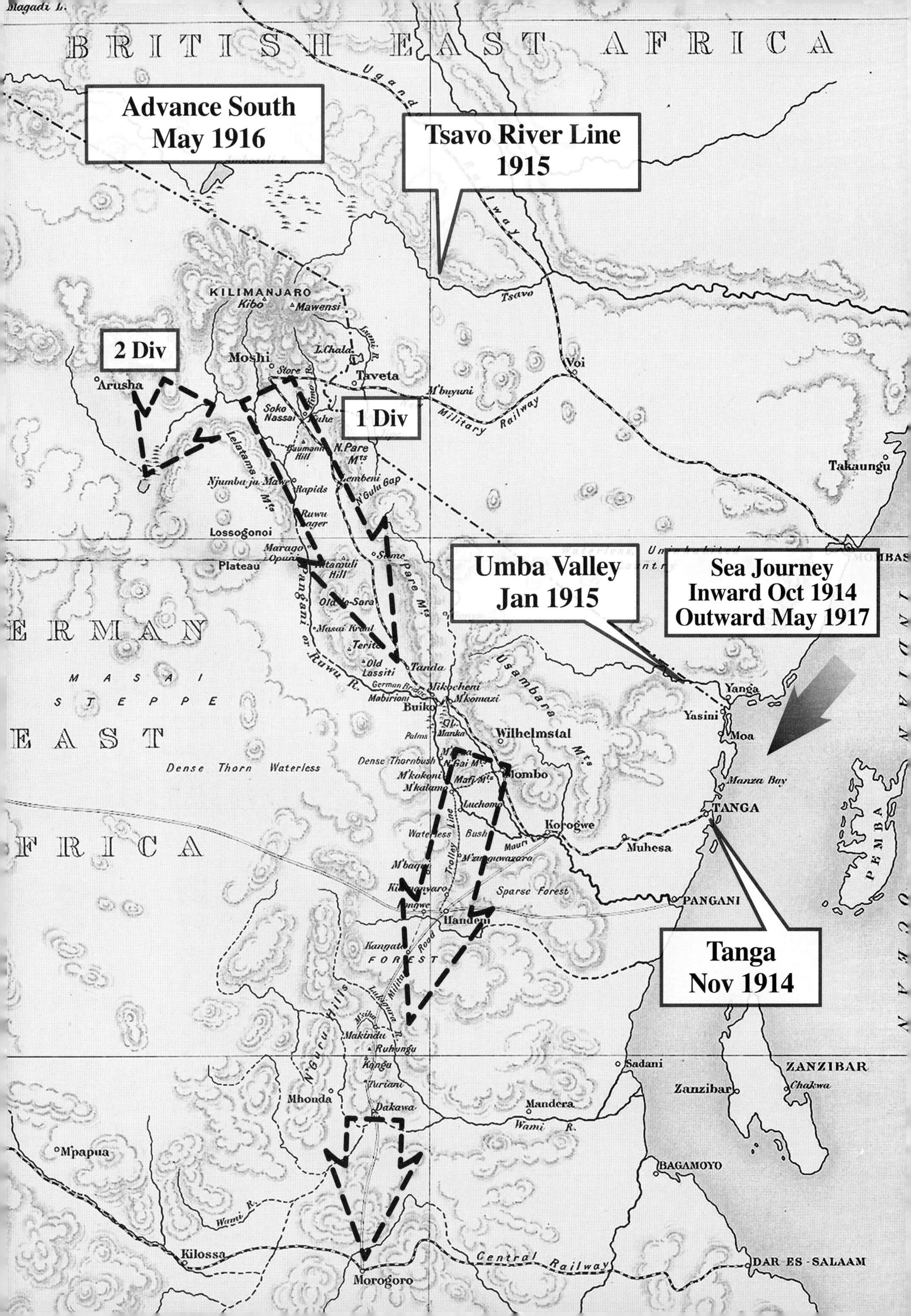

BRITISH EAST AFRICA
Advance South
May 1916
Tsavo River Line
1915
KILIMANJARO
Kibo
Mawensi
2 Div
Moshi
Arusha
Taveta
Voi
Tsavo
1 Div
Military Railway
Soko Nassai
Kahe
N. Pare Mts
Lembeni
N'Gulu Gap
Njumba ja Mawe
Rapids
Lossogonoi
Plateau
Takaungu
Umba Valley
Jan 1915
Sea Journey
Inward Oct 1914
Outward May 1917
GERMAN
MASAI STEPPE
EAST
AFRICA
Dense Thorn Waterless
Old Lassiti
Tanda
Mikocheni
Buiko
Usambara Mts
Wilhelmstal
Mombo
Yanga
Yasini
Moa
Manza Bay
TANGA
Korogwe
Muhesa
PANGANI
Handeni
Tanga
Nov 1914
Kangata
FOREST
Makindu
Kangu
Turiani
Mhonda
Dakawa
Sadani
ZANZIBAR
Zanzibar
Mandera
Wami R.
M'papua
BAGAMOYO
Kilossa
Central Railway
DAR ES SALAAM
Morogoro
PEMBA
INDIAN OCEAN

As the German's withdrew southwards they laid waste to everything of value from crops to houses and most significantly they destroyed the railway lines, bridges and rolling stock. This destruction helped to make the supply situation even more critical. It was the specialist Indian Army Railway and Engineering Units that were to rebuild this infrastructure and new trains and rolling stock had to be imported. Motor cars and lorries were adapted to run on rails.

their operational mobility using porters to carry their logistics – the Field Company (FK) concept of operation emerged. This was a self-contained micro-army that travelled light, was hard-hitting, using machine guns, and could live off the land. Each FK had three platoons of sixty and some twenty German officers and NCO's. Integral to its whole were its transport and supply capability, including 250 porters. They also used significant numbers of armed native auxiliaries. The 2,500 Askari or Schutztruppe were dispersed in these FKs throughout German East Africa.

Havildar Nandbir Thapa 3rd Kashmir Rifles.

Lt Col Paul von Lettow-Vorbeck led the German forces from the outset – he was a resourceful and highly admired leader. His father had been a Prussian general from Pomerania. Lettow-Vorbeck was forty-four in 1914 and had learnt his practical bush-fighting craft and native population control from ruthlessly suppressing an uprising in German South West Africa. He became the outstanding commander of the war in East Africa and was a post-war hero figure to many Germans, British and Africans alike. Whilst he succeeded in avoiding capture and in tying up significant resources through his tactics of a quick skirmish and withdrawal, his methods and use of terror to ensure local population support, combined with laying waste to vast areas of Africa, were fanatical in the extreme and caused disproportional devastation and suffering to Africa and its people. This factor is often overlooked by his admirers. Effective leadership on the British side did not emerge until the appointment of the South African General Smuts in January 1916. He inspired and drove the men to the very limits of existence. Smuts was personally courageous with stamina greater than the proverbial ox but was repeatedly 'out manoeuvred' by Lettow-Vorbeck as he sort to implement his own personal brand of mobile warfare learnt in the Boer War fighting the British!

The tropical climate and topography dominated the war. The lack of water and food, the difficulties of communication, logistics and transport were all big factors. The absolute killer issue was the combination of malaria (see Appendix D for description), dysentery and festering abscesses on tired, thirsty, exhausted and hungry bodies. So bad were the conditions that the hardy South African soldiers captured by the Germans on the Somme battlefield told their captors that 'they would rather endure a winter in France than face the disease and hardships of campaigning in German East Africa'.*

The topography was exploited to the full by the German tactics of ambush (using well-sited and mobile machine guns, often mule-

---

* Footnote: see Charles Duffy through German Eyes: the British & the Somme 1916 p49).

Alec took this picture of the interior of Pathan House, somewhere near Peshwar. The gentleman in the foreground is Col (retired) Aslem Khan.

packed) and withdrawal often along railway lines – after destroying them. All these factors combined to devastating effect causing enormous casualties. Manpower just melted away as the British Empire's lines of communication became catastrophically and repeatedly over extended. Especially devastated were the whites of European extraction and the Indian Troops – The Loyal North Lancashire, whose casualties were some 70 per cent (from 901 men in March 1916 to 265, fourteen weeks later). At the end of December 1916 most troops who had fought throughout the year were withdrawn from the theatre. There was nothing left of them but a few cadres – a good example of this was the Rhodesian Regiment with only twenty-five fit men, even though they were all locally recruited, or the Baluchis depleted to seventy-two (Lt Cooke's diary 05.02.17 notes both these battalions were in theatre for less than a year). Against this background the 2nd Bn Kashmir Rifles performance with a strength of some 280 at the end of 1916 (Cooke's diary 30.12.16), looks better. True comparisons are difficult as reinforcement drafts complicate the story and some soldiers who recovered were returned to operations.

The Kashmir Rifles started the war at one-and-half battalion strength, totalling 1,109 men, and drafts sent out from Kashmir added a further 909.

Very few who started must have been there at the end so casualty rates over the whole period (30 months) were colossal. Lt Col Lyall's 2nd Bn Kashmir Rifles Regimental diary entry for 8 February 1917, at Morogoro, states that Army Medical Board had found 90 per cent of the remaining 280 that were still with the battalion unfit for further military operations (there were more unfit men at various stages of medical evacuation). The Kashmir Rifles, along with the remainder, were all sent home but not without another drama as the GOC (General Officer Commanding), General Hoskins, wanted to retain them 'as they fight' and he sought to combine the fit remnants of both battalions into a 300 rifle-strong force. The men did not recover quickly enough and finally embarked for India at the end of April 1917. Hoskins continued to plead for the other battalion-and-a-half of Kashmir Rifles, but was turned down. No other external soldiers were in theatre on active service for so long a period.

The new troops were drawn from tropical Africa and were hurriedly deployed as Hoskins, the battle-hardened new GOC, had to rapidly rebuild and expand military capability while the 'hero' Smuts was back in Britain telling everyone that the campaign was won, East Africa was occupied and the battles were over. The experience of 1916 had also re-taught the commanders that pack animals could not operate in such conditions (100 per cent loss a month) and so in future all operational logistics would be provided by porters – many hundreds of thousands were recruited locally and they too died in their tens of thousands in 1917 and 1918, again from malnutrition and disease. Edward Paice in *Tip and Run* devotes a whole chapter to what he calls the 'suicidal system of supply' describing how almost every able-bodied East African male became involved (on both sides) and stating this as one of the greatest and least-known tragedies of the First World War.

For the Kashmir Rifles the 2½ years of fighting centred on the railway lines – the essential means of strategic supply and the arteries of East–West communications. From late 1914 and throughout 1915, it was particularly concentrated on the Mombasa to Nairobi line, with defensive operations to keep the Uganda Railway open for the British. In March to July 1916, focus switched to the Tanga to Kahe line, with offensive operations to deny the Usambara Railway and the Trolley Line to the Germans and then rebuild them as fast as possible for logistics. In July to December 1916 they moved to the Morogoro to Dar es Salaam line and carried out further offensive operations to deny the Central Railway to the Germans and then use it for allied logistics.

Alec Kerr was in theatre from December 1914 to December 1916, when he spent the final four months of his tour recovering from malaria and other tropical diseases during a casualty evacuation journey that retraced his and the regiment's steps across both East Africa and all the way back to Kashmir.

Whilst the story that follows is told mostly through pictures and seeks to show the bravery, determination and martial spirit of the Kashmir Rifles, but one should also appreciate that this so-called sideshow was in truth a massive war in its own right – its cost to Great Britain has been described as the equivalent to the entire defence budget of 1914 which was then at 4.16 per cent of GDP and would therefore in today's money represent some £70 billion. Even more importantly, it was as great a tragedy to the peoples of East Africa as the highly publicised Western and Eastern Fronts were to the Europeans. Here, too, total war brought famine, decease, social disintegration and misery.

Opposite: Haramukh from Tragbhal Pass
The track climbs stiffly through pine and deodar forests, the first pass at 11,800 feet on the journey to Giligit – a journey of high passes and guest camps. In 1890, 300 mules and their drivers of the Expeditionary Force, perished in a blizzard. This view looking back south over the Vale of Kashmir is stunning. This is towards snow-clad Haramuhk.

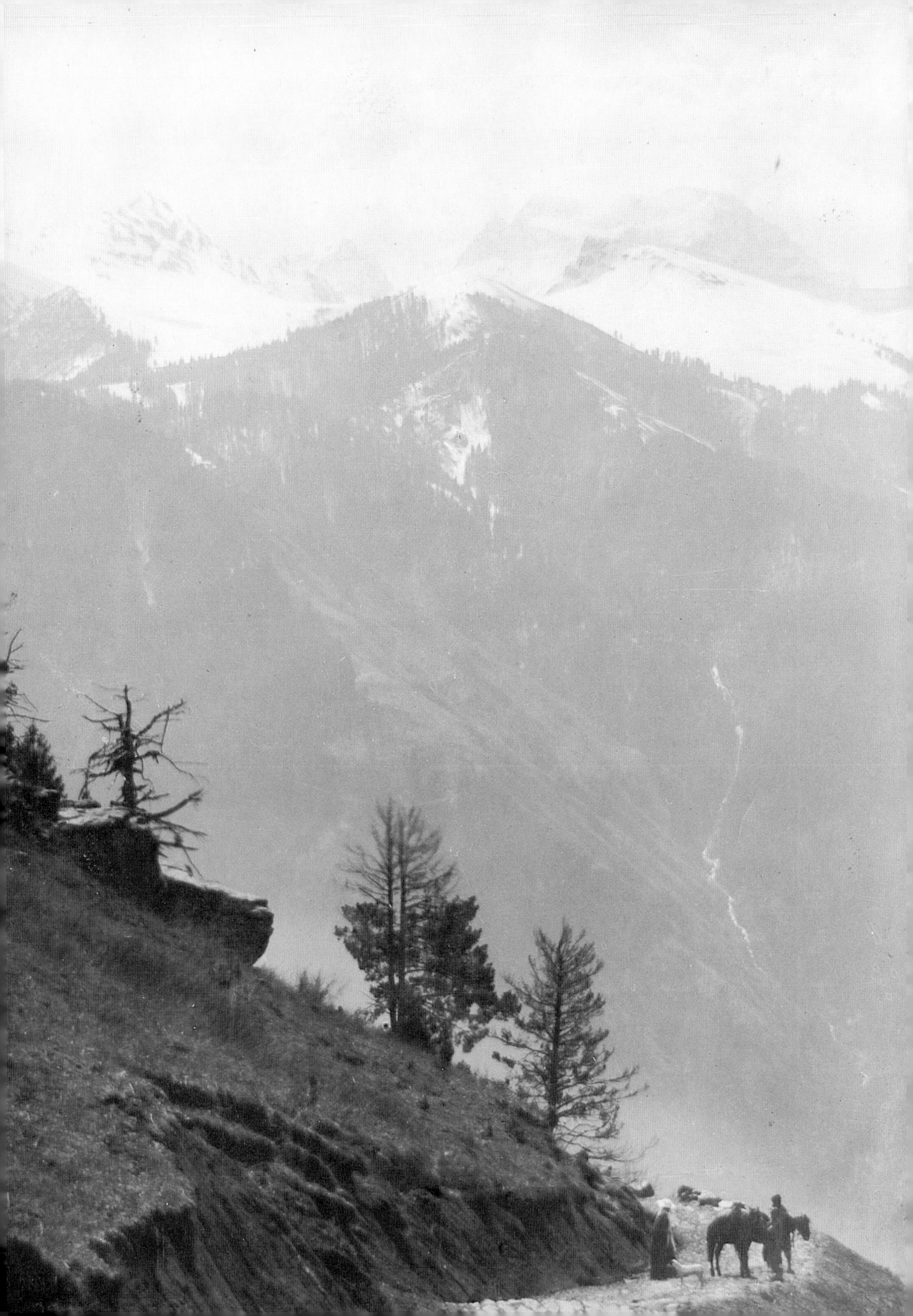

Footsteps of the old journey from Srinagar to Gilgit
Minimarg and Haramukh from the Burzil Pass 13,775 feet, now in Parkistan.
Taken by Captain Alec Kerr, 1912
The Author followed this route and photographs taken in 2010 are on page 170.

The Kashmir State Forces Mountain Battery that was deployed to East Africa and stayed on in 1917 after the Kashmir Rifles returned. It was a direct fire weapon.

1

The Kashmir Rifles

'...as among the most valued of all soldier races of northern India... with their good behaviour, courtly manners, high courage and physical endurance.'

Lt Gen Sir George MacMunn DSO, Armies of India (1911)

The Indian Princes, who ruled their own states under the British Raj retained small armies of their own and these were collectively called the State Forces. The Kashmir forces were the largest of these private armies. At their courts these Princes or Maharajas were guided in their policies by British Residents or Agents. The total establishment in 1914 was about 22,000 men. A British officer was detached from the Indian Army to act as Military Adviser with other officers as Assistant Military Advisers. Many of these formations were very small and their purpose was more about ceremony (gun salutes) and prestige within the concept of state rule in British India than serious professional soldiering.

The Kashmir Rifles were an exception and had a real military purpose for both local frontier defence and the wider national defence of the Raj. They also had a long martial history and tradition that predated the British. Jammu and Kashmir is the most northerly state of India and has borders with Afghanistan, Russia (Turkistan) China and Tibet. In British history it is the northern tip of the story of the 'North West Frontier'. The region is dominated by the highest

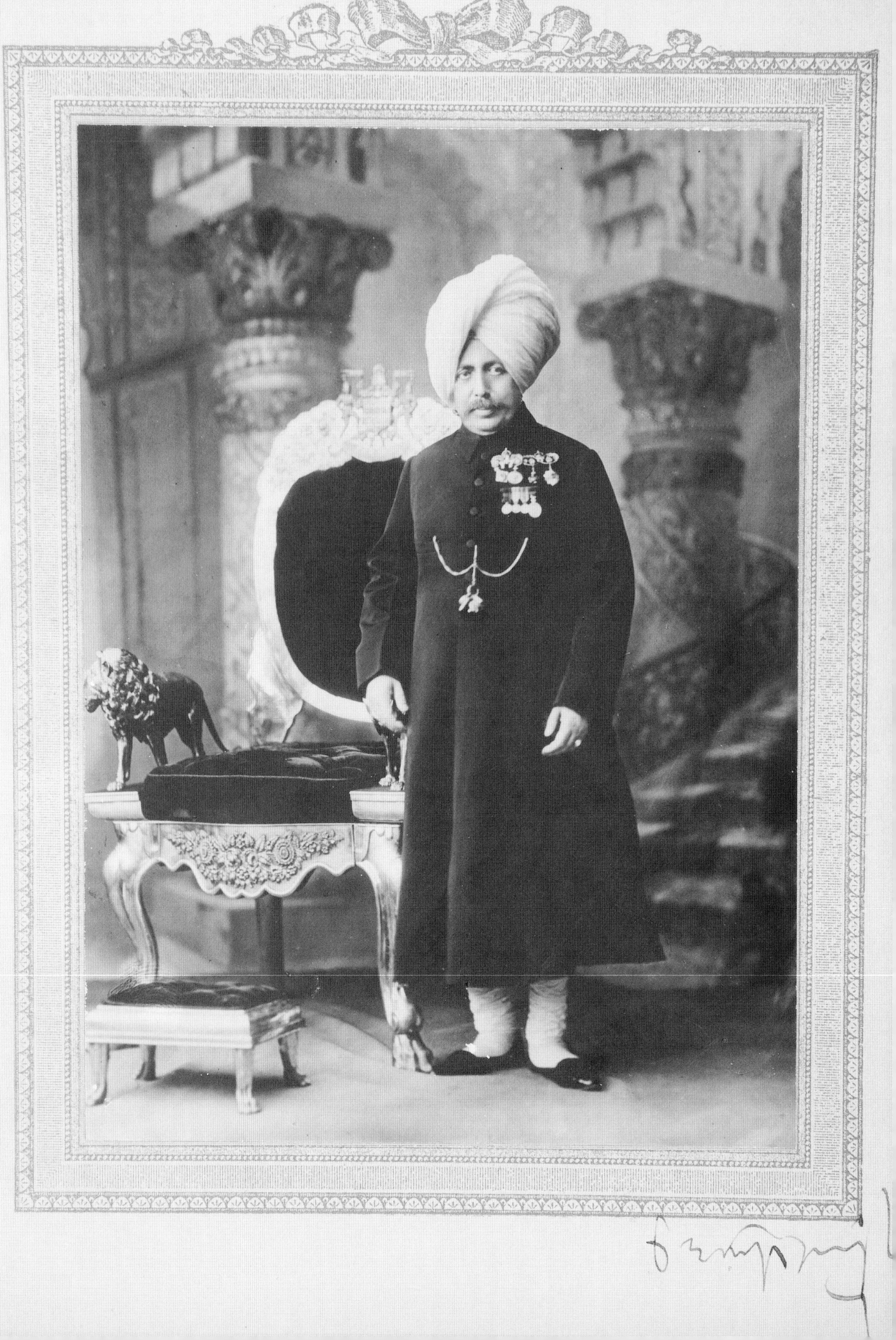

The Kashmir Rifles

mountain ranges in the world. It is the western end of the Himalayas and faces the Pamirs to the north and the Hindu Kush to the west. The great rivers of the Indus, Jhelum, Chenab, Ravi, Tawi and Sutlej all flow from it in a south westerly direction.

The Dogra armies of Kashmir can trace their ancestry back to Maharaja Gulab Singh, the founder of the state of Jammu and Kashmir, who first raised a company of soldiers in 1820. During the following decades the armies through conquest greatly expanded the state and by 1846, through the Treaty of Amritsar with the British, it was confirmed and covered 84,000 square miles. This was by far the largest of the princely states.

The Kashmir Rifles' proud tradition as fearsome and noble warriors can be traced through a series of battle honours including Ladakh 1834–1840, Baltistan 1840, Tibet 1841, Gilgit and Punial 1846–1860. At these battles the fighting qualities and reputation for courage and endurance of these men was established, so much so, that successive British writers and thinkers described them 'as among the most valued of all soldier races of northern India... with their good behaviour, courtly manners, high courage and physical endurance'.

Following the Second Afghan War major policy changes occurred that led to the strengthening of British defences in the north west – the British feared a Russian advance at worst and meddling influence at best. Fortifications were improved, railways extended and roads built. For the Kashmir State Forces it meant greater integration with the Indian Army and supervised training from carefully selected British officers. These 'Imperial Service Troops' were to be better fed, equipped and trained. The cost of this fell on the state of Kashmir and the result was a steep reduction in overall troop numbers from over 20,000 in 1888 to less than 5,000 by 1914. These were structured and spread between just three KR Infantry Battalions, the two Mountain Batteries, the Lancer Squadron and the supporting services.

Successive Maharajas and their families took a very close and personal interest in the regiment's affairs. Money was always tight and equipment levels were considerably lower than the Indian Army. Many of the Kashmiri officers were drawn from the families of the local chiefs and had titles such as Mir or Malik, coupled to the town or place they came from. Maj. K. Brahma Singh the Kashmir Rifles' historian has told me that these leaders were not literate and failed to keep records of their history and according to Lt Cooke's diary entries were reputedly casual about payment to their soldiers for

Opposite: The Maharaja gave this signed photograph to Alec in 1919.

From Satwari Camp looking North to Jammu and the Pir Panjal Mountain Ranges – the Trikuta Hills.

their services. The first battalion was named 'Raghupratap', Alec's first appointment was their Assistant Inspecting Officer, the second was titled 'Body Guard', and the third, 'Raghunath'.

The British presence amongst such a proud regiment was well established by the time Alec arrived in 1912 but it had not always been an easy relationship for the British, who did not initially understand the Dogra culture and concept of discipline. Brahma Singh writes in the regimental history following a period of high desertion in about 1890 (this followed the creation of the Imperial Service Corps):

> The Dogra concept of discipline was borne out of a sense of self respect and pride in the cause. That discipline did not affect a soldier's individuality nor crush his initiative. He did what he was required to do willingly and with a sense of purpose... under the British concept the soldier lost his identity and he was treated with disrespect as a necessary aspect of training [imagine the abuses that the drill instructors must have hurled on him]. All in all he was made to feel inferior and stupid under the new environment. Besides he

The Kashmir Rifles

Above: The Shergarhi Palace.

Below: Baramulla.

'I Can Never Say Enough About the Men'

Above: Shah Hamadan Mosque.

Below: Srinagar and the Hari Parbat.

must have felt insecure. His officers had been sidelined and the command virtually taken over by the British Inspecting Officers... the human touch had gone as everything worked like a machine under rules and regulations.

It is interesting to gauge where the balance may have been struck in this clash of martial cultures, however what is clear is that a year later the Agent, Colonel Durrand, in his despatch to the Resident in Kashmir made reference to the 'cheery spirit with which the men and officers faced their work and to the ready cooperation which the British officers received on all occasions from their Kashmiri brothers in arms'. But perhaps more important than words were the successful deeds in military operations that followed with the capture of the fortress at Nilt as part of what came to be called the war on the roof of the world, then a few years later with the Chitral Campaign of 1895 and the Tirah Expedition of 1897.

The Jhelum Road that was built for wheeled vehicles in the 1880s – according to Dr Duke seventy-four men died in its construction – Maj. Lyall had one of the first cars in Srinagar in 1917.

The pattern of life that Alec was welcomed into was based on a rotation of the three infantry battalions through the three major cities of Jammu, Srinagar and Gilgit. Gradually accommodation had been improved, medical facilities developed, further education provided and patterns of recruitment by ethnicity and religion established.

Militarily the modernisations of the battalions had slowly taken place and were based on the rifles' model from the British Army. Inspecting Officer's reports emphasised the high levels of fitness and musketry, as well as the personal qualities of the men, and by contrast they were critical of the signalling – so one might surmise that raising the game here was Alec's key task in 1913.

Perhaps the most interesting aspect of life, especially when viewed from today with our ease of travel by car, helicopter and aeroplane, is to consider the challenge of maintaining the garrison battalion at Gilgit to the far north of Kashmir separated by the highest mountain range in the world. Jammu the southernmost city was the winter capital and Srinagar the summer one. The reason for this was the

The great Nanga Parbat (naked mountain) towers above Bunji – it was often hidden by cloud. At 26,660 feet it is the ninth highest mountain in the world and some say that in the absence of foothills, the most dramatic. It was first climbed in 1953 and had taken many lives. The views of Nanga Parbat must have characterised the whole four-week journey and Alec was to spend two years in this bungalow.

Himalayan snow line which cut off Jammu from Srinagar for many months every year along the Pir Panjal Mountains and it completely shut out Gilgit further to the north, where the key pass the Burzil at 13,700 feet was closed to all but the most intrepid traveller from mid-September to mid-June, or put the other way was open for just 3 months a year. Even today this frontier poses unique military challenges and soldiers face temperatures of minus 50 degrees Celsius, one of the coldest places in the world. Successive policies were enacted to maximise Gilgit's self sufficiency and minimise dependence on external supplies. In the early 1900s some 10,000 ponies and pack animals were needed to transport the supplies, a

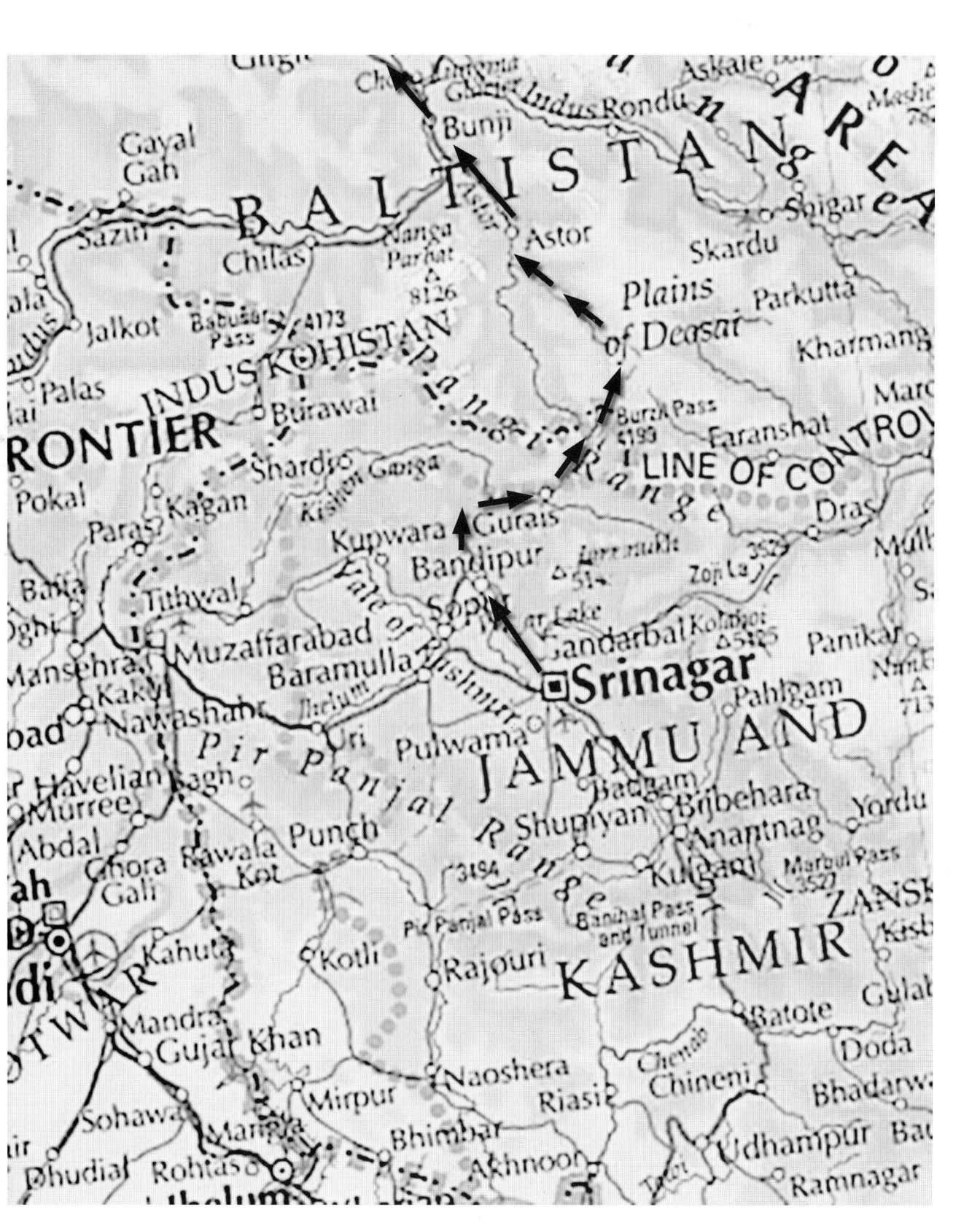

The 240-mile or four-week trek from Srinagar to Gilgit that Alec made to join the 1st Bn, between 28 September and 24 October 1912. This route was only passable during the Summer months.

The staff of the Gilgit Agency and local leaders and their sons, outside the Agent's residence in Gilgit, 1914.

huge cost which the state could ill afford.

As Alec was posted to the 1st Battalion at Gilgit he had to make this 240-mile journey from Srinagar as part of a small planned convoy – his service record suggests it was between the 28 September and 24 October 1912, so right at the end of the open or snow-free period. Whilst Alec did not keep a record he did take some photographs and labelled them – these I have pieced together and by using the descriptions from Trevelyan's book, the Golden Oriole, describing a similar journey but made in the same months of 1929.

Life in Gilgit must have been extraordinary even by the extremes of Empire given its isolation and the smallness of the British community. Trevelyan's descriptions are worth reading from the predictable elements like shooting and polo to the unpredictable stories of their relationships with the Mirs and Rajahs. Such a small community of British had to work with the existing social, cultural and political order, and exercise what is sometimes today described as 'soft power'. Alec's photographs show the beautiful gardens around the few bungalows, with Nanga Parbat towering overhead, the Durbar of 1914 and the annual Gilgit event on the polo ground, called the Jhalsa. There are just eight British faces amongst the

Above: The annual shoot at Gor – a two-day trip from Gilgit and quite near Bunji. The chukor were driven by beaters: 'they came so fast and low, they took your hat.'

Below: The 1914 Durbar on the Polo ground at Gilgit. 1st Kashmir Infantry are middle right and Gilgit Scouts in the foreground (they were locally recruited militia founded in 1913).

Local leaders, left to right: Ishukman, Nagar, Hunza, Punial and Ghizar.

local Mirs, Rajahs and their sons; other pictures show shooting the Chukor (partridge) at Gor and remarkable scenery shots of dramatic mountains and snow. However, this way of life was about to be shattered by the events of 1914.

The 2nd Bn and half the 3rd Bn were sent out to East Africa as part of the hastily formed Imperial Service Brigade –an emergency and expedient measure, earlier calls on the Indian Army to support the European war against the Germans had already reduced the garrisons of India to a minimum and had taken many of the best-equipped and trained to form the Indian Corps of two Infantry Divisions and a Cavalry Brigade. In fact scraping the barrel has been a commonly used description for the troops of the Imperial Service Brigade, most of whom did not have the military pedigree of the Kashmir Rifles.

Their equipment limitations compared with other units appear

The Gilgit Scouts: Ghazan Khan and Mohad Ali.

great with no machine guns, no modern Lee Enfield rifles (they had the incredibly ancient Martini-Henrys and were issued with the Lee Enfield on mobilisation, and had little time, or chance, to become familiar with it), no field telephones and no pistols for their officers. The manpower for the Kashmir Rifles came from a mixture of Gurkhas and Dogras. There were some 1,100 in all, split into 715 for the 2nd Bn and 376 for half of the 3Bn. During the operations they were divided many times in different ways. Overall there were 542 Gurkhas, 294 Dogras and 255 Punjabis. The Punjabis were all deployed in the 2nd Bn. The reason that only half of the 3rd Bn was sent reflects the difficulties in finding enough reinforcement troops from across India, as some troops needed to remain for local defence – they were officially the other half to 3rd Gwalior Infantry to make up a composite Battalion.**

The official history shows they embarked separately, the 2nd Bn

THE GILGIT AGENCY 1930

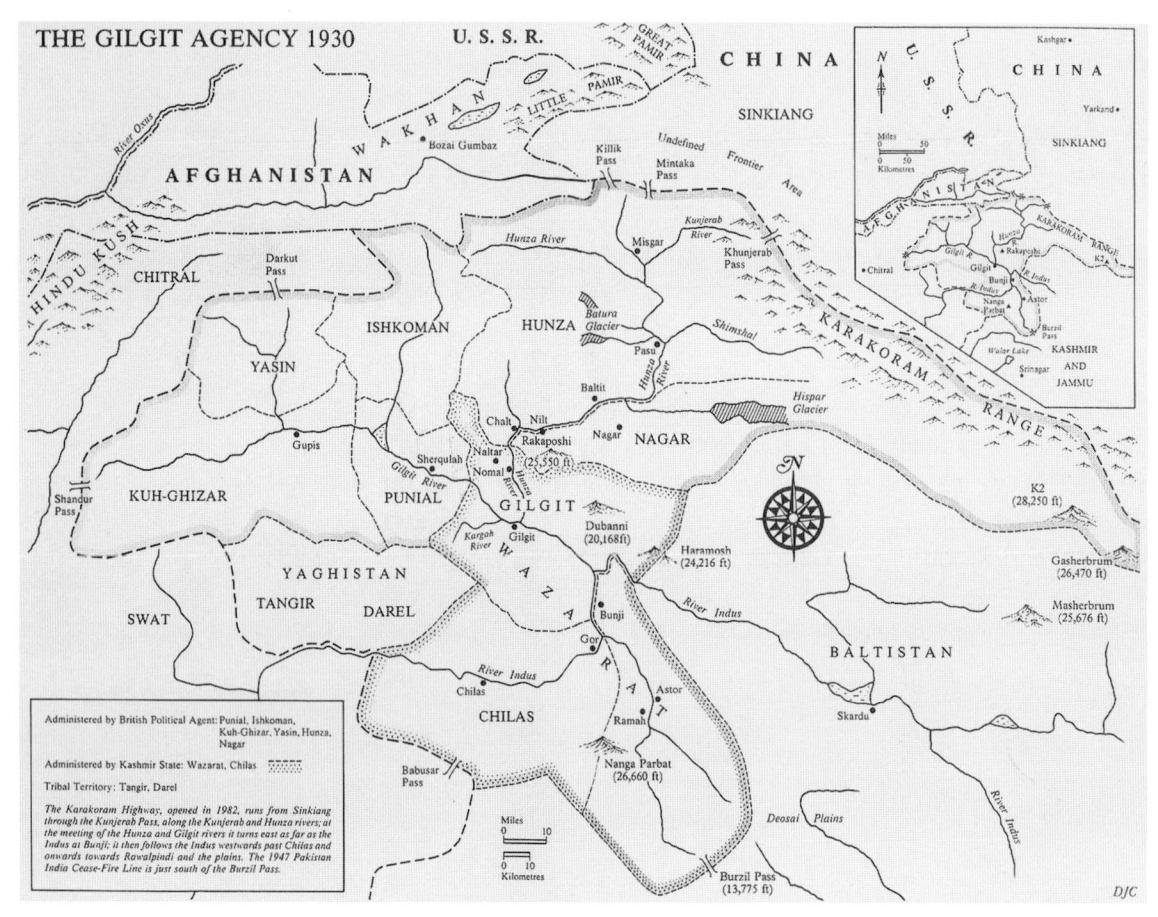

The Gilgit Agency was reckoned to be 15,000 square miles (1.25 times the size of Wales) with a scattered population of 165,000. It was part of the self-governing state, Kashmir and Jammu of British Empire, ruled by the Maharaja. The British kept a Resident at Srinagar and an Agent at Gilgit. The British Political Agent administered Punial, Ishkoman, Kuh-Ghizar, Yasin, Hunza and Nagar. Kashmir State administered the Wazarat (Gilgit Village) and Chilas direct. Tangier and Darel were described as Tribal territory. Yaghistan was the inspiration for Kipling's Man Who Would be King.

on the *Khosru* and the 3rd Bn with the Gwalior Infantry on the *Barjora*. The Kashmir Rifles had forty-four and twenty-four official camp followers, and six and seven private ones respectively. No riding horses and three pack mules each. There were no transports. The two British officers with the 2nd Bn were Captains Ames and Hanson, and those with the 3rd Bn were Lyall and Money.

The journey from Kashmir took several weeks. The orders for the 3rd Bn were received on the 15 September and mobilisation was complete by the 26 September when they entrained from Satwari Camp, near Jammu***. The train journey took five days to arrive at Deolali (near Bombay). They pitched camp on the 1 October and were inspected by the GOC on the 2 October.

Alec was stationed further north at Gilgit with the first battalion guarding the frontier, the journey from Gilgit to Srinagar took three or four weeks on a horse – it was to take him several more weeks to make the arrangements to join the expedition.

There followed three days of manoeuvres and the battalion's practised 'Advance Guard' and 'Reconnaissance of the Enemy Position.' On 7 October they entrained for Bombay and embarked on the *SS Bajora*. The convoy of fourteen vessels left on 16 October, and during the interval they had bathing parades, rowing practices and musketry instruction. On board there was a routine of physical training and lectures. These were completely disrupted and even stopped for four days by the sea-sickness that affected 70 per cent of them. There is a note to say that some of the latrines were not working and had to be closed.

They arrived off Mombasa on 29 October exhausted and one imagines keen to return to dry land.

Havildar Ata Ullah 2nd Kashmir Rifles.

****

Major (Retired) Brahma Singh wrote:
The question of how and why people from such far off lands went and fought for the British cause in East Africa is applicable not only to the people of Jammu and Kashmir but all Indians. They can certainly not be termed as mercenaries as they were fighting as members of the Army of their own country and fighting under orders of the Indian government. It so happened that their country was at that time ruled by the British and as true and disciplined soldiers they were, by tradition, loyal to the government of the day. I doubt if they ever thought of the cause for which they were fighting. As a matter of fact all through history the Indian soldier has mostly fought as a matter of duty towards his ruler rather than any particular cause.

It might interest the reader to know that in the famous Hindu Epic- The Mahabharata – depicting the fight between the good and the evil, a large number of warriors sided with the wrong cause, knowing fully that it was wrong, only because their king was associated with it.

Devoid of the cause the Indian soldier's motivation emerged from the martial status conferred on his community by society. The Indian soldiers from the martial races fought for their community's prestige, honour and name. This fact was well exploited by the British in India and consequently only men from the recognised martial races were enrolled in the fighting arms of the Indian Army. Besides in order

'I Can Never Say Enough About the Men'

to create competition between the martial races in valour, spirit and acumen, the fighting arms, composed of martial races, were organised on communal or regional basis. So the Indian soldier, even as he fought in Africa, was motivated by his duty towards his ruler and for the honour and prestige of his community. The State troops for the prestige of the Maharaja out of their unflinching loyalty for him.

In this connection I may mention that in those day Kashmiris (people from the Kashmir Valley, both Hindus and Muslims) were considered non martial and, therefore, not enrolled in either the Indian Army or the State Force. The State Force was composed of Dogra Hindus, and Dogra Muslims (as Muslims of Jammu province were then known) and some Gorkhas especially recruited from Nepal. The troops that went to fight in East Africa were Dogras (both Hindus and Muslims) and Gorkhas. So technically speaking these troops should not have been referred to as Kashmiris like they were in most official reports. But in those days, as also till the end of the British rule, the Jammu and Kashmir State was mostly referred to in British circles as just Kashmir for short. Consequently people not too knowledgeable about the State's geography and demography would call every one belonging to the State as a Kashmiri. In those days of course there was no confusion as every one knew what the other meant. But now after a lapse of about hundred years the perspectives have changed beyond recognition and while the events are being viewed as part of history, an explanation of this nature would seem necessary.

******

** The use of Punjabi here is due to the fact that the Muslim Dogras from Jammu Province were enrolled as Punjabi Muslims, even though they were in reality Dogras. Thererfore, the class composition of 3rd Battalion was Gorkhas (Gurkhas) and Hindu Dogra in the proportion of 50:50 and for the 2nd Battalion it was Gorkhas and Muslim Dogra again in the ration of 50:50. Battalions with Gorkhas in their class composition were selected probably because Gorkhas were known to be good fighters in the jungles and mountains.

*** The Jammu Cantonment was located at a place called Satwari, about 4km to 5km from the city. The cantonment still stands at Satwari *See picture page 28.*

2

Captain Alexander Kerr and the British Officers

> Sepoys of the Indian Army accepted as a matter of course that their Sahibs would lead them in the literal sense.
>
> Gordon Corrigan, *Sepoys in the Trenches*

In peace time each Kashmir Rifle battalion had just one attached British officer and on mobilisation this was increased to two, and for the 2nd Bn Kashmir Rifles, three with the arrival in 1915 of the machine guns.

The pre-war officers were selected and drawn from the Indian Army, from the best talent available on grounds of both military competence and proven ability to lead, inspire and to get on with the local and prevailing Kashmiri military's, social and religious customs. The Indian Army was rightly tough on those British officers who did not have a natural feel for and respect for their Indian soldiers.

After the debacle of Tanga the senior British officer was Major R.A. Lyall, Alec was his captain and then later Lt G.H. Cooke joined and took on the maxim guns. These three all arrived at different times Lyall from the 3Bn, Alec from the Ist Bn and Cooke from a civilian life.

Lyall came from a very prominent and long-serving Anglo-Indian family that could boast two Lieutenant Governors, one of the North West Province and the other the Punjab. The family and these governors had used the Haileybury (formerly the East India College) route into the East India Company and political prominence. Lyall himself was not just a soldier and had recently seen service as the Political Agent at Kurram and, like Alec, had pressed his case in 1914 for action and the chance to lead Indian soldiers on military operations. During the East African theatre of operations the Kashmir Rifles battalions were often mixed and matched so Lyall who was initially with 3rd Bn Kashmir Rifles and was then transferred to the 2nd Bn.

Cooke's background was very different in that he had started life in India in business (having been educated at Queen's College, Taunton) and was a soldier volunteer in September 1914 with the Maxim Gun Company. He arrived in East Africa in October 1914 as a Lance Corporal and on 1 October 1915 transferred to 2nd Bn Kashmir Rifles as a 2nd Lieutenant. His diaries and letters are very complete and liberally express his strongly held feelings on many subjects, especially his frustration with his immediate British officers commanding (OCs), Lyall and Kerr; he also expresses his admiration for the Kashmiri soldiers. He had a demanding task as he had to learn on the job and he took his studies and soldiering very seriously. Throughout 1915 he learnt the language and cultures of his men – this was a key theme of the Indian Army: the British officer learnt, enjoyed and took pride in the language, customs and traditions of their regiment, and if he couldn't or didn't then his military career was unlikely to develop and his card was marked as not suitable.

The British Officer in the Indian Army evolved a very special role and relationship with his men which can be difficult to comprehend from a modern standpoint. A typical regular Indian battalion had a total of about twelve officers including an MO (Medical Officer), and those on leave and courses. In the Kashmir Rifles (State Forces) it must have been even more extraordinary with the British influence being exercised by so few. Gordon Corrigan, who had served with the British Gurkhas, wrote in 2006 in his book *Sepoys in the Trenches*:

> The Indian Army operated by using the British Officer as the instigator and promulgator of policy, while the Indian Officer executed it. The British Officer was seen as being above tribalism and had no vested interest in extending favour to one man rather than another. The British Officer was educated and could make sense of operational orders written in English. The British Officer was impartial. There was a touching – and nearly always justified – faith in the

honour and integrity of the British Officer who, while he might not always come to the decision that the soldiers would prefer, would at least come to it without fear or favour... in the main he took pains to get to know his men's language and to understand and respect their customs and culture.

Such a system then could only work if the Indian officers were really competent and if the few British officers could live up, not only to this reputation, but also to the one of leading from the front. Corrigan continues: 'sepoys of the Indian Army accepted as a matter of course that their Sahibs would lead them in the literal sense' – the British officer therefore needed great physical and personal courage. Their isolation from the general British community was extreme and especially so in a place like Gilgit or on independent operations when they must have lived at very close quarters with their brother Kashmiri officers and men. If they had not been competent and respected it is difficult to imagine how these British-led operations could have worked. Alec Kerr is interesting in that his story is not exceptional and that his social background, education, values and ways of thinking are typical of that era.

Alec was born into a traditional Scots and military family. His father, grandfather and great-grandfather had all served in India with the Madras Presidency, his uncle had won a VC at Kohlapur (1857) during the Indian Mutiny and his great-great-grandfather's brother had been killed at the siege of Calcutta in 1756. It was not uncommon for these long serving traditions in the Indian Army however with five consecutive generations this would have been worthy of David Gilmour's description of the 'Dolphin Family' in his book *The Ruling Caste*. The Kerr family were an ancient Scottish border clan that could directly trace their ancestry back to William the Conqueror and were caught up in many of the battles and skirmishes between England and Scotland.

They were in the retinue of the Bruces at the battle of Bannockburn 1314, survived

Alec Kerr at St Andrew's, Scotland, the home of golf, at about 1888. Note the golf club, a St Andrew's long-range putter, which the family still enjoys.

Five generations of Kerrs

Alec's great-grandfather. His two great gandfathers were **General Thomas William Kerr** 1768–1825, who served with the Blackwatch before transferring to the Ceylon regiment, where he fought campaigns to capture Ceylon and some years later was the GOC and acting Governor. And **General Sir Alexander Murray McGregor (above)** who had fought with Wellington in Spain and was his Quartermaster-General.

Alec's grandfather was **Colonel Alexander Boyd Kerr** of the 24th Madras Native Infantry 1810–1867. He was a cadet at Addiscombe in 1826.

Alec's father, **Colonel John McGregor Kerr** of 3rd Madras Light Cavalry 1838–1915. He was born in Palaveran, educated at Loretto in Scotland and returned aged 17 as a Cornet. He served until 1885 and was commandant of his regiment.

Alec's uncle, **William Alexander Kerr** (9th of Abbotrule) 1831–1919 served in the Bombay Presidency and when on secondment formed the South Mahratta Horse and led this native detachment to retake the Fort at Kohlapur and won the VC. This picture now hangs in the main entrance hall at Sandhurst.

Flodden 1513 and throughout the sixteenth and seventeenth centuries were one of the leading protagonists in what was called 'reiving' (inter-tribal raiding and plundering). In the eighteenth century they had been in force on both sides at Culloden 1746 (the Jacobite Rebellion) and the last great land battle on British soil.

Soldiering, duty and honour was therefore in Alec's blood and it is thus unsurprising that he followed a military career. It is difficult to say that he chose this path, as both his younger brothers were soldiers too and as Evan (the youngest) stated '...life followed a preordained plan rather like a tram'.

He was christened Alexander Nairne Kerr and was born on 7 June 1882 at Secunderabad, Madras; he was to live to aged eighty-two, and as the eldest son was to be the 10th Kerr of Abbotrule – a minor Scots title with the land near Jedburgh long since sold. His mother was also from an established Scots family called Nairne who were landowners at Dunsinan, near Perth, the site of Macbeth's castle made so famous by Shakespeare.

Alec, as he was always called, grew up in India and came back with his family when his father retired in 1886. They lived initially in Scotland and then finally settled in Folkestone. He was educated at Marlborough, a famous English public school in Wiltshire, with a strong tradition of service both to the Church and the Empire, he played fly half for the rugby fifteen and went on to the Royal Military Academy Sandhurst. We were always told that he was stretched on a rack in order to meet the minimum height requirements! He achieved good marks and passed out near the top of his intake. There was great competition for the Indian Army with its higher pay and generous pension and only the first twenty or so of each intake were placed.

Of his early life there are sadly few stories. His younger brother Evan, writing in his common place book, talks of his aggressiveness and of the caddies at St Andrews (the home of golf) calling him 'curry pooder'. He does not seem to have liked horses, in spite of his father's cavalry influence, and the family was obviously short of funds. Field Marshal Sir Frederick Haines (Commander in Chief, India 1876–81) is said to have provided the obligatory nomination to support his entry to the Indian Army, his father Colonel John MacGregor Kerr (3rd Madras Light Cavalry) had worked for many years on the General's staff.

I have wondered why he chose the Dogra Regiment and believe that when the three Presidencies of the East India Company were progressively reformed following the Mutiny into one Army, Alec

Alec

Alec's Forefathers

Alec (10th of Abbotrule) 1882–1964 was born in India and educated at Marlborough. He was only 20 in 1902 when he followed the family tradition of service to India that had started with his Great-Great Grandfather's brother, Charles Kerr (5th Abbotrule), who aged 18 was killed in service with the Honourable East India Company in 1756 at the defence of Calcutta. Alec's son John Kinloch Kerr (11th Abbotrule) served with the Dogras in the Second World War. Both John Kinloch Kerr's sons served with the British Army in the 1970s. Thus, the Kerrs of Abbotrule have a service record that spans 200 years and seven continuous generations.

would consequently not have felt so obliged to enter the successor Madras Regiments. Furthermore the North West Frontier enjoyed the aura of action, whereas the southern regiments had not had a war for several generations and in the language of the time were considered less martial – so perhaps his choice of the Dogras with their fearsome warrior reputation reflected these trends and possibly the family advice from General Haines – certainly the Dogras were very well thought of and considered a crack regiment.

His official record of army service reads as follows:

2Lt	Attached to Royal Sussex	18 Jan 1902
	Attached Kings Royal Rifles	
Lt	38 Dogras	18 Apr 1904
Adjutant	38 Dogras	7 Jun 08 to 6 Jun 1912
Capt	38 Dogras	18 Jan 1911
	Attached Kashmir Rifles	1912–20
Major		18 Jan 1917
Lt Col	2/17 Dogras	4 Jan 1927
Service Completed		4 Jan 1931

Alec went straight from Sandhurst to India and, as was the custom for those joining the Indian Army, he was initially attached to a British regiment spending two periods of over six months. The first was with the Royal Sussex Regiment and the second with the Kings Royal Rifles before being posted to the Dogras* on 9 April 1903.

He had two periods of Active Service. One of short duration in 1908 with the 24th Sikh Pioneers North West Frontier – the Mohmand Expedition of 1908 where Alec as the machine gun officer gained valuable experience in their deployment in action. Following which his officer commanding, a Major Gilbert, has written this testimonial:

> I have much pleasure in informing you that Lt Kerr worked the machine guns always to my entire satisfaction and managed his men with judgment and tact. I formed a very high opinion of Lt Kerr's

---

* Dogra was a term used for people living in the Jammu province of Jammu and Kashmir and the hilly regions of Punjab – now known as Himachal Pradesh. While the State Force were mostly Dogras (both Hindus and Muslims) belonging to the Jammu region, the Dogra Regiment of the Indian Army was composed of Dogras (only Hindu) from the hilly regions of Punjab. The affinity was, therefore, not only neighbourly but also ethnic. The Raghupratap was composed of 100% Hindu Dogras. (Information courtesy of Maj. Brahma Singh)

Alec (third from right) during a six-month attachment to the Royal Sussex Regiment, displaying the fabled British sense of humour in fancy dress, Dalhousie 1902.

soldiering qualities and I consider him an officer of worth and promise and congratulate you on... such an officer. I shall be obliged if you could attach this letter to Lieutenant Kerr's record of services. I have the honour to be Sir your most obedient servant etc.

The other was in East Africa fighting the Germans between the years 1914–16 with the Kashmir Rifles, which is fully described in this book.

Another question which one might ask is why did Alec volunteer for the Kashmir Rifles? A posting that would take him to the very northern edge of the British Raj at Gilgit, where the British community was tiny, perhaps eight people, and the area vast and isolated (the Gilgit Agency was larger than the whole of Wales with a population of 165,000). The Dogras were near neighbours and had close training links with the 1st Battalion Raghupratap so it is likely that he would have heard wonderful tales of friendships, beauty and

Above: In 1905 Alec (six in from right with the terrier) attended the Musketry School at Changla Gali, he is seen here sitting, wearing blues with his terrier, six in from the right, with other students and the instructors. It was here that Alec learnt the rudiments of the Vickers Maxim .303 machine gun that has been called one of the most indispensable weapons of the century. Alec also learnt several languages: Urdu, Punjabi and Pashtu.

Below: As commanding officer of the 17th Dogras, around 1930.

adventure – the romance of Kashmir.

However, I suspect there were also several practical reasons including extra pay and military experience at a more senior level, which in due course would be sound preparation for command. Certainly his experiences with the Mohmand Expedition of 1908 would have further developed his confidence and certainly would have helped his application to the Kashmir Rifles.

In 1920, after his eight years of life with the Kashmir Rifles, he returned to his parent Regiment the 17th Dogras and completed a typical series of appointments all on the North West Frontier, culminating in command of the regiment in 1927. He went back to Britain for a long period of leave in 1922 and met and married Eve. She did not like the heat of India and after command in 1931 he retired to Perthshire, Scotland where he built a house and where Eve's family had also heralded from, and lived a quiet life concentrating on golf and gardening, perhaps his two lasting passions (his name is on the board to this day at the Gulmarg Golf Club). This along with a daily press ups kept him fit right to the very end. He also gave considerable time to the Red Cross and was active in Perthshire local life. He never spoke of his war to his son John and if he did collect papers and books on the war in East Africa these never survived his death or were ever mentioned in family discussions. He did, however, keep his photograph albums and these record his life and experiences of both India and East Africa, and are a key source material for this record. John, his son and only child, followed his father into the Dogras and so became the sixth generation to serve India.

In an age of post traumatic stress disorder it is interesting to speculate what impact the war in East Africa may have had upon him. Certainly the Kerr family had absorbed much of the culture and values of service in India over many generations – they were very comfortable with structure, order and deference, they thought in terms of social hierarchies, of correctness and of loyalties, they were frugal, self-contained, practical, patient and quietly determined. Perhaps, above all, they loved India. The modern expression 'team player' would also fit but, of course, in those days you had to be or the structure and approach to leadership would simply not have functioned – otherwise how could so few have led so many.

John was brought up as an only son in a very Victorian way to elderly parents who were both in their forties when they married, but perhaps the clue to the war's impact on Alec comes from the comments of his brother and junior officer, Lt Cooke, who on their return to India in his private diaries comments that he never

Lt Col R A Lyall, DSO.

Note from John Lyall on his father Lt Col RA Lyall DSO "My father attended the Royal Military College Sandhurst where he failed to qualify high enough for the Indian Army and joined the Gordon Highlanders. In 1897 he was involved when the Gordons were attacked by Afridi tribesmen near the entrance to the Khyber Pass. He collapsed with a violent attack of fever and was rushed to hospital in Peshawar and celebrated his 21st birthday in his hospital bed. He then volunteered for the 34th Pioneers attached to the China Expeditionary Force which was known as the Boxers. In 1903 he was placed with the Foreign Department of the Government of India as a Political Officer and was posted to Kurram until the First World War broke out in 1914."

He immediately joined 3rd Kashmir Rifles and upon return from Africa went to Palestine with the Kashmir Rifles serving under General Allenby and fought at the Battle of Gaza.

Alec Kerr.

speaks. This is in sharp contrast to the fun-loving young man of pranks and high jinks of his subaltern days as conveyed by the picture of Alec dressed as a girl at a Royal Sussex Regimental fancy dress party (see photo).

Certainly I remember a man of great self-discipline, politeness and quiet charm who was often being directed by a busy, noisy and humorous wife. So my concluding thought is that perhaps he did turn inward on himself as result of these war experiences and like so many never shared the burden.

3

The Battle of Tanga
2–5 November 1914

> He proved himself a capable leader and was most distinguishable in the way he led parties in the right column. His coolness and ability to carry out tactical movements in the confusion and excitement of action and the hours after it was very creditable.
> Capt Hanson on Lt Col Raghubir Singh in 2nd Bn War Diary

> I should like to take this opportunity of saying that all through the actions up to the time of his being wounded he handled his regiment very ably and skilfully and with much personal bravery.
> Captain Money on Lt Col Durga Singh in 3rd Bn War Diary

Alec Kerr was not present at this battle. He was on route travelling to join the 2nd Bn Kashmir Rifles from the 1st Bn. He had kicked up a fuss and did not want to be left out of the action, fearing, like so many brave or perhaps foolish young men, that the 'war would be over by Christmas' and that he would miss the action. The Kashmir Rifles were to perform impressively at Tanga and in marked contrast to many Indian Army units and especially in contrast to Army Command.

Tanga was the northernmost port in German East Africa it was, and remains today, an important centre for communications. Strategically it was the key to the Northern provinces which was then the region of greatest prosperity.

'I Can Never Say Enough About the Men'

Captain and later Major Money who lead 3 Kashmir Rifles. Some of his records survive in the Regimental Diaries. His account of Tanga is particularly useful and his complements about Lt Col Durga Singh are very telling. He went on to Palestine after the East African Campaign.

The Royal Navy had command of the seas and the Germans were having huge difficulties supplying their forces. The high command back in Germany decided to largely 'write off' their colonies and Col Lettow-Vorbeck, who had only recently arrived as the local commander, was planning a campaign whose strategy and purpose would emerge as the absorption of as greater proportion of British and Empire resources as possible and for as long as possible.

The British plan was muddled from the outset with rival thinking between the Colonial Office, Army Headquarters India and the War Office in London. What emerged was absurdly ambitious given the forces available, the enormity of the task and the German self belief: 'To bring the whole of East Africa under British authority.'

The Indian Expeditionary Force B was hastily scraped together and then dispatched from Bombay on 16 October 1914. It consisted of two brigades, the 27th Bangalore, under Brigadier R. Wapshire, and the Imperial Service Brigade under command of Brigadier M.J. Tighe. The former brigade had the 'Regular' troops and the latter were a diverse collection of 'State Forces' formations. The Kashmir Rifles were of the latter. Structurally the force suffered from virtually no artillery and a staff who had only assembled on mobilisation, and who had not developed and honed their methods in training. Equipment shortages were scandalous and the Kashmir Rifles had no machine guns and no field telephones. Some aspects of mobilisation worked efficiently like the indenting for the new Lee Enfield rifles, entrenching tools and field service clothing, whereas others did not, notably the 'unaccountable delay of the foreign minister in the transmission of recall papers to Gurkhas on firlo [leave]'.

The overall expeditionary commander was Maj. Gen. Aitken, who along with his two brigadiers, was a typical product of the conservative and over-confident Indian Army system. Their training and background would not have included what today is called amphibious warfare, let alone military service on another continent against a disciplined, well-trained and well-equipped enemy, capable of delivering considerable firepower. The immense task of welding these disparate, under-trained and ill-equipped units into an effective military formation would have taken months even in ideal conditions – instead the generals, at best, had a couple of days in India at the holding camp near Bombay called Deolali, and then 2,000 miles of Indian Ocean in fourteen ancient transports, which today might be better described as coastal craft.

The two weeks' sea journey was foul and the troops were tossed around in these small, stinking hot boats in overcrowded conditions.

The 1,109 men of 2nd Bn and half the 3rd Bn Kashmir Rifles, September 1914, Satwari Camp, Jammu.

There was inadequate food and water – morale suffered and all on-board training ceased. 2nd Kashmir Rifles' war diary records: 'these vessels being light roll considerably, some 70% of men are seasick'; Miller in the *Battle for the Bundu* concluded: 'After a fortnight of retching the Indian Expeditionary force was hardly in a state of combat readiness.'

On 31 October Gen. Aitken and his staff landed at Mombasa and held a conference at Government House with Sir Henry Belfield, the Governor. The decision was to land and capture Tanga, and then advance up the railway towards Mount Kilimanjaro and link up with Brigadier Stewart's 'Indian Expeditionary Force C', who were attacking and reclaiming sovereign territory hundreds of miles north in the Kilimanjaro area. Serious opposition was not expected and the lack of military intelligence and thorough preparation and planning were soon to become very evident. The British over-confidence in hindsight is simply staggering.

The GOC Aitken was so convinced that there would be no opposition and that the Germans would immediately surrender that he initially landed only a small proportion of his available force and made no contingency. Consequently he failed to organise any beach reconnaissance of suitable landing sites and failed to plan disembarkation to achieve any momentum. He apparently retired to read a book and let the activity just unfold. The consequence, apart from being very slow, was a muddle – with troops from different brigades and different units becoming entangled within an atmosphere of confusion. Today's Sandhurst instructor might say there was a complete lack of grip!

The Regiment was issued the Lee Enfield rifle a few weeks after mobilisation in September 1914 and did not receive machine guns until March 1915.

The sequence of events makes pitiful reading. The force arrived off Tanga and disembarked in dribbles by lighters onto beaches over a mile to the east of the port during 2nd and 3rd November. Patrols and then an advance from the 13th Rajput and the 61st Pioneers, were sent forward to take Tanga itself; however there was a complete lack of urgency and a single Askari company hurled them back in panic and disarray – meanwhile the build-up of forces from the beachhead progressed slowly. In sharp contrast Lettow-Vorbeck used this time with vigour to entrain reinforcements from nearby and to enable those further away to start the journey (150 miles from Kilimanjaro). On 3 November Gen. Aitkin with his confidence still unshaken made a more detailed plan for an advance through the thick scrub to capture Tanga with most of his forces; however as he still left his inadequate artillery on the boats he was not expecting to need them.

The full-scale advance and attack started at 12.30hrs on 4 November with the Kashmir Rifles centre and right and the 2nd LNL centre and left. The Kashmir Rifles acquitted themselves with distinction, demonstrating classic fire and manoeuvre tactics which enabled them to penetrate further into the town of Tanga than any other unit. The Germans defended vigorously, they brought to bear fifteen machine

The railways were of vital strategic importance to both the British and German forces. There were three main lines running East to West: the British 'Uganda Railway' (Mombasa to Nairobi), the German 'Tanga Line' (Tanga to Kilimanjaro) and the German 'Central Railway' (Dar es Salaam to Lake Tanganyika.

guns across the front and reinforcements continued to arrive and counter attack. Casualties started to be taken by the Kashmir Rifles, the LNL and the 101st Grenadiers. Some 600+ Indian Troops from the 63rd Palamcottah Light Infantry and the 61st Pioneers who were on the left of the line, also took casualties from this effective fire, and when, with most officers 'down', the latter troops panicked and fled the mile or so back to the beachhead, where they mingled and caused further panic and confusion amongst the 3,000 civilian porters and labourers.

These events progressively caused Gen. Aitken to wobble and, after considering his options, he decided to withdraw his forces to a compact beachhead perimeter. The two most competent regiments, the LNL and Kashmir Rifles, were ordered to hold the beachhead and so enable an orderly withdrawal and evacuation to take place. Re-embarkation was, by contrast, dramatically quicker and there was no German attempt at intervention, for unbeknown to the British they too were wobbling – Lettow-Vorbeck was writing his own order to withdraw and according to Mienerherzhagen (the British Intelligence Officer on the staff) the bugle call for their

The enemy: a parade of the Germans and their fellow Askari troops, known as the Field Commando (FK). They were a fearsome fighting force.

withdrawal was actually sounded. Ross Anderson in the Battle of Tanga states the German actually withdrew. The British orderly exit was completed by 15.30hrs on 5 November – the LNL and Kashmir Rifles were the last out.

Casualties were some 12.9 per cent for the British and 11.6 per cent for the Germans. The Kashmir Rifles percentage was less than half this, in spite of having engaged in close combat, urban fighting and the capturing of several machine guns – seventeen killed and forty-three wounded, with two missing. It was a German victory, not only by dint of occupying the battlefield and Tanga at the end of play, but especially by the level of casualties inflicted. The German's 11.6 per cent casualties amounted to 145, which compared favourably to the British Empires, 800.

This chaotic disaster was hidden by censorship from the British public and the obvious lessons were not learnt by the military command, and so were largely repeated a few months later at Gallipoli. The hasty withdrawal and Gen. Aitkin's panicky order

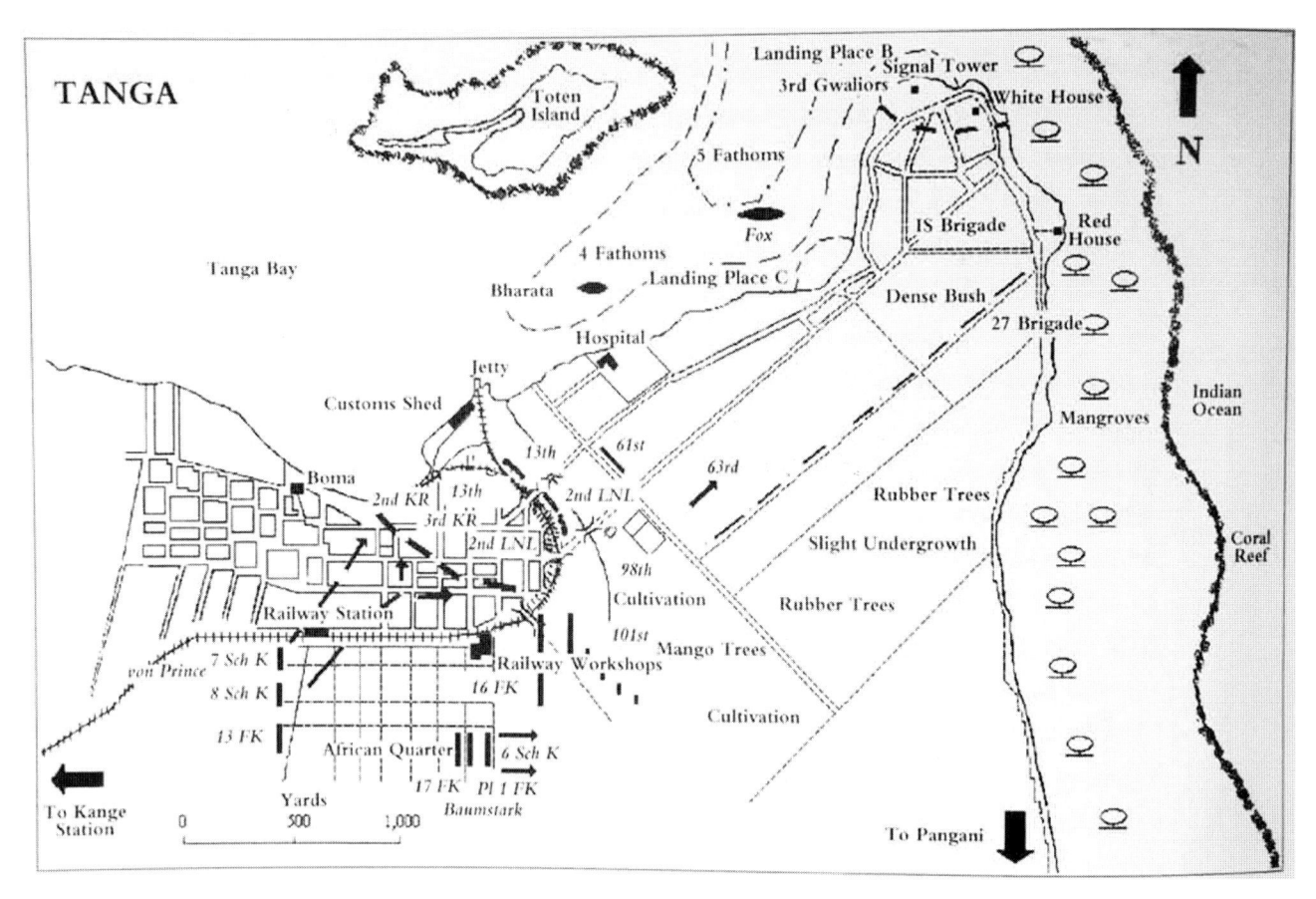

Map of Tanga 3–5 November, 1914, the Kashmir Rifles advanced the furthest into Tanga.

to leave equipment behind meant that the Germans were able to replenish their stocks from the British Empire – eight precious machine guns, 455 rifles, 500,000 rounds of ammunition, and other medical and food stores.

The battle for Tanga is often remembered for the problems that bees caused to both sides. These bees had very powerful acidic stings that caused arms, legs etc to swell to twice the normal size. It seems that the wild bees were disturbed and threatened by bullets 'whizzing' amongst them. Whilst the bees completely knocked out machine-gun teams on both sides and turned the 98th Infantry retreat into comic farce – the Kashmir Rifles were able to use their puggarees as protection and so remained in action.

Two days later on 7 November the force arrived off Mombasa and Gen. Aitken was duly sacked. Wapshire, the other brigade commander, took over and was promoted to major general.

Some of the war diaries for the Kashmir Rifles have survived and the following extracts are edited and recorded below:

'I Can Never Say Enough About the Men'

The railway cutting where Subedar Randir Singh showed great leadership in spite of severe wounds as the commander of D Coy 2KR at Tanga. He was responsible for the capture of the machine gun.

The statements in the Kashmir Rifles' War Diary at Tanga

Capt Hanson 4 Company, 2Bn Kashmir Rifles
Advanced three companies (Coy) up and one in support – to their right was the sea and to the left was 3rd Bn Kashmir Rifles, at about 14.00hrs on 4 November.

Lt Bala Sahib brought a message to push on [towards Tanga]. The enemy soon opened heavy fire, accurate at first but as the KR firing line warmed into action the enemy's fire grew wild. The advance of these four company's [under Capt Hanson] was uninterrupted and on arriving at the clearing before the railway line, enemy could be seen in flight beyond.

  The enemy machine gun was still working but especially on account of the steady pressure of D Coy under Subedar Randhir Singh, who was especially notable in his handling (and was wounded), this was silenced. After the fall of the Coy Commander his NCO carried on (section commanders 78 Jagat Ram, 80 Surju, 2393 Hoshiar, 60 Balbahadar). At about 3pm the whole railway line for some 50 yds from the sea was occupied by the Kashmir Rifles, there were some other detachments of Regiments on the left. By the enemy machine gun B some 10 men were killed in the house.

Havl Mahdu and another man each bayoneted enemy here, around this spot there were some 25 dead enemy were found, all natives except one (some say two), up to this time only 2Kashmir Rifles were present in the firing line.

Major Ames 4 Company, 15.15–17.15hrs
These companies close in and provide support for 2nd Bn Kashmir Rifles and then operate in the firing line between Capt. Hanson 4 Company and the Loyal North Lancashire. As soon as the enemy opened fire, he thought it advisable to push forward at once.

These Coy's advanced forward with great dash to within about 60yds of the railway line. He then sounded the charge and we dashed for the railway embankment. [Jemd Bal Bahadur distinguished himself here]. The enemy [Europeans] jumped out of their trenches and bolted, 5 or 6, being shot on the run. We found the far trench of the railway embankment full of abandoned accoutrements and a maxim. We stopped in the embankment trench for some 10 minutes and then advanced into the town.

At this moment some 2 Coys of the North Lancashire's appeared on my left and advanced with us. There was heavy maxim fire down the street and from the houses. Shortly afterwards some 3 lines of men on the left of the North Lancs were seen retiring precipitately. At this time some 3 Coys of 2Kashmir Rifles, with large parties of North Lancs and 13th Rajputs had reached the market. About 250 of them, on the left including some 3KR under Capt Money, also Subdar Mardan Ali F Coy 2Kashmir Rifles made a bayonet charge and gained some ground amongst the houses and market. Finding that the troops on the left had retired Major Ames withdrew his men to the railway line. Adjutant Rahmatallah Khan greatly distinguished him self in conducting this withdrawal, he was ably assisted by Subadar Kesri Singh.

At about 6PM the GOC IS Bde gave orders for a retirement to the line of the civil hospital and then at 11PM a further retirement to the base position.

Commenting in the 2nd Bn Kashmir Rifles regimental diary Capt Hanson went on to review the hard ship of the day as follows.

During the above movement Major Ames was hit twice, whilst under heavy maxim fire. His orderly's ruck sack being riddled at the same time. Major Ames reached the railway embankment, where he fainted from loss of blood and fell to the bottom amongst a swarm of bees 5 men helped him down the line under severe fire half carrying him

Kessi Singh was noted for his deeds in the with drawl to the Railway Cutting from the town of Tanga. The Kashmir Rifles found their left flank exposed.

to the beach, where the SS LaiSang promptly responding to a signal sent a boat and carried him off under fire to the ship. (Next morning whilst lying recovering in his bunk a shell from a German gun passed through the cabin).

Capt Hanson's 4 Company 15.15–17.15hrs
About this time those on the *SS Khosru* saw some 50 of the enemy bolting for the all they were worth along the harbour side. The right of the 2Kashmir Rifles advanced from house to house and along the sea shore. There was sniping from all directions but few casualties. A party of the 13th Rajputs joined us under a Captain Seymour (wearing spectacles) who took one street whilst Capt Hanson followed another. The column under the later finding themselves in a cul-de-sac emerged to the right. There was a good deal of firing round the Kaiser Hotel, where Capt Seymour climbed to the balcony and tore down two "Tanga" flags.

The advance here stopped short of the commissioners house and finding the sounds of firing to be all to the left rear, a withdrawal was ordered to the embankment where a halt was made. During this withdrawal and the later part of the advance some of the houses under which our men were moving were struck by shells from HMS Fox, a large one fell between two lines of our men. During the withdrawal 3 men were wounded including Capt Seymour. Havildar Sohan dressed his wounds and was conspicuous on other occasions.

Three killed 466 Havl Haria, 602 Naik Rahamdad and 1587 Bhimal Singh

The 2Kashmir Rifles worked all this day with full kit—waterproof sheet, blanket, 1 & 1/2 days rations, emergency rations, 200 rounds, filled chagiuls and water bottles, behind entrenching tools and kukris - this great weight in the heat, the worst of physical condition, was excessively trying to the men who also had the fatigue of entrenching themselves the previous night. Many men suffered from attacks of bees during the advance.

When writing up a list of officers and ranks and file recommended for awards for gallantry in action at Tanga he mentions the following, who have not been mentioned in this text:

Subedar Chattar Singh – for his leadership and bayonet charge of the captured machine gun.
Sepoy 891 Ahmdallah Khan, 1115 Raisla for taking a hut and setting it on fire.
Sepoy 1091 Billu and Naik Attar Singh for assisting the wounded Capt. Seymour.
Naike Bal Bahadur for leading to furthest point into the town.

The battle for Tanga is often remembered for the problems that bees caused to both sides. These bees had very powerful acidic stings that caused arms, legs etc to swell to twice the normal size. It seems wild bees were disturbed by the bullets 'whizzing' amongst them.

> Subedar Mardan Ali for leading his men into the native bazaar under heavy fire.
> Sepoy Saif Ali... Major Ames Orderly who whilst grazed in two places but helped the wounded Major.
> Sepoy Bhagwan Singh for also helping Major Ames.
> Sepoy Hari Ram for dashing the enemy machine gun and shooting the last man of its crew.
> Havaldar Tez Bahadur 357 and 358 Havaldar Karabir for leading the bayonet charge into the railway cutting trench.

The final entries of Capt. Hanson in the war diary are significant in that they record the thoroughness of the defensive positions that are prepared for covering the withdrawal:

> At 10 am on 5th Nov the whole 12 Coys of the KR's being placed under command of Colonel Macpherson, with Capt Hanson as Adjutant. The following Company Officers were attached as Double Company Officers. Capt Money (2KR), Capt Wemys (Royal Scots), Capt Marshall (36 Sikhs) and Capt Dento (3rd Gwaliors). [This is remarkable as being the first time Indian State Troops have been on service with British officers as OC Commanders.]
> At 2.30 PM Kashmir Rifles ordered to retire from the right, this was done expeditiously and unnoticed by the enemy. Men wadded into the sea and boats took them to any steamer or lighter indiscriminately.

Some 160 kits. 28000 rounds of ammunition, all entrenching tools, all medical equipment, most of the heavy signalling kit, some 800 blankets, were discarded or thrown into the sea by order. Some five rifles of men killed in action only were left behind, the remainder were brought in.

Report by Captain Money on action 4 November 1914 at Tanga, embracing the part taken in these operations by the 3rd Kashmir Imperial Service Rifles, 4 Companies from the time of disembarkation.

3 November 1914
The 3rd Kashmir Rifles under Lt Col Durga Singh Bahadur IOM proceeded to disembark onto lighters from the HT Barjora at 2pm and were landed on the beach ¼ mile west of the signal tower by 4pm.
The regiment halted at this rendezvous with the 2nd KR and 4 Companies of the 3rd Gwalior Infantry at 6pm, when orders were received from the signal tower for this force to form the outpost line on the right flank from the signal tower inclusive to the right of the Loyal North Lancashire Regiment's outpost line – the 3rd KR extended the outpost line from the left of the 2KR (who had the extreme right of the outpost line) to the main road running from the beach through the jungles to Tanga. On the left of this road the 3rd Gwalior Inf extended the line to the right of the Loyal North Lancashire's (LNL). During this night in outposts, the 3KR had one Coy A in the piquet line, one Coy B with Supports and two Coys C and D in reserve. The night passed without incident.

4 November 1914
At 10am, the 3KR with one Coy of the 3rd Gwalior Inf assembled at the undergrowth behind the 3KR outpost line, preparatory to taking up their positions in the centre of the IS (Imperial Service) Brigade, with 2KR on their right and the LNL on their left. The orders for the 3KR were to take up the line with the right on the road leading to Tanga, before in a ... in the outpost line of the 3rd November with their left on the road, on the right of which the LNL was the directing flank for this Brigade. Before leaving this preparatory rendezvous position, the orders of the GOC IS Brigade had been issued that the force would advance on Tanga.

Before the advance of the whole force started, the position of the 3KR, in linking up the extended line, was as follows. A Coy on the right, B Coy in the centre, C Coy on the left. These three Companies formed the firing line. The supports were D Coy on the right directly behind A Coy, with one Coy of the 3rd Gwaliors Inf behind B Coy

Whilst the bees completely knocked out machine-gun teams on both sides and turned the 98th Infantry retreat into a comic farce – the Kashmir Rifles were able to use their puggarees as protection and so remained in action.

– the supports were also extended.

The advance started at 11am and continued without incident until we arrived through the thick jungle, in the outskirts of Tanga, about one mile, I should think from the railway cutting. The 3KR arrived at this position at 1pm, where we halted with the LNL on our left and with 2KR slightly in our rear and on our right. At this time I sent an orderly to Major Ames and Captain Hanson SSO's to 2KR, describing our exact position on a map, also the position of the LNL, the 27th Brigade on the left again of the IS Brigade. We advance again at 1.30pm, when sniping fire started, and in a few minutes rapid firing started on our right. Up to this time the 3KR had only one slight casualty – a sepoy wounded in the hand from the sniping. When 2KR started firing on the right I noticed that they had got rather ahead of us, about 200yds, Colonel Durga Singh ordered up the two Coys in the support to close up on the firing line. The 3KR advanced well by rushes through this country, infested with village huts. Slight jungle and we noticed that the enemy native troops did not stop in front of us, but chased off to their rear. By 2pm, the 3KR had arrived at the railway cutting, by which time both Companies in the support had reinforced the firing line. I further noticed that in this advance from 1.30pm to 2pm that a few shots had been fired at us from the rear. And it was imparted to me that the German native troops had had a few men left behind the lines, but fortunately their fire was not good and no casualties happened. I further noticed that in this advance of the 3KR, whenever they opened up a steady rapid fire, no response was offered from the enemy native troops. On arriving at the railway cutting, we did not remain intact, as 2 Coys of the 2KR had crossed over to our left and in crossing over the cutting by the bridge, the 2nd one from the sea. Companies of the 2nd and 3rd KR got together. After crossing the railway line we advanced into the town, up through the bazaar. At this time 2.30pm the position was as follows. – 2KR on the right had advanced about a ¼ mile ahead of us and we were in touch with the LNL on our left and had half a Coy their left with us in the Bazaar. The 3KR pushed on and were in front of the Bazaar in Tanga at about 3.30pm. I noticed that very severe firing was going on to our left and it seemed to me as if the Germans were making a counter attack , though we could not actually see them as we were in the thick part of the town. I then noticed the LNL were retiring in the direction of the railway cutting and I pointed this out to Colonel Durga Singh. If we had wheeled to our left through the streets in the direction of the open space, where the LNL had originally adjoined. We should have come under fire of the enemies maxim guns and pom poms. So I informed Col Durga Singh to retire his regiment to the railway cutting as it was the only way by which we could keep touch with our left, our right being secure, as there were no enemy between us and the 2KR. It was at this time that 3KR suffered most of their casualties three men being killed and a good few being wounded and they suffered more casualties from sniping, which took place from the upper stories of the houses in Tanga. It was when crossing the railway line that I regret to say Colonel Durga Singh was wounded, he was taken to the rear by the stretcher party – I should like to take this opportunity of saying that all through the actions up to the time of his being wounded he handled his regiment very ably and skilfully and with much personal bravery.

From 4pm to 5.30pm, until the orders were received from the GOC IS Brigade to retire to a position near the German Hospital the 3KR mixed up with the men of 2KR and the 13th Rajputs held the Railway cutting East of Tanga.

At 6.30pm the 3KR were in position with the 2KR on their right, and the 13th Rajputs on their left – the 2KR extending off to the sea directly in front of the German Hospital across the road, and the 3KR extending on from their left to the right of the 13th Rajputs. Our orders were to hold on to the position for the night but during the night 3KR received orders to move back to their original position of the early morning. On arriving there they continued the same outpost line of the night before with the 3rd Gwalior Infantry 4 Coy's on their right in the position where the 2KR were the night before and with the Loyal North Lancashire's on their left. This night on the outpost line passed without incident.

5 November 1914
The 3KR continued to remain in the front line and were in this

The evacuation following the withdrawal, 5 November 1914: as the Kashmir Rifles had fought so well they were chosen to hold the perimeter – the general panic led to the order to leave behind materials, including sixteen machine guns, 455 rifles and 600,000 rounds of ammunition; General Aitken, unsurprisingly was removed from command.

position when covering the retirement of the force with 2KR and on their right the Loyal North Lancashires on the left.

Two signallers of the regiment at the top of a tree on the right of our position saw 3 German Officers and 40 native troops moving from the German Hospital through the jungle parallel to our line and this was reported to HQ in this action of the morning 5th November the 2nd and 3rd KR were under the direct orders of Colonel Macpherson 37th Dogras. We were slightly attacked on the right by I think the reconnaissance party of the enemy, above mentioned, and rapid fire was soon very soon poured at a range of about 800 yards. By the early afternoon we received orders to retire from the left of the 3KR, the Loyal North Lancashire Regiment covering the retirement of the KR – on reaching the beech we embarked.

Signed Capt ETD Money SSO to 3KR

Selected extracts from the Kashmir Rifles War Diary after Tanga

After Tanga the Kashmir Rifles went ashore at Mombasa and camped on a football ground by the yacht club and the war diaries reveal many of the daily challenges that were to characterise soldiering at a company and individual level.

Jemadar Milkha Singh C Coy was particularly conspicuous for leading his men into the enemy trenches and through the town – he helped Captain Seymour mount the balcony and remove the flags.

Porters unloading stores at Tanga.

11 and 12 November
Day spent in distributing kits and replacing the Tanga losses. Some 160 kits were obtained from the 101st Grenadiers, 830 blankets and cooking pots from the Mombassa ordnance depot. 50 water bottles and much private kit was purchased in the town. The following deficiencies were not replaced, about half the signalling kit, all heavy entrenching tools, blankets, stretchers and 30 rucksacks.
Regiment set out from camp. This late start was occasioned by having to detail coolies to their respective loads, and also to not having realised the difficulty of performing even a short march in the heat of this country.
The route followed a 3 foot track for about 3 miles where it emerged on the Mombasa–Gazi road. There was little wind and the heat terrific, coolies and men soon began to straggle...

At Tanga, Mahden Ali led F Company 2nd Kashmir Rifles in a bayonet charge under heavy enemy fire gaining ground and houses around the market place.

There are many mentions of water shortage, dirty wells, coolie problems and heat exhaustion—all of which would dominate their future in Africa. At Ghazi on the 14th November the war diary makes two points:

The coolies had never previously been subjected to discipline apparently, and any attempt on the part of sepoy guards to keep them in their places provoked quarrels. They threw their loads and sat down when ever it pleased them. Some 200 were too feeble to carry a 20lb load. They are being well organised now and some of these difficulties may disappear. Our men were warned not to strike them, lest, as was possible, they would disappear into the jungle.
The men of 2KR are essentially hill men. They were warned of the climate and conditions of the march, but still some, principally the Gurkhas wore thick waistcoats. Their accoutrements are not suited to this country, all the weight of their kit rested on the back, in the rucksack. This contained the usual rations etc, but also a cape and water bottle, and on the first march some carried a blanket. The rucksack only serves to heat and to keep the air off the back, also the weight of the extra kit they are designed to carry in the hills is no longer required; haversacks are being indented for to replace them. They carry the entrenching tool and a kukri. It is not the weight of the kit that proved trying to the men on the march, but rather the change from their hills, to a tropical plain such as they have never before experienced.

Commenting on the camp at Gazi (20 miles north of Jasin) the diary states that in order to make a camp safe good fields of fire are essential and the tall grass is cut clear for 300–400 yds. On the surrounding countryside the comment is that there is dense bush with stretches of open which is covered with grass as high as a man. It is impossible to move with flankers and roads are mere tracks. On the 15th November it goes on to say...: 'Men have the first chance of arranging kits, washing clothes properly since they left Bombay a month earlier.'

At this stage it is worth pondering what the men might have been thinking. Here they were one month later, 3,000 miles away from the hills and their former lives of Kashmir, fighting another man's war. They had been propelled into the twentieth century with a series of unimaginable experiences – a long hot railway journey, an ocean crossing complete with a week of sea-sickness, being dumped in a Mango swamp and then fighting a bloody battle, being stung by giant bees and were now being marched into a tropical heat hell with dirty water and feeble coolies.

Sadly there are no records of their thoughts and feelings, however, in Gordon Corrigan's great book *Sepoys in the Trenches* he tells some interesting Gurkha[*] stories of their journey and experiences to and of the European War:

> Many of the soldiers were nervous about embarking upon this expanse of water which stretched to the horizon and for all they knew beyond... the Gurkhas were particularly intrigued as to how a ship could find its way: there were no landmarks, nothing to follow, just a vast expanse of kalo pani that stretched in all directions as far as the eye could see. Some rifleman thought that there must be rails laid on the sea bed along which the ship progressed on wheeled stilts. The conundrum was resolved when one British Officer took a party to the rear of the ship and pointed out the wake. That he said is the ships road which it follows until it reaches its destination....

Alec arrived just before Christmas on 20 December at Mombasa to find most of the 2nd Bn Kashmir Rifles guarding and retaking the soputh-east corner of the country, the coastal plain below Mombasa. The ½ Bn of the 3rd Bn Kashmir Rifles and a Coy of the 2nd Bn Kashmir Rifles was inland guarding the railway near Tsavo and Voi. Alec was to serve in both places.

---

[*] It is interesting to note that the Gurkhas (spelt as Gorkha in pre-British India) were the only element of the Jammu and Kashmir Rifles that were hill men. The major component was from the plains of Jammu and quite used to the heat, but not perhaps such intense humidity. (Information courtesy of Maj. Brahma Singh).

4

The Umba Valley operation and the Battle of Jasin January 1915

> Their ammunition had finally run out. Lt Col Raghubir Singh was dead. Captain Hanson, his second in command, had been left with no choice but surrender.
>
> Charles Miller, *Battle for the Bundu* (p.143)

The performance of the Kashmir Rifles at Tanga made them an obvious choice for deployment to the threatened south east corner of British East Africa, to protect Mombasa, the vital sea port and railway terminus. The village of Jasin is on the coast and further south and just over the border into German East Africa.

General Wapshare, the GOC, decided in December that Brigadier Tighe, the brigade commander in the South East, should lead a force of 1,800 men and six machine guns to recapture this corner of British East Africa that had fallen under German control. The feeding of 5,000 displaced fugitives was also proving a strain and a further reason for military action. This operation was referred to as the Umba Valley and as transport was non-existent some 5,500 carriers or porters were to be employed and the supply line would be fed by sea, using the small port of Goa. This was a notoriously unhealthy area, beset with tsetse fly, the killer of the horse, mule and oxen, and also beset with anopheles mosquito (malaria), the killer

The River Umba in full flood… many experienced their first malaria attacks in this mosquito infested swamp.

and debilitator of man. For an added challenge the River Umba was in high flood from the heavy tropical rains.

Early operations went well, surprise was achieved and by Christmas Day British territory was cleared of all the German forces. Alec Kerr landed at Mombasa on 20 December, ready to take up his new appointment as a Special Service Officer with 2nd Bn Kashmir Rifles. He was thirty-two, a substantive captain and machine-gun trained.

Alec reached the front line at Umba Camp on 23 December, two days ahead of the reinforcement draft that he had brought out from Kashmir to replace the losses in manpower at Tanga – he had disembarked from the SS Kilwa at Majhreni and on 24th was supervising working parties. On Christmas Day, Subedar Bhagwan Singh disembarked at Vanga from the SS Bajora (the same vessel that had brought out the 2nd Bn two months earlier) with the draft of 119 men.

The Regimental diary goes on to say:

> …these men were equipped as we were on first landing, carrying 60lbs kit and wearing vests, shirts and thick waistcoats. We were given no opportunity to adjust their kit at Mombasa, neither was Captain Kerr who brought the draft out, informed of the nature of the climate and country to work in. The surplus kit was prepared for return to our base at Mombasa.

In depth defensive positions were created, not only to retain control of the area in the likelihood of a major attack, but also to secure the

The Kashmir Rifles

port of Goa. Logistics by sea were essential to the overall defensive position. Troops were rotated through the main positions at Umba Camp and across the River Umba, and just into German East Africa at Jasin – this camp was cited on the western edge of a small fishing village near the River Suba. Today, it is a small collection of mud huts just a few yards into Tanzania and farming, rather than fishing, is the key occupation. The map in Horden's official history has the site a few yards west of the village and the word 'camp' is firmly used to describe it. One can imagine a similar structure and set up to the neighbouring post at Samanya, which Alec Kerr's photograph reveals as a basic defensive structure made from thorn bushes, some wood and sisal. It would have provided minimal protection against both rifle fire and artillery. The official war diary does mention a beacon tower at Jasin and Alec's photograph of Samanya is taken from the top of such a tower. The post could accommodate up to four companies and at the time of the German attack on Jasin it had two in residence it was some 4 miles to the North and East.

The rotation of troops through the camp at Jasin had already seen the arrival of four KAR companies and the departure of two that were acutely suffering from the Umba climate. The 2nd Bn Kashmir Rifles was spread between Umba, Samanya and Jasin where there were two companies, commanded by Colonel Raghbir Singh, with Captain G.J.G. Hanson and a further company of 101st Grenadiers was attached under Captain J Turner. There was also a small outpost at the sisal factory with a detachment of forty.

Early attacks at one or two company strength were successfully repelled and Von Lettow-Vorbeck decided to raise the stakes and attack at daybreak on 18 January 1916 with all available resources. Edward Paice in *Tip and Run* states the size of German force as 244 Europeans, 1,350 Askari and 400 Arab levies; on the British side, in Jasin, he states there were 138 men from 101st Grenadiers and 144 from the Kashmir Rifles with a KAR machine-gun detachment. Reinforcements (three companies of the KAR) were sent from Umba Camp, and Alec Kerr was ordered to send a company-and-a-half commanded by Maj. Haidar Ali Khan. Both sets of reinforcements were beaten off, taking casualties and unable to relieve Jasin.

The small force of forty at the Sisal Factory fired their last rounds and then charged out with bayonets and kukris; twenty-nine of the forty made it back to Umba Camp.

The garrison at Jasin fought bravely and effectively. In the process of their determined defence their accurate fire stopped the repeated German attacks and in one assault alone, when repelling the elite

Haider Ali Khan as CO of the 2nd Bn. Like many officers he was from a notable family – his title was the Ghakkar of Mirpir. Capt Hanson wrote of him after Tanga:
He conducted the advance of D Coy after the fall of the Coy Commander. Later at Jasin he tried to reinforce the garrison and along with the KAR was beaten back.

'I Can Never Say Enough About the Men'

13 Fk (Fieldkommando), killed three prominent officers within ten minutes. However, once the lone machine gun packed in and once their ammunition was expended, and following the death of their inspiring commanding officer Lt Col Raghbir Singh, their situation became desperate and morale suffered.

After a long isolated night without water, hoping and praying for reinforcements, the German artillery bombardment resumed with added intensity, Capt. Hanson, the senior British officer, reluctantly decided to surrender and all firing ceased at about 08.00hrs on the 19 January. Brahma Singh in the regimental history states that of the 135 Kashmir Rifle prisoners, 115 were wounded – this is not surprising given the very limited protection they would have had from the German artillery and bullets in such a close space. The official history states twelve killed and thirteen wounded.

Capts Hanson and Turner were taken before the German Commander Von Lettow-Vorbeck, who congratulated them on their defence and in a gallant gesture returned their swords. He released them on parole, on the understanding that they would not fight again during the war.

Conditions at Jasin were ghastly for both sides and Miller's very full account emphasises the failure of the reinforcements to break through the German cordon, the great heat and the running out of ammunition and water. Certainly the German position above the bank of the River Suba commanded the ground and made reinforcement across the river impossible. Furthermore, had these reinforcements got through and given the growing scale of Lettow-Vorbeck forces (he had brought up and deployed nine Field Companies in total and two 75mm field guns), a different outcome seems unlikely.

The German firepower was so intense that they too ran temporarily out of ammunition. German casualties were growing and the discomfort was so great that at one stage Lettow-Vorbeck's field officers urged him to break off the action, but he was shrewder and reckoned that it must be a greater hell in the camp. Miller goes on to say: 'a light plantation railway literally became a conveyor belt, moving large numbers of wounded and dying Germans and Africans to the rear'.

Lettow-Vorbeck's victory was a little hollow for he had used a quarter of his entire army's ammunition (200,000 rounds) and thirteen of his twenty-two officers present were casualties, including four key senior officers killed – it was a defining moment – he realised, that given his limited resources and given that Royal Navy's blockade would continue to strangle his re-supply and reinforcement, he

Lt Col Raghbir Singh who commanded 2KR with great distinction and bravery at Tanga and who was killed a few weeks later at Jasin. Capt Hanson wrote in the Regimental Diary:

'he proved himself a capable leader and was most distinguishable in the way he led parties in the right column. His coolness and ability to carry out tactical movements in the confusion and excitement of action and the hours after it was very creditable.'

Samanaya Post established from 26th Dec. Alec commands the post during the battle

Umba Camp Established 23/24 Dec Alec arrives on the 23rd and superintends working parties.

Draft of 119 arrive by sea 25th Dec

German advance and attack

Operations around JASIN January 1915.

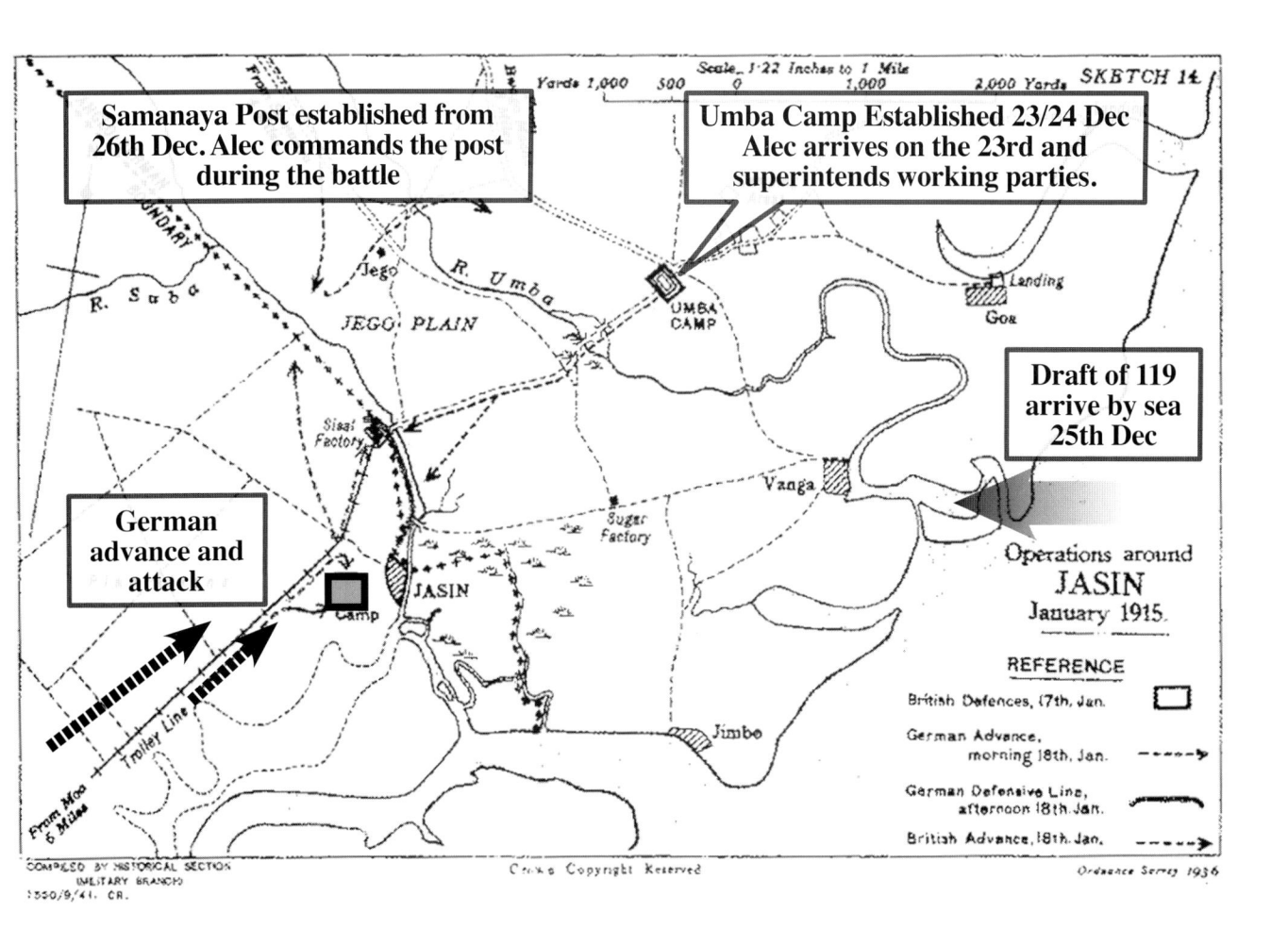

REFERENCE
British Defences, 17th Jan.
German Advance, morning 18th Jan.
German Defensive Line, afternoon 18th Jan.
British Advance, 18th Jan.

German Askari troops travelling by train.

Samanya Post, the camp at Jasin was probably similar.

could not achieve victory in a direct staged battle, and it led him to develop a new strategy and the emergence of what Anderson calls the 'bush leader' and not the guerrilla leader that he has so often been described as by other writers and historians. Anderson goes on to define this as 'the conduct of defensive and delaying operations in the bush and he was the master of the timely counter-attack.'

After this setback the Empire forces were withdrawn and the defensive line maintained to the north of the mosquito-ridden Umba Valley. During 1915 the Kashmir Rifles were rotated through outposts on a defensive river line between the towns of Tsavo and Mzima.

They had again fought well and were showing themselves to be brave and hardy soldiers, more than able to take on the German Askari, it is perhaps entirely fitting that in the months ahead several of the senior generals were to be 'moved on'. There is a revealing story of Maj. Gen. Wapshare's departure (Miller, p.101):

> on his way down to the coast… he spied some cock ostriches from the train, pulled the communication cord and in the presence of a train loaded with passengers disembarked, lay down on the veldt quite unembarrassed and proceeded to bombard the ostriches, securing a cock and hen. And all of this in a game reserve!… some 20

passengers assisted him in dragging the two huge birds back to the train ... where Wappy sat for the rest of the trip plucking them.

Umba Valley was notorious for its mosquitoes and so many Kashmiri soldiers must have received their first exposure to this East African malaria strain – malaria of a different strain to their Kashmiri homeland.

The 2nd Bn left Umba Camp on 1 February and travelled by boat (the HT Barala) from Vanga Bay to Mombasa and then by train to the railway town of Voi arriving on 5 February at 18.00hrs.

Alec Kerr was transferred to the 3rd Bn Kashmir Rifles on 3 February, this 1/2 Bn had been rushed as reinforcements from Voi to Umba on 24 January and stayed until the entire force was withdrawn – embarking at Gazi on 12 March for Mombasa and on by rail to Voi where they joined 2nd Bn on the Tsavo River line. Alec was evacuated on 8 February by sea with fever (probably malaria, the first of his many attacks – he was to have fifteen in 8 months during 1916, see Appendix D for description of malaria) and next appeared in the diary for 24 March at Voi, about to move to Tsavo Post.

Alec's photographs of the fortified post at Samanya, 4 miles north and west of Jasin are of great interest. They show the professionalism of the Kashmir Rifles. Note the substantial defences built round the camp, the drainage ditches, tent layout and its overall orderliness – the war diary of 17 January says that the very heavy rain filled the trenches to a depth of 2 feet. The camp was in regular communication by telephone with the HQ at Umba Camp and there is reference in the diary to statements like 'telephonic orders received...'.

The war diaries describe the building of the camp (entrenching), the clearing of fields of fire and the construction of a bridge over the River Umba. Of particular interest to an infantry soldier there are reports of aggressive patrolling, ambushing, listening and reconnaissance. The diary entry for 29 December continues to ention work on fortification.

The diaries also describe the bridging of the River Umba under the instructions of Maj. McClintoch Commander RE, who accompanied the column and developed the fortifications.

Tanga and Jasin were serious defeats for the British Empire and it created a significant strategic pause, compounded by Kitchener's directive from Britain of no offensive actions.

As 1915 unfolded the British East African population became increasingly infuriated by the large military presence, its ineptness

Bhagwan Singh
He came out with Capt Kerr and the draft of 119 men.

its takeover of colonial social life and above all its inability to stop German raids. All in all morale was very shaky and was to remain so until the arrival of Gen. Smuts. Importantly this gave the Germans time to build up their strength, to mobilise their entire colony, to make plans and so prepare for a long war that would absorb disproportionate resource from the British Empire.

5

1915
Patrolling the Tsavo River Line

'...the worst affliction of all, however was the arthritis of apathetic gloom that crippled every limb and joint of the British East African military body throughout 1915...'

Charles Miller, The Battle for the Bundu (p.137)

The continuing poor performance of the British Empire's forces meant that the best of the fighting troops had to carry the brunt of the operational load, much of this fell to the Loyal North Lancashire's, a portion of the King's African Rifles battalions and the Kashmir Rifles.

They were greatly helped by the local militias that had been hurriedly formed in late 1914 – the most notable of these was the East African Mounted Rifles (EAMR). Gradually during 1915 the King's African Rifles were also further developed into a fighting force but their full potential was not realised until their rapid expansion in 1916–17 and wide-scale deployments.

A notable arrival from the trenches in France during January 1915 were the Baluchis who quickly adapted to East Africa and became the other Indian regiment that won great praise from the British, and a grudging from the South Africans. They were also joined by a Rhodesian battalion and, from Britain, the 25th Bn of the Fusiliers:

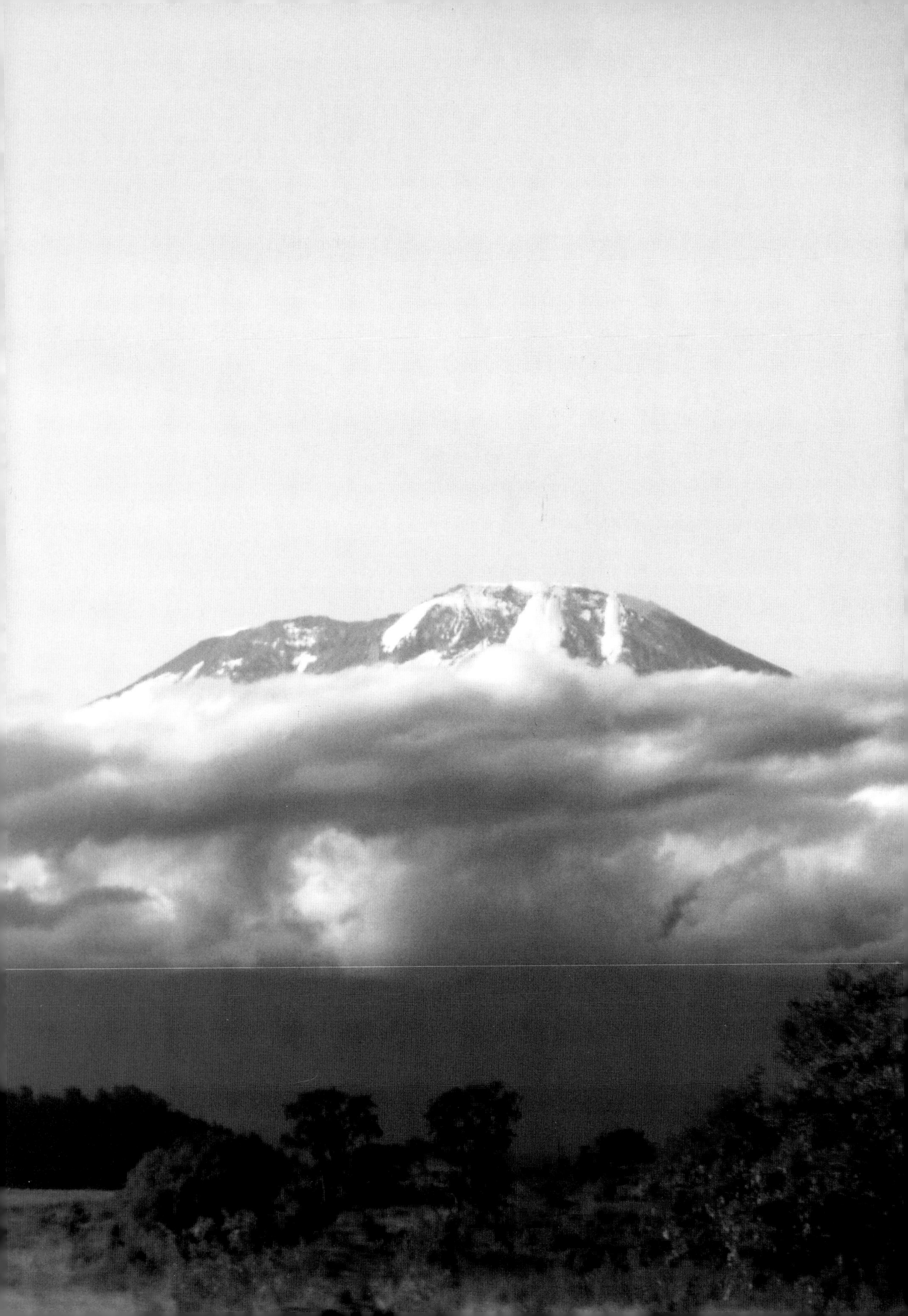

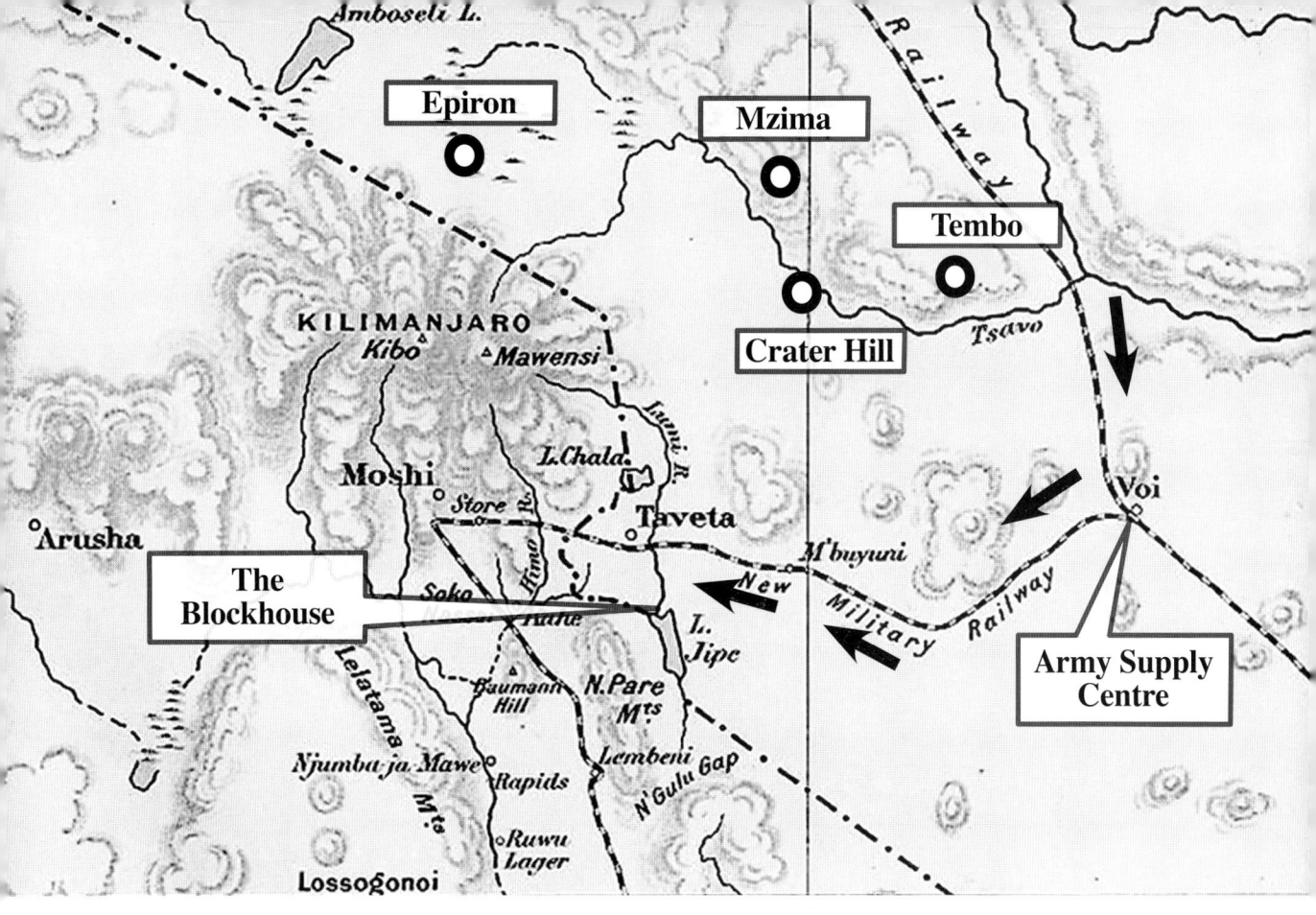

The 1915 River Line Posts. The advance of Kashmir Rifles between February and March 1916 using the railway and 'the blockhouse', where Alec was sent on a recce to clear the left flank of the advance and was fired on at 10 yards and lived to tell the tale!

Opposite: Kilimanjaro dominated the landscape and the lives of the Kashmir Rifles through out 1915 and on the long march south in 1916.

an extraordinary unit developed from the Legion of Frontiersmen and populated by wild types from across the Empire.

The Germans had seized land from British East Africa between Lake Chala and Lake Jipe (near Kilimanjaro), and mounted fighting and raiding patrols both to the north and east. The northern ones were to threaten Nairobi and the eastern ones to disrupt the British extension to the railway. These raids were very good for both German morale and for developing Askari fighting qualities. To counter these incursions, the British conceived a defensive strategy based on the Tsavo river line. A number of bases (posts) were set up from which counter patrolling and fixed piquets were established. These fixed bases along the River Tsavo needed constant re-supply from their main depot at Voi. The main artery for supply to Voi was the railway that ran from the seaport at Mombasa to Voi and then on to Nairobi.

During 1915 the British East African railway was extended from

'I Can Never Say Enough About the Men'

The Kashmir Rifles had been criticised by the Inspectors of the State Forces for poor signal skills and by 1914 had remedied this. Here is Alec at Tembo Post with the signal section using the heliograph.

Voi westwards towards Mount Kilimanjaro. The construction was led by the Indian Army, Engineer's Pioneers and a specialist Railway Company. Alongside the railway a water pipe was built to take water from the Bura Hills westwards. The Germans built strong defences between the Pare Mountains and Kilimanjaro, known as the Taveta Gap, and it was from here they mounted their fighting and reconnaissance patrols deep into British territory. The stretch of railway west of Taveta was completed in early 1916, in a great hurry after the battles that blooded the South Africans and was consequently very twisty and trains could only pass slowly.

The Kashmir Rifles' war diaries are very limited in their descriptions over this period, they tend to just report facts and do not give any impression of the hardship and boredom that pervaded the

British troops, Capt. Money 3rd Kashmir Rifles repeatedly writes 'nothing of importance to report' or 'constant patrolling maintained' and Lt Cooke's personal diary does not start until his attachment with the Kashmir Rifles, which commenced on 1 October 1915. However, there are some references in the Hordern official history and Brahma Singh's History of the JAK Rifles.

Typical German raids were about twenty strong with a mix of Askari, German officers and a few porters to carry the explosives. Occasionally large-scale fighting patrols of perhaps 300–600 Askari were mounted. Maj. Lyall and a detachment of 2nd Kashmir Rifles at Epiron in March lost eleven killed or captured. Three such attempts in June and July caused little damage or delay, and some writers state that the Germans never discovered the all-important water pipeline that ran buried alongside the railway. This type of defensive soldiering was very wearing on the soldiers and morale was greatly boosted when there were successes, like the capture of a German brass eagle insignia near Mzima in July, and great sadness when there was loss of a comrade's life, such as when the acting Lt. Col. of 3rd Kashmir Rifles, Gandharab Singh, was killed in an ambush. There was also an unfortunate incident on 14 December when Cooke's diary states 'lion killed and ate one of the 3rd Kashmiris near Tsavo'.

Indeed, there were many animal incidents reported from shooting deer, actually more often missing them, to on 2 December when Cooke writes 'a message came in to say that the patrol from Crater Hill had been attacked by a rhino and had killed it. According to the account of the native scouts they must have fired a tremendous number of shots.' The next day he mentions that it was a large beast with 23-inch horn. He also comments on the local hyenas howling at night and digging up the dead and buried.

The physical conditions were tough and Cooke makes frequent observations of sickness amongst his brother officers including one death from blackwater fever (on 5 November, Maj. Leeke of 4th King's African Rifles). He reports Alec suffering on several occasions from malaria and others with blackwater fever. Of himself he describes an early attack of malaria on 20/21 January 1916 'have felt fearfully unwell these last few days have no energy at all – am afraid my last 4 ½ years in the tropics without any kind of leave is beginning to tell – I have also felt my heart a good deal lately going up to the piquet's.' Whilst there are no formal sickness records for the Kashmir Rifles, other regiments' make interesting reading. Miller (p.137), writing on the Queens Lancashire's, states

Detraining the Rhodesian stores and mules.

that by October 1915, 836 have been admitted to hospital and only 278 have not – resulting in a typical scenario of one-third of the Battalion being unfit for active duty at any one time.

Cooke's diaries at Tembo Post describe repeating daily routines of up at 0430hrs to mount the hill piquet, inspecting rifles and ammunition, commenting on mail arriving; excitements seemed to be about pot shots at dick-dick (a small antelope). A snooze from 0500hrs to 0600hrs, rifle and ammunition inspection at 0900hrs, Hindustani lessons in the afternoon, and bridge piquet inspection in the evening. Visits from officers on re-supply were a social highlight and the number of companies at a given post varied according to the threat and the latest military operations. At one moment he comments that he, as a lieutenant, is in command of 800 men and 1,000 carriers. There is mention of trips (leave) and training (use of machine guns) at Nairobi, which was only a short journey by train to the north.

There was plenty of time between incidents for chat and reflections. He writes on the 25 November 1915:

I was talking to Chitty [visiting officer probably from the KAR with Intelligence experiences] who remarked that having fought with and against natives for so long he would never give a native a chance

The Kashmir Rifles

of surrendering – he says the mutilations they do when they get the chance is so terrible that he would rather finish off a wounded native with his boot or hip knife than give him a chance to recover.

It would be easy to get the impression that the British officers were all good friends and had similar high sense of duty and commitment; Cooke's diaries are full of his feelings about others and they understandably change and contradict over the months. Cooke's background as a soldier was untypical, as he had not attended Sandhurst, as already discussed. He was, therefore, deprived of the subaltern banter, pranks and camaraderie that is such a feature of a mess full of young men; Kerr and Lyall, his other two British officers, in the Battalion were of the 'old school' and steeped in Indian Army ways and of course were ten to fifteen years older. His diary is often an outlet of frustrations as he learnt 'hands on' the officer's way of life in a very unusual regiment: the Kashmir Rifles. One such critical, and perhaps, justified entry is about an officer from the Carrier Corps, called Connelly:

Seypoy Ridal Sing Gurung 2nd Kashmir Rifles.

> ...he rather gets on my nerves he does not do a dam stroke of work he leaves it all to Sgt Clissold he seems to have the idea that he is of immense importance. Instead he is a damn nuisance, chucks his things about the mess and never thinks of moving them but still I suppose we can not expect much else from a man who was at home when war was in full swing and yet came back to a civil job out here and even then did not turn out to do his whack until the government sent for him and told him to get out and do his bit – he then chose a non combatant job as a full Lieutenant with his full civil pay and rations – he would.

Re-supply was mostly by porters and gradually some wheeled vehicles were used – each produced their own dramas and breakdowns. Unsurprisingly, the recruitment feeding and general management of the ever-growing force of porters, carriers and road builders created regular incidents. At the end of January 1916 Cooke writes about one 'there was trouble in the porters camp – the boys who had been promised or said they had been promised to be sent home in six months refused their food... the result of this little show down was that 6 men had to guard them.'

On 20 December 1915 he wrote 'Major Lyall rang me up on the phone from Mzima and said the Colonel had told him the duties here were very heavy and asked me to send him a list. He also told me that we were to get 2 machine guns.' A few days later Cooke watched and heard a British aeroplane drop two bombs on a German

The Kashmiri Mountain Battery was part of the State Force deployed to East Africa.

patrol some 10 miles south of Crater Hill, thus heralding a new year with its full-scale offensive operations against the Germans and their East African Empire.

In spite of the relentless and tiring nature of these defensive operations they did succeed and the volume of railway traffic steadily increased throughout 1915. Of course this was merely the prerequisite for the proposed offensive of 1916. The testament to their achievements is in the statistics: in October 1915 15, 146 train miles were covered and in February 1916 this increased to 38,206.

The Germans' mobilisation of their colony reached its peak during this time and by the beginning of 1916 had rough parity with the British forces. The exact number is disputed, even amongst German sources, however the bracket is some 15–20,000 Germans and some 3,000 Europeans. These were concentrated in the Kilimanjaro area with smaller numbers elsewhere, including the south and west to face the Belgian and Portuguese forces and, of course, a substantial body to defend Dar-es-Salaam. Von Lettow-Vorbeck was convinced by the extension of the railway that an attack south from Kilimanjaro would be the British strategy for 1916 and accordingly he prepared some strong defensive positions in the Taveta Gap.

Meanwhile, 1915 is remembered by many for two naval incidents: one on Lake Tanganyika's amongst small craft and the other for

The Kashmir Rifles

the cruiser Konigsberg. Whilst the Royal Navy had almost total command of the sea, the Germans challenged this in 1914 with the armoured cruiser Konigsberg. She was determinedly pursued and took shelter by hiding in the vast shallow and muddy Rufiji Delta (November 1914). Her boilers had broken down and Captain Loof moved them for repair 100 miles across land on sledges to Dar-es-Salem and back, it took 1,000 men and three weeks. Loof arranged for the secondary armament to be dismounted into a strong defensive position.

The Royal Navy put the delta under state of siege, as their ships with deeper draughts could not get within range. Finding the exact location was not easy and both air reconnaissance and foot patrols were used. In July 1915 they sent a force of monitors (small flat bottomed un-armoured boats mounting up to 4 x 6-inch guns), there followed an 11-hour duel with airborne spotter planes; the Royal Navy fired so many rounds (1,000+) that they damaged the bulkheads of the monitors!

After the Konigsberg had settled into the mud working parties dismantled the ten surviving guns and took them ashore by raft, these too then made the same journey to Dar-es-Salem, where the shipyard and railway workshops improvised mobile gun carriages. Their redeployment as field artillery was typical of the ingenuity the Germans deployed to counter the effects of the Royal Navy blockade. They also manufactured their ammunition, explosives and medical supplies.

The Kashmir Rifles were soon to be on the receiving end of the heaviest artillery in East Africa. However, before this could happen the British needed to reinforce the theatre. The build-up was only possible thanks to the railway line extension from Voi and the water pipeline from the Bura Hills. It started in November 1915 when the word got out that the South Africans might provide large-scale assistance and that General Sir H. Smith-Dorrien would command them. Recruiting in South Africa had been very successful and eventually five mounted regiments, eight infantry battalions and five batteries of artillery units proceeded to East Africa in December 1915 and January 1916. By early February the total of all forces in theatre was calculated as 27,350 men, seventy-one guns and 123 machine guns.

The experiences of operating in East Africa during 1914–15 should have taught the allies many lessons about the difficulties of conducting operations and the competence of the German Askari, however at Salatia Hill (the Taveta Gap) on 3 February 1916 the

'I Can Never Say Enough About the Men'

new South Africans arrived and went into battle two brigades up with similar levels of over-confidence as those that went before at Tanga, only this time they were relatively untrained raw recruits. Again the British Empire's forces took a severe bashing and failed to take the ground.

On 23 February General Smuts from South Africa finally arrived* in Nairobi to take command and to lead the coming advance.

On 23/24/25 February 1916, 2nd Kashmir Rifles left their various posts on the Tsavo river line and marched to assemble at Tsavo itself, before entraining at Voi for the Bura Hills, arriving later that day at 1630hrs. The biggest dramas en route came from wildlife interfering and threatening the men; both a rhino and an elephant were killed and eaten. The Bura Hills were very beautiful and a green oasis. The British had built up a huge base at Mbuyani a few miles further west and alongside the railway, which Cooke describes on 4 March after a visit whilst 2nd Kashmir Rifles were waiting to be called forward:

> Mbuyani is an enormous camp – it is strange to find away out here in the waterless plain where few white men have ever been thousands of men, horse, foot, artillery, aeroplanes, motors, trains simply seething with activity.

After the Konigsberg had settled into the mud, working parties dismantled the ten surviving 4.1" guns.

---

* **General Smith-Dorrien was ill and never made it to the theatre of operations.**

6

The Advance South towards the Central Railway

> We had a lot of hard marching, short rations, and bad water and I can never say enough about the men.
>
> Capt. Alec Kerr

This phase of the Kashmir Rifles' story is the one with the most supporting documents. There are significant personal accounts from the battalion war dairies, Cooke's diary and the wonderful descriptions from the book *Marching on Tanga*. It is possible to truly sense and understand the hardship from these original materials.

The decision to appointment Smuts to command the British East African forces can probably best be described as political. It was a clever move for it strengthened South African Prime Minister Botha's hand in dealing with the anti-British and unreconstructed Boer community whose memories of the recent brutal war were still fresh in their minds. Smuts had been an enemy of the British, an inspirational commando leader and was a national Afrikaner hero. The immediate effect of his appointment was an instant surge in recruiting the South African volunteer army and the long term impact was to isolate the more extreme Boer communities, and so enable Botha to anchor South Africa to Britain.

Smuts' appointment marked him, at forty-six, as the youngest British lieutenant general anywhere in the world. He had lead-

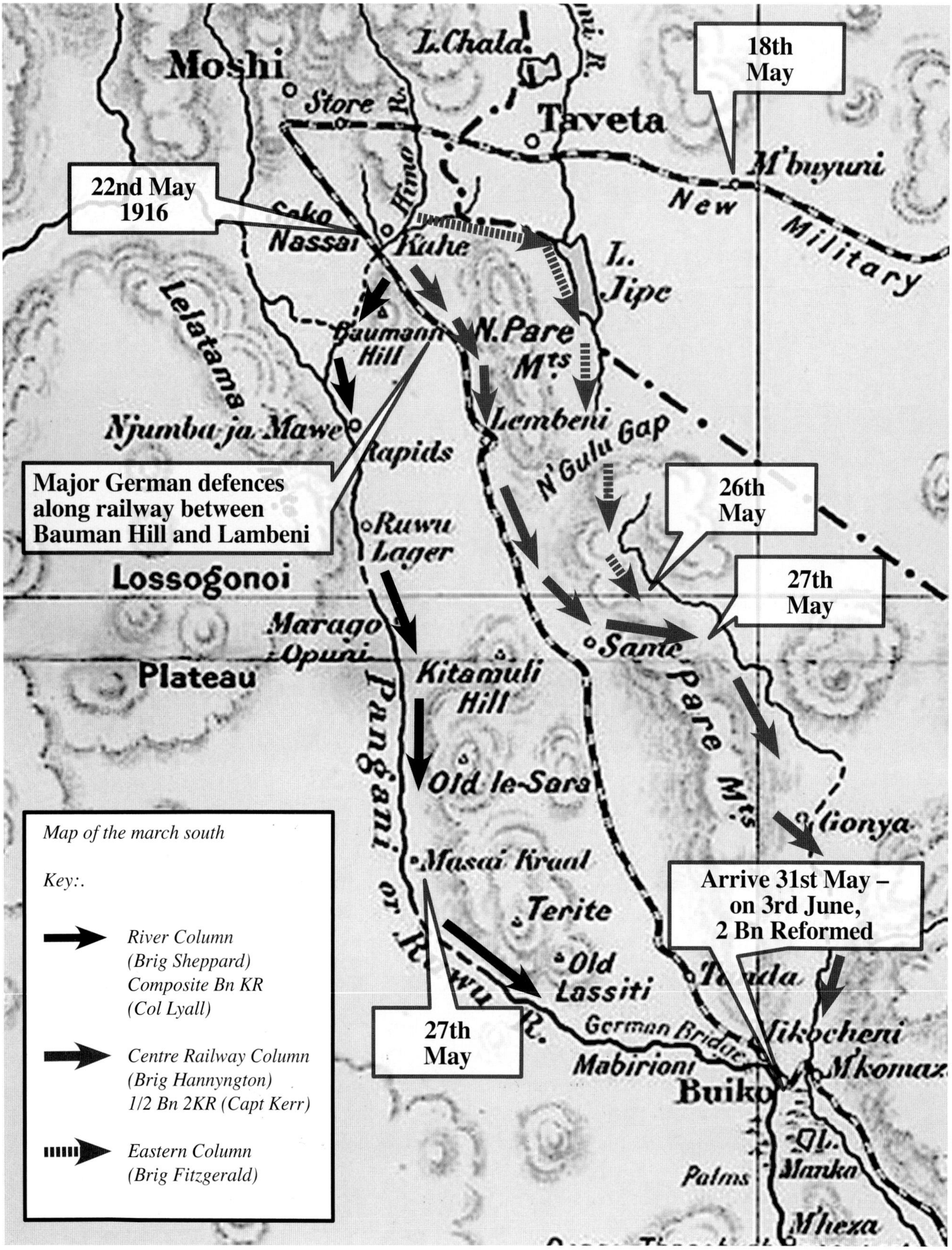

18th May
22nd May 1916
26th May
27th May
27th May
Major German defences along railway between Bauman Hill and Lambeni
Arrive 31st May – on 3rd June, 2 Bn Reformed
Moshi
L. Chala
Store
Himo R.
Taveta
M'buyuni
New Military
Sako
Nassai
Kuhe
L. Jipe
Lelatama
Baumann Hill
N. Pare Mts
Lembeni
N'Gulu Gap
Njumba ja Mawe
Rapids
Ruwu Lager
Lossogonoi
Marago Opuni
Plateau
Same
Kitamuli Hill
Pangani or Ruwu R.
Pare Mts
Old le-Sara
Gonya
Masai Kraal
Terite
Old Lassiti
German Bridge
Mabirioni
Buiko
M'komazi
Palms
Manka
M'heza
Map of the march south
Key:.
River Column (Brig Sheppard) Composite Bn KR (Col Lyall)
Centre Railway Column (Brig Hannyngton) 1/2 Bn 2KR (Capt Kerr)
Eastern Column (Brig Fitzgerald)

ership qualities by the bucketful: energy, decisiveness, confidence, grasp, drive and personal bravery, but his fighting experiences were all as a relative small force commander, leading a horse-borne, long-range raiding commando unit of about 300 men, travelling light and living off the land. His tactics were all about boldness, mobility and seizing opportunity. How this mix of leadership and military experience was going to work out was of course uppermost in the minds of the military and civil community in British East Africa. They generally welcomed him but had reservations.

Smuts inherited a campaign plan and only tinkered at the edges, on the one hand he was impatient to get on the offensive and on the other he and Prime Minister Botha did not want, and could not afford, a politically heavy butcher's bill. He split his forces either side of Mount Kilimanjaro in a wide enveloping manoeuvre – one part largely horse borne attacking from the north and around the west of the mountain, and the other attacking from the east along the axis of the extended railway – the Kashmir Rifles were in the latter party in a supporting role covering the left or southern flank.

The Kashmir Rifles were not intimately involved in these bloody and exhausting battles and marches, during which the newly arrived South Africans had their arrogance and over-confidence forcefully rammed back down their throats. Instead Lt Cooke's diary speaks of the build-up and the disappointment:

Lt Cooke volunteered in India with the Maxim Gun company - he was commissioned and attached to 2KR. He served from October 1915. His diaries are a major part of this history. He went on to serve in Palestine with 3KR.

27 February, Bura
Kerr returned from Mbuyani with the news that we [4 Coys and the MGs] are to join up with the half battalion of 3KR and form a battalion and then join a brigade with the Baluchis, Rhodesians and Lancashire's – Major Lyall is to command our battalion, Money to be adjutant and Kerr and Proctor 4 Companies each...

he goes on to say that they were not going to move for about a fortnight.

In fact they promptly moved forward to the front, passing through Mbuyani and Serengeti. On 7 March they were warned off to attack at Salatia which caused Cooke to comment in his diary 'my anxiety was that I should be an example to my men'. He goes on next day 'we formed up behind the ridge in the sun waiting for the order to move forward to attack Salatia but it never came'.

The Kashmir Rifles crossed the Latema battlefield on 15 March and Cooke says 'everywhere there are signs of the struggle and some of the dead are still lying about in putrid condition while

The blockhouse incident at Kingarunga by Lake Jipe, 22 March 1916.

others in shallow graves do not pass unnoticed'. He goes on 'Lyall is appalling he can't make up his mind about anything and does not know a thing about MGs yet tries to arrange their disposal in a faltering indefinite sort of way'. On the 17th the Kashmir Rifles were withdrawn and replaced in the frontline by the Rhodesians and Cooke comments 'that it was good to get a bath again and to leave the smell of the dead behind'. He records Lyall's promotion to local lieutenant colonel.

These diary entries are particularly significant with regard to the command structure of the Kashmir Rifles for it so clearly states a British officered one with Lyall promoted to a local lieutenant colonel. Whilst this may seem entirely logical from a clear lines of communication point of view it should be remembered that these soldiers were Kashmir State Forces, paid for and totally loyal to the Maharaja and officered by their own. It could have been a difficult moment but these were well-disciplined soldiers united by fighting both the Germans and the tropical conditions they had developed strong bonds of mutual respect.

The Kashmir Rifles

Kangarunga – the Blockhouse Incident

By 22 March the Kashmir Rifles were covering the left flank of the westward advance before it turned south into the heart of German East Africa, with Lake Jipe as their southern boundary. The Kashmir Rifles continued to be in reserve and missed the main fight, however there is one interesting incident that is described in both the official war diary and in Cooke's private one.

Lyall in the regimental diary states orders were received to make determined effort to seize the bridge over the Rufu River at Kangarunga about 8 miles south of Taveta. The bridge was believed to be held by one enemy company (100 rifles or so and one machine gun), the only approach to the bridge was found to be a narrow winding path through dense grass and banana plantations, and both flanks to the position were covered for miles by impassable papyrus swamp. The bridge itself was invisible but a blockhouse guarding it on the enemy bank of the river was located and found to be occupied. The next day at 0745hrs two guns of No. 8 Field Battery arrived and took up position. At noon Capt. Kerr with one company went down to the bridge to reconnoitre under cover of the battery. Cooke's diary then describes the Kangarunga Blockhouse incident in which he and Alec are nearly killed:

Parad Singh distinguished himself leading Number 2 Company in support of the Punjabis as they counter attacked the 3rd Field Kommando, the German Askari, at Handeni.

> Up at 4.30 to stand to – bitten to death by mosquitoes all night. At 1030 moved out towards the first footbridge across the Rufu river with 2 Coys [Lyall states one Coy] and my MGs under Kerr. Scouts had reported seeing blockhouses near where the bridge had been and said it was empty. Kerr afterwards said he misunderstood them – a mistake which nearly cost us both our lives. After going for about a 1 ½ through a swamp track Kerr and I who had gone forward with a few orderlies, having left the guns and Coys behind suddenly came in sight of a blockhouse with a river about 15 yards wide in front of it. Kerr had just reached the edge of the water and I was a few yards behind him when the blockhouse opened fire on us Kerr dropped where he was and had little cover – I was on a slope facing the blockhouse so I made a dive for the ground but found myself still exposed to fire at about 30 yards range. I eventually got to a small dip and waited there with Kerr's orderlies and could see Kerr about 10 yards from the blockhouse and knew that as long as he did not move he was all right – I got back through the grass and sent men to watch our flanks as I expected an ambush and then sent back for more men. The few with us had scattered from which they could see nothing. My idea was to form a frontal and flanking fire at the blockhouse and so

'I Can Never Say Enough About the Men'

get them away. As however I was getting up to the men Kerr came in by himself having got up and come back.

How these people missed us I cannot imagine – the guns Calcutta Battery opened fire soon after the rifle fire started and that probably upset the Huns nerve. Kerr then cleared off and left me down in the swamp with a Coy – he went back to get the guns onto it – after about an hour and a half the guns started that is about 2.00pm and then ceased. It then struck them that it would be as well to see where they were shooting and Young of the Battery came down with a telephone and registered the shots. They fired about 20 rounds between 3.30 and 4.00pm and we then went forward again to the blockhouse but no fire was opened up on us.

We sent a man in to ford the river but he dropped into deep water about the middle and got out with difficulty and not far away there was the swell of crocodile. We returned to the hill at 5.30 and learned that Kahe had fallen.

This was the perspective of a young emergency commissioned officer having his first experiences of an advance to contact.* The 2nd Bn war diary written by Lyall (signing himself local lieutenant colonel) concludes:

> Reconnaissance seemed to show that the enemy had abandoned the position on the south side of the river. General Tighe, commanding the 2nd Division, visited the position in the morning. Over the coming days patrols were sent out to gage enemy location and strengths, a temporary bridge was built and the new Divisional Commander General Shepperd visited and inspected.

A few days later on 28 March the battalion entrained and returned to Mbuyani, the main base, for brigade training and a small amount of leave until 17 May. The Germans had been kicked out of British East Africa and time was needed to plan and prepare for the next offensive. The heavy rains had come and the railway needed extending to Kahe. Additionally Smuts was keen to reorganise the diverse army on more logical lines. As the Kashmir Rifles had had little of the real fighting this narrative does not provide a sense of what had happened, especially the intensity and casualties of the fighting and the success of Smuts' campaign in forcing the Germans out of British territory and in securing the Uganda railway. Overall it was a victory and Smuts was heralded a hero in both Britain and South Africa.

---

* **Remember that he would not have enjoyed the formal training and preparatory experiences of a Sandhurst regular officer.**

Smuts' plan was to advance south with two thrusts. The mounted troops of the South African 2nd Division on a wide sweep south and west (this had already reached Kondoa Irangi on route to Dodoma, a key town on the German Central Railway) and for the infantry to march south on foot to Handeni, cross the River Wami and on to Morogoro, also on the Central Railway. He hoped to use this flanking manoeuvre to get behind the retreating Askari and then force them to do battle, inflicting heavy casualties that they could ill afford. He promised his troops a tough but short campaign!

These were lovely grand plans but would they deliver in East Africa with its tropical rains, diseases and hostile landscape and roads? After all this was not the relatively easily traversable bush veldt plains of South Africa. The conditions were wonderfully described by H.L. Pritchard, who later wrote this in the history of the Royal Corps of Engineers:

> Imagine a country three times the size of Germany, mostly covered by dense bush, with no roads and only two railways, and either sweltering under a tropical sun or swept by torrential rain which makes the friable soil impassable to wheeled traffic; a country with occasional wide and swampy areas interspersed with arid areas where water is often more precious than gold; in which man rots with malaria and suffers torments from insect pests; in which animals die wholesale from the ravages of tse-tse fly; where crocodiles and lions seize unwary porters, giraffes destroy telegraph lines, elephants damage tracks, hippopotami attack boats, rhinoceroses charge troops on the march and bees put whole battalions to flight. Such was German East Africa in 1914-18.

With hindsight it is very easy to say that these were overly ambitious plans that did not give due weight to the tropical conditions and the risk of over-extended lines of communication, but the date is April 1916 and the British Empire's forces had been in theatre for over two years and had hard first-hand experience of these challenges. The question must be posed how did this concept of operations survive the scrutiny of experienced staff officers? Perhaps the debacle of Tanga could be reasonably explained by the years of peace and written off to inexperience, but this can no longer be a credible excuse after two years of conducting operations in theatre.

Edward Paice (p.196) believes the explanation is the need for a quick, low-casualty victory for political stability in South Africa, which the Smuts' enveloping strategy looked like it might achieve, if the Germans would stand still for long enough. Perhaps another, and less glamorous, explanation is that the obvious first sweep south was bound to focus on the Tanga railway line for communication and the Pangani River for water – these points meet at Buiko, so to try and envelope the enemy at this clear choke point would have been perhaps obvious to the Germans too. As to what next, Smuts may have thought that he would decide that once Buiko was taken. The intelligence assessment of where Lettow-Vorbeck might withdraw suggested westward to Tabora along the Central Railway and into the Askari recruiting heartland, which again makes sense of the advance south with a view towards the Central Railway line and Morogoro.

My own view is that Smuts was a charismatic and instinct-based leader with un-bounded self confidence and belief – he had always taken risks, travelled light, relied on speed and lived off the land – so why change his modus operandi now? This was the way he knew how to fight. He would have said go for it, keep your options open and not placed due weight of emphasis on logistics.

Advance to Buiko and then on to Msiha 18 May to 30 June 1916

Smuts reorganised the 1st and 3rd Divisions into three columns which he named the River Column, Central Column and Eastern Column, and they were commanded by Sheppard, Hannyngton and Fitzgerald. The Kashmir Rifles were split between the River and Centre Columns. Initially Lt Col Lyall had 1/2Bn of 2nd Kashmir Rifles and 1/2 Bn of 3rd Kashmir Rifles on the Pangani River. The other half Bn of 2nd Kashmir Rifles were with Capt. Kerr and were on the Central or Railway Column. The combined battalion was often referred to as the 'Composite.'

Cooke in his diary on 17 May says 'we move out tomorrow for the Promised Land at 8.30am – Col Lyall unwell. The BO [British Officer] allowance of kit is 40lbs mess, 40lbs tentage and 40lbs kit which is very generous all things considered. We passed through Serengeti at 11am – it was just an overgrown wilderness'. The daily march was about 10 miles and there are descriptions of crossing the Himo River and the camp at Store, where the British railway had now joined the German Tanga Line. He goes on 'in fact all the way from Bura the road to German East Africa is marked by little batches of the graves of those who have fallen by the way - road and dust fearful'.

The smiling faces of the Kashmir Rifles, early in the advance south.

The Kashmir Rifles were often on half or no rations and digging for water was a regular occurence. When close to the River Pangani with its swamps the attacks from mosquitoes prompted Lt Cooke to comment 'the men were absolutely done, it was a poisonous spot, infested with fly and mosquitoes and many of the men just lay down where they halted and slept.'

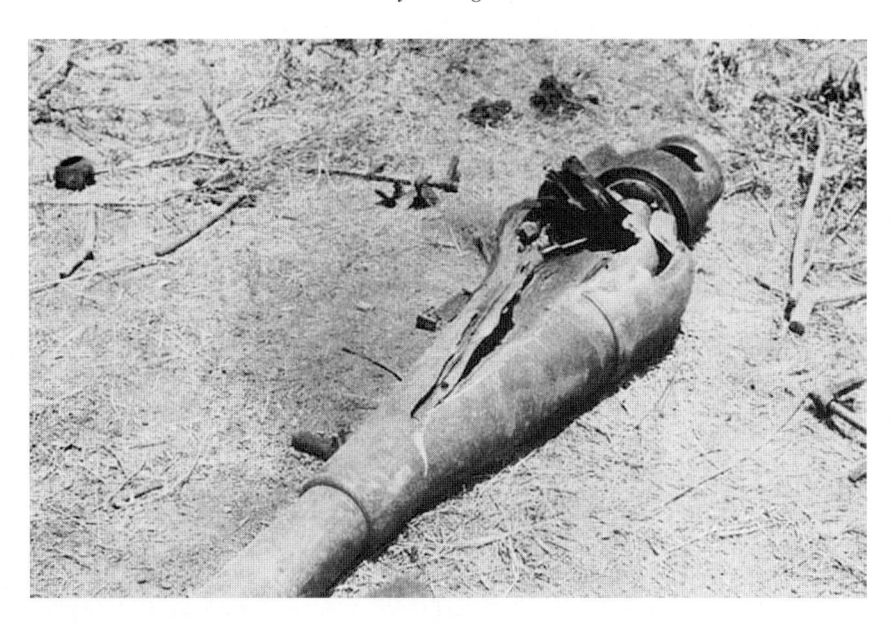

In a typical and brilliant way the Germans redeployed the 4.1" guns from the battlecruiser Konigsberg. The German tactic was to lay waste, ambush and withdraw along supply lines.

On 22 May at Kahe the division of the Kashmir Rifles between the two columns took place and the daily records of Lyall and Cooke both follow the River Pangani column – the two columns were to meet up some 10 days and 100+ marching miles later at Buiko.

Immediately the going gets tough and the regimental diary entries are very brief and factual – possibly reflecting the exhaustion. On the 23rd it just states 'party was sent to cut bush and make road' and for the 27th 'a long and trying march with no water'. Cooke was more colourful with:

> we crossed the Tanga Moshi railway just below Kahe about 2 am and our progress became slower as the track faded and we had to cut our way. We camped on the east of the Pangani river near Massende about 10 am – I was just about done to the world when I was sent straight out with 100 men to cut a road with the 61st Pioneers under Robinson – I managed to get a cup of tea and a biscuit before leaving – we cut parallel to the Pangani – I returned to camp at 230pm had a meal but failed to get any sleep.

On the next day he mentions General Smuts' visit and another road cutting party, he goes on:

> orders were then received to push on at once. I was very glad to get a peg of whisky and some chocolate from one of the 17th Cavalry

The Kashmir Rifles

Officers Ibbotson while halted – it was just getting dusk as we moved off again and the column was soon lost in the bush in the dark – it was about 10 am when we halted having luckily struck water and the men were absolutely done – it was a poisonous spot infested with fly and mosquitoes and many of the men just lay down where they halted and slept – we must have covered more than 20 miles going as slowly as we were – we had been on the trek since 4am.

The pattern of operations was to rotate the 'advance guard' between the fighting arms – 2nd Rhodesia Regiment, 130th Baluchis and the composite battalion of the Kashmir Rifles. The squadron of the 17th Cavalry also were pushed forward. There were several minor incidents, skirmishes and few casualties on either side. There are descriptions of receiving Maxim fire in ambushes and the first rounds of the Konigsberg's 4.1-in. guns firing at ranges of about 10,000 yards.

Cooke writes on 30 May at Mabrioni (just west and slightly north of Buiko on the banks of the Pangani):

Jemanda Ali Bahadur 2nd Kashmir Rifles.

> Had a rotten night on account of mosquito only one shot fired but too tired to worry about it – Col Lyall was absolutely finished with fatigue. Up at 4.00 am ready to move off at 5.30 am but order cancelled as no rations since a day before yesterday. Rations arrived about 7.00 am and we fed and moved off at 8.30 am.

Cooke goes on to describe an artillery exchange just north of Buiko when the Germans found their range and had bracketed them when they were saved by a counter-battery bombardment from the 27th Mountain Battery. He goes on to say on 31 May 'here the animals had their first drink for nearly 48 hours'. Cooke also witnessed at a distance the Germans blowing up the railway lines and other facilities at Buiko and seeing the last train leave.

The story of this advance is wonderfully told by Brett Young, the regimental doctor of the Rhodesians, in his book *Marching on Tanga*. He is very complimentary about the Kashmir Rifles and records many scenes of great natural beauty and incidents of the Kashmiri building Bandas, as well as fishing for small blue barbell, and of course treating the wounded. On p.71 writing about outbreaks of malaria during this time, he states:

> So great was the number of new cases that morning that I took special stock of the quinine to see if I could deal with the regiment in what I took to be a proper way, giving everyman in it a regular prophylactic

'I Can Never Say Enough About the Men'

dose. I found that if this were done I should soon be tapping my reserves. The risk of being stranded without any was too grave to be taken on.

On p.103 he continues with:

And now arose more urgently than ever the question of evacuating these wounded men, and those sick with malaria or dysentery who were pouring into our tents each day. We had come down the Pangani far too fast for our communications. Rations were already diminished by half and likely to be scarcer. The railway had been so well destroyed that our trains ran no further than Kahe our starting point, and there the nearest casualty station lay. The only way in which our sick men could return was on empty supply lorries, unsheltered from the sun, toiling with the utmost weariness through vast sandy stretches and thick bush, jolted without mercy in deep nullahs, sleeping under cold stars along the fever swamps of the Pangani. But it would have been worse if we had left them to languish by the river, for already our tents were overflowing and at any moment we might be moving on and they would have been at the mercy of any prowling company of askaris from the Pare......such was the purgatory our wounded men faced; and later on, when the line had been lengthened again, their case was harder still.

On 31 May the columns arrived at Buiko and Brett Young describes a week of forced rest in the pestilential spot, the death of large numbers of horses, cattle and mules from Tsetse fly and reveals the casualty state of the Rhodesians on p.113: 'in a fortnight the regiment had lost a quarter of its strength; the Baluchis too began to show the effects of their sudden excursions into the mountain's unfamiliar cold'.

Charles Miller in his great book, The Battle for the Bundu, seeks to capture the horror of this experience on p.17:

The most widespread sickness on the drive down the Pangani was malaria, of whose symptoms death was not necessarily the most violent, although it was common enough and sometimes welcomed. Other manifestations included chills, heat stroke, epileptic seizures, delirium tremens, cardiac failure and insanity. The British suffered much more from malaria than did the Germans, partly because their relative newness to the tropics made them less resistant, partly because their knee-length shorts and short sleeved shirts were a standing invitation to the anopheles mosquito. [The Schutztruppe's more sensiblelong sleeves, ankle length trousers and puttees did a great

Alec with Kavirondo porters and stretcher bearers.

Both Brett-Young and Cooke comment on the success of the Kashmiris at fishing to supplement the faltering supply of rations. Here Lt Col Lyall looks on as the Kavarondo porters do their bit.

They marched until they collapsed, many doing so on reaching Misha Camp.

deal to hold malaria at bay.] Quinine was a helpful prophylactic but it could only do so much, and stocks were often in short supply owing to transport snarls. Mosquito netting, which ripped like tissue paper, was slightly better than worthless, but could never be used when most needed: on night sentry or patrol duty. The British soldier in East Africa who escaped Malaria in some form was almost a freak.

Everyone also caught dysentery – amoebic or bacillary or both – from contaminated food or the waters of the Pangani and other rivers; East Africa had the highest dysentery rate of any theatre in the First World War. The most noticeable symptom was uncommonly virulent diarrhoea: more than one British unit could be followed by its miles-long trail of bloody faeces. Also common was blackwater fever, so called because it turned ones urine black, although advanced cases vomited themselves to death. There was also relapsing fever caused by ticks; its symptoms could resemble malaria. Small cuts often expanded quickly into livid, suppurating jungle sores as big as a fist. The afflicted airs were almost enough to make a man welcome a bullet.

Other ailments, caused by insects, seldom killed but were troublesome enough. The jigger flea burrowed into a man's toe and laid several million eggs. If the eggs were not extracted with a knife or a safety pin, the toe would presently rot. Literally thousands of British, Indian and African toes were amputated on the march to the Central Railway. The bott fly laid its eggs in a soldier's arm or back.

The Kashmir Rifles

The egg soon grew into large white maggots; unless removed they would die and form festering abscesses. Army surgeons often pulled out as many as four dozen of these from a single patient.

In Christopher Thornhill's story of his experiences, called *Taking Tanganyika with the East African Mounted Rifles*, he tells of a dramatic incident at a waterhole when his mate Fred lay down next to the mules to drink:

'God what shall I do? I have swallowed a young eel or something. Could see it quite plainly swimming about – then suddenly it made a dive for me. No, I haven't swallowed it!' And Fred put his hand in his mouth. 'Wow! It has got hold of me!' And Fred was tugging at a slimy, black, slug-like insect which seemed to have a firm hold on the inside of his mouth and he was apparently in great pain. Soon blood started to flow from his mouth in profusion. It was some time before I realised what had happened. 'Don't tug at it,' I said 'it only catches hold with the other end when you get the one end loose and each time it grips it cuts your skin. You have got a leech and if you wait a moment I will get it out for you.' 'Won't it crawl down my throat?' gasped Fred, blood now trickling down to his tunic... I rubbed the leech well with salt and without much difficulty was able to remove it and held it up for Fred to see.

Havildar Sharma 1st Kashmir Infantry.

He goes on to describe the leech's life cycle and its effects on livestock.*

The 2nd Rhodesians were decimated by disease during these first three weeks of the advance (140 miles/210km in 10 days – Ross Anderson (p.124) *The Forgotten Front*), the raw statistics tell a shocking story, with the regiment losing 300 from 525. The Kashmir Rifles were clearly also losing men but the Regimental Diary does not report sickness as an issue until 30 June, approximately a month later when at Misha Camp.

On 1 June Cooke writes at Buiko, 'had a glorious nights rest and was glad to hear there was a days halt'. On 3 June the 2nd Kashmir Rifles reformed as a whole under Brig. Sheppard and was renumbered No. 3 Column, with the objective of Handeni. The 1/2 Bn of the 3rd Kashmir Rifles joined Brig. Hannyngton's No. 2 Column and continued the advance along the railway.

---

* Leeches would most surely have been a strange phenomenon to the British, but the Indian troops must have been quite used to it. Assam and Burma (which was part of India until then) are full of leeches and most Indian soldiers must have had a good experience of leech bites. (Information courtesy of Maj. Brahma Singh)

General Smuts the allied commander had learnt his military trade fighting the British as a commando leader in the Boer War. Whilst there is no doubt that he was personally brave and an inspirational leader, he did push himself, his men and their animals and equipment beyond endurance. He ended up suffering from malaria and his army disintegrating around him in December 1916. His reputation, however, remained.

The obvious military challenge for Brig. Sheppard and No. 3 Column was to cross the Pangani which at this point was described as canal-like, 100 feet wide and 14 foot deep, with a 4 knot current. The practical problem was food, exhaustion and supplies; the pause that Smuts was forced to accommodate to allow the supply line to catch up was one week, but in practice this was not enough because the Tanga railway line could not be opened up quickly following its destruction by the retreating Germans. Smuts was pressing hard as he thought he saw the chance to force a decisive action.

2nd Kashmir Rifles as rearguard crossed the river on 6 June by pontoon bridge and raft without accident, although Cooke says there were many amusing scenes getting the mules and bullocks across. They marched some 7 miles south and then were moved on a further 4 miles during the night to join the 27th Mountain Battery, where they entrenched as trouble was expected. Half rations and road cutting characterised the next few days until 9 June when the brigade went into action near Mkalmo, where the Trolley Line commenced and ran south to Handeni (this was a narrow gauge shuttle tramway for moving farm produce).

The Kashmir Rifles

The Germans had developed a prepared position (3 FK) and attacked westwards with 1, 5 and 16 FK. The 130th Baluchis and the 29th Punjabis under Col Dyke were heavily engaged in dense bush, and 2nd Kashmir Rifles were the rearguard. No. 8 Coy under Subd Hakim was sent forward on the right to escort the Mountain Battery and No. 2 Coy under Subd Parshed Singh, with 2nd Lt Walshaw, was sent to reinforce the 29th Punjabis on the left flank and was credited with repulsing the counterattack from 3 FK. The engagement was characterised by heavy rifle and machine-gun fire, but with minimal fields of fire the fighting continued until after nightfall when the regiment received orders to dig in where it stood. No water was obtainable during the day and little food.

The total British casualties were fifteen killed and thirty-three wounded, mostly from the Baluchis. Eighteen enemy dead were counted and four prisoners. The Kashmir Rifles expended 5,000 rounds and the 130th Baluchis 18,000. Brett Young in *Marching on Tanga* describes in graphic detail his experiences during this action when his medical teams were overrun by the counterattack of 3FK:

> Whilst the bullets flied they only killed a few it was the tropical climate that was doing the far more serious damage. The columns had entered one of the more lethal 'fly belts' that the Germans had kindly recorded on their maps which of course was known to the British and naturally ignored by Smuts whose self belief was total. The impact on the transport horses, mules and cattle was appalling and by July had become 100% a month. The suffering was horrific, it started with a swelling in the chest and is characterised by frothing muzzles and massive weight loss. The only treatment was the revolver.

The impact of this was to put further strain on the supply lines which now completely broke down. The Kashmir Rifles and Sheppard's brigade marched on and it took until 18 June to reach Handeni. Lt Col Lyall's diary entries become very short and daily repeat the words '...half rations and have to dig for water'. From Smuts' perspective he knew he had to press on hard as there was no water between Buiko on the River Pangani and the Lukigura, the next river south and still 39 miles away.

Lt Cooke's diaries are dominated by the need to find and dig for water. On 14 June he describes a personal conversation with Brig. Sheppard, who had come down to see his successful work digging for water:

Tired and weary the Kashmir Rifles... it was not just the endless marching, it was the constant call for road cutting, using the Kukris, the day often started at 0300hrs, with little time to rest.

5.30 he was very pleased – I walked back with him and he pointed out Handeni Hill to me as the aeroplanes passed over us to bomb it and told me that the reserves were going to be brought up before taking Handeni and also that we [meaning the Brigade] had now led the advance for 220 miles – the camp was attacked by bees and many were badly stung.

On the 16th he writes 'we made a wonderful advance with the armoured cars reaching the Kondoa Irangi road about 3.00pm'. Sheppard pressed on and the brigade entered Handeni unopposed on 18 June. Smuts pressed Sheppard on and so the troops marched on Mwejimbu on the 20th and Kangata on the 21st. The Regimental Diary notes half rations and very little water of poor quality.

The 2nd Kashmir Rifles' strength was recorded in Lt Col Lyall's official regimental diary on 23 June as 446 Indian Ranks and four British officers strong – they were at little over 50 percent strength, in spite of repeated drafts of fresh soldiers from Kashmir and were about to launch their weary bodies into an attack. Smuts had intelligence that the enemy were preparing a defensive position on the Lukigura and therefore made plans for his forces to get behind the position and force a significant engagement.

7

The Battle of Lukigura
24 June 1916

'We knocked spots off the swine and finished off with the bayonet...'

Capt. Alec Kerr

Lukigura was in many ways the high point of General Smuts' strategy. It was virtually the only time his forces managed to execute his manoeuvre and pin down concept of his operational strategy. The Kashmir Rifles manoeuvred behind the enemy, cut them off and brought into action enough firepower to actually kill and wound the enemy with bullets and bayonets.

The battle was a classic with intelligence identifying the enemy position, and a distracting force, including machine-gun fire from armoured cars, that kept the Askaris' attention for nearly 24 hours, which then enabled the Advanced Guard to march through the night and attack from the flank achieving that ultimate military goal of surprise.

There are several eyewitness accounts of this battle and they largely agree on points of detail: there is a very short account in Horden (the official Military Operations account), Cooke's diary has some useful confirmatory evidence, and the descriptions of the night march are valuable in From Hobo to Hunter by C.E. Stoneham (the author

The Battle of Lukigura.

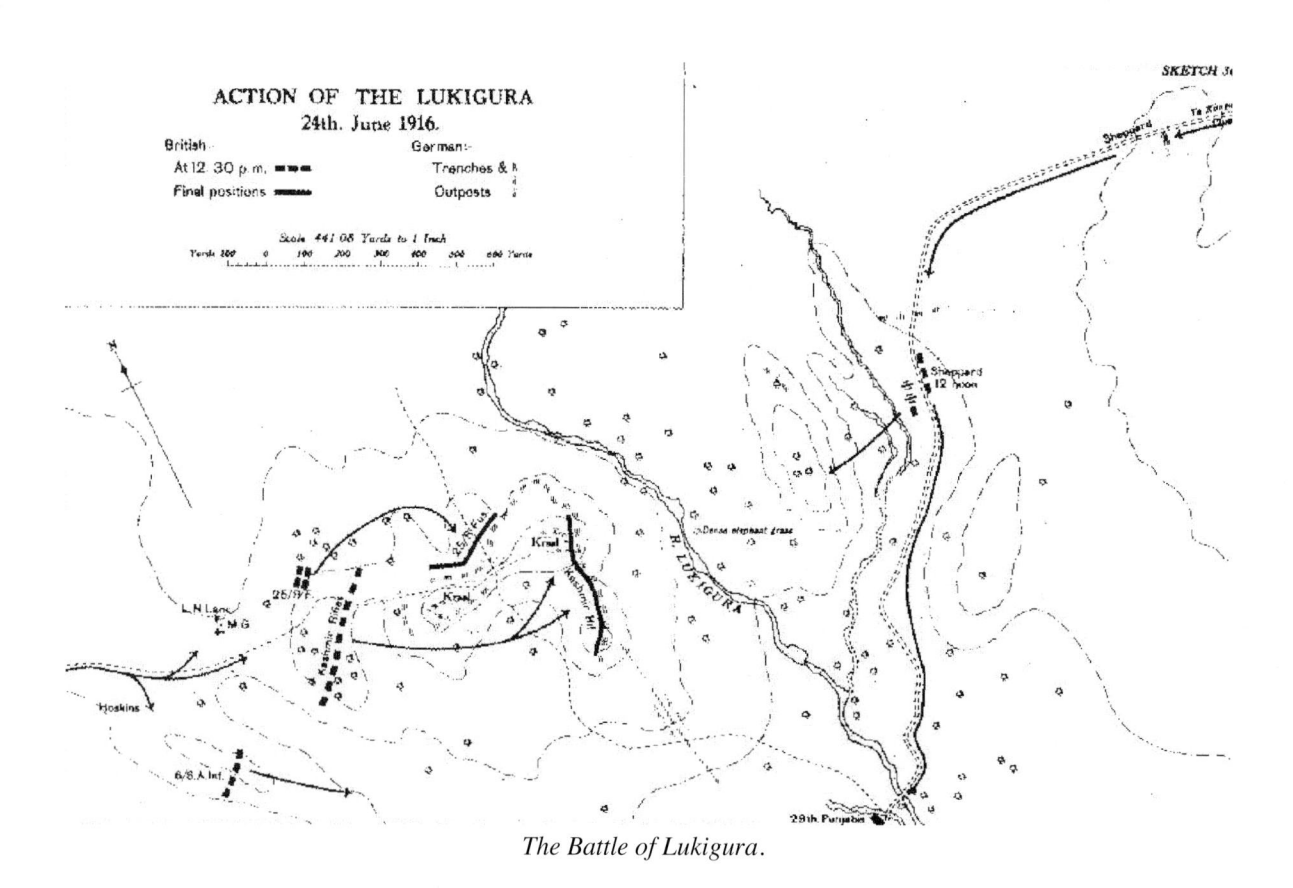

Major Sir John Willoughby (of Jameson raid fame and who had given the armoured cars to the war office) acted as the decoy and gave covering fire from the Kangata Road during the Battle of Lukigura.

The 4 Leyland Armoured Cars that supported the advance south. They were primitive with limited ground clearance and very poor off track mobility. They were withdrawn from Africa.

The 4.1" Naval guns from the sunk German Cruiser Konigsberg that were remounted on wheels. This gun was blown up by the retreating Askari and 2nd Kashmir Rifles posed for photographs on 2nd September 1916 south of Morogoro near the Ruvu river crossing. Cooke states " the river was 60yards wide and full of shells and rifle grenades thrown away by the retreating hun."

Early aeroplanes arrived at Mbuyuni, East of Kilimanjaro in February 1916 as part of the strategic build up prior to the advance South. The BE2C with 70hp and 60 mph, from 26 Sqn were used for reconnaissance and to bomb German defensive positions, especially the 4.1" guns, with poor results. However they terrified the natives and were a great tonic for morale although the pilots seldom flew when sober. Cooke wrote "every Hun these days lives in fear of air bombs apparently lives under bushes with funk holes."

The Rolls Royce Armoured Cars of No1 Squadron the Royal Navy under Lieutenant Commander Whittall - they were sent out to East Africa with no spares and half the force was cannibalised to keep the remaining 6 working.

had been a soldier with the 25th Royal Fusiliers), but for once the best all-round account is from Lt Col Lyall's entry in the Battalion War Diary. There is also a paragraph in Captain Kerr's letter (see Appendix A). However, as a taster to what is ahead, Cooke captures the moment of assault with these words: 'as soon as the advance guard reached the ridge there was a terrific fusillade offered —rifles, machine guns & pom pom gun of sorts. It seemed as if nothing could live...'

However, the correct place to start recounting the battle has to be Stoneham with his narrative of the build-up, written some forty years after the event:

Jem Kalu distingushed himself at Lukigura attacking on the right flank.

> It was forced marches all the time. Twenty miles, thirty miles, twenty five miles – day after day we slogged through bush and plain without food or covering, for it was months since our transport had been able to come near us. We wore shirts and shorts, well enough in burning sunshine, but little protection against the chill of high-veld nights... We were thin as skeletons and rotten with malaria. Several times I marched all day with a temperature of over hundred degrees. In warfare the impossible is always being accomplished – we were doing it then.
>
> The General [Smuts], in a speech made from the back of a staff car told us we had beaten the best record of the French Foreign Legion. In my company were three men who had served with that force and they thought so too. But we were not enheartened. Everybody was weary, hungry and diseased...
>
> It was the worst night march I have ever endured. In a single file on a narrow winding bush-path we plunged straight into a welter of wooded hills, divided by sudden, rocky ravines. There was no moon, but in East Africa starlight is very bright on a clear night, and, except while penetrating tall grass or scrambling in and out of dongas we could see our whereabouts plainly. The great trouble was our intense fatigue. For weeks we had been trekking an average of 20 miles a day through burning heat and blinding dust, with barely enough food to maintain life, and now we were worn out. After twelve hours of marching during the day I thought it doubtful we could reach the place of camping - that I should go all night was beyond possibility. But I marched another 30 miles in spite of that. I stumbled along in a sort of coma, the heavy pack and cumbersome rifle weighing me down. The rifle is an intolerable burden, because wherever you carry it you are lopsided. Askaris are fond of carrying it across the nape of the neck with a hand on each end, but this posture a European feels crucified. The only thing to do is to keep shifting it from shoulder to other, where it upsets the balance of the pack and chafes the skin

*In spite of all the hardship the men of Kashmir Rifles just keep going
Left to Right: Havildar Giandar, Sepoys Hafiziullah, Mirchand and Tula.*

under a layer of sweat and sand.

The rough path kept turning and twisting like a corkscrew. It was overgrown with grass and I could not see where to place my feet to avoid jolts and tripping. We seemed always either going up or down, and both were bad: the down hill part driving sore, blistered toes into stiff boots and climbs straining aching muscles to the limits of endurance. We moved in fits and starts, for the column was continually held up by difficult dongas and the guide's uncertainty. Guides never know where they are going and always arrive somewhere they had no idea of when they started. They then claim they have been aiming for this all along. This guide led us into a hornets nest in the finish.

We kept going to sleep on our feet, which meant falling heavily over unexpected obstacles. I remember the man in front of me falling headlong into a donga, myself landing on top of him, and two others pilling into the mix up – four of us rolling amongst rocks, with rifles and equipment groaning and cursing, until we managed somehow to untangle ourselves and go on.

The 30 miles we covered before daylight might just as well have

The Kashmir Rifles

been a hundred- it is not the distance so much as the conditions that count. At dawn we were strung out along the side of a hill when firing suddenly broke out in front.

Lt Col Lyall's War Diary entries now follow and are, of course, are less descriptive and written in daily sequence:

23 June 1916
The regiment was camped by itself 250yds north of the Handeni—Kangata & Nderema—Kangata roads with a piquet of one company with the two armoured motor maxims at the cross roads. The morning was spent in fatigues digging water holes for the Brigade which was expected during the course of the day. At noon orders were received that the regiment was to march with a force under General Hoskins at 4pm. Rations for the 23rd were received at 2.20pm and as much food as possible in the limited time was cooked. The Regiment marched for the rendezvous at 3.45pm (Kangata village 1 1/2 miles distant) 446 Indian Ranks & 4 British Officers strong. All wheeled transport & all weakly men were left in camp with orders to join the Brigade transport in the morning of the 24th. No cooking pots or followers accompanied the Regt. The force was composed and marched as follows—Advance Guard Capt Kerr (Comd) 2nd Kashmir Rifles (1/2Bn)—Main Body Divisional Signal Coy, 2nd Kashmir Rifles (1/2Bn) Loyal North Lanc Machine Gun Coy, 27th Mountain Battery, 25th Royal Fusiliers and East African Mounted Rifles. Followed at 4.35pm by the Force Reserve.

The force marched without halt until midnight & then lay down in order of march until 3.00 am at which hour the march was resumed. The track followed passed thick bush & forest with occasional open spaces of shoulder high grass & was very trying for flankers & advance scouts.

24th June 1916
The march resumed at 3.00 am and a river forded half an hour before day break. At about noon when the head of the main body had reached the edge of some very thick cultivation some Belfields' Scouts with advance guard reported seeing 2 enemy Askaris & a piquet was suspected on a ridge with grass at the foot & dense cultivation in the middle of the ridge flanked by forest & bush on both sides. Capt Kerr was ordered to make good the ridge with the advance guard. The 4 Coys forming the advance guard got up to the cultivation & the crest of the ridge on the left without a shot fired & then heavy rifle and maxim fire began showing the enemy were in force. The two maxims under Lt Cooke were sent up in support of the advance guard & later one by Sub Bal Singh was sent up on the right with orders to turn

Jemadar Bal Singh who came out with a reinforcement draft was from 1KI and at Lukigura he led his Coy in the charge yelling like a banshee.

The Germans lost 34 killed and 54 captured, it was the high moment that for Smuts must have vindicated his strategy... the low was soon to follow.

the enemy's left flank 2Lt Walshaw went with this Coy & was joined later by Jem Kalu's Coy which has been watching the right flank during the first advance.

The firing grew in intensity & the enemy opened up with a pom pom & a sort of mortar. The 25th Royal Fusiliers were ordered up in support on our left and at 1.30pm firing died away and it was reported that we had made good the ridge with the enemy on another ridge a few hundred yards in front & on a hill to our left flank.

At about 2.00pm a further advance was ordered. Capt Kerr led the advance supported by the 25th Royal Fusiliers & some LN Lancs machine guns. 2Lt Walshaw & his two companies had in the meantime worked round the right and gained touch with Capt Kerr's 4 Coys. Shortly after the second advance began the enemy developed a heavy machine gun & rifle fire & Capt Kerr arranged with Major White (25th Royal Fusiliers) to deliver a bayonet charge with the Fusiliers in support. Owing to the extension of the line & difficulty of controlling the men in the bush, Capt Kerr found difficulty in starting the charge & it was only when the Fusiliers came up that the whole of the left and the centre of the line charged and took the ridge at the point of the bayonet. This charge swept over at least two enemy

The Kashmir Rifles

maxims and the pom pom which were captured intact, and swept the enemy to the back of the hill on the left & a third ridge.` Several enemy Askaris & white men were bayoneted in the charge. The machine guns came up & the right of the line with some Fusiliers charged on the right flank without getting home & the enemy were driven in disorder off the ridge & hill into the valley beyond. After a short period orders were passed to cease firing as the Ist Brigade were expected in the direction taken by the enemy. General Hoskins was good enough to express an opinion on the spot that the 2nd Kashmir Rifles had done 'very well indeed' & to give the regiment one of the German Machine Guns captured. After firing ceased the regiment was assembled & eventually camped on the captured ridge. The enemy endeavoured to shell the camp with long range gun & continued an hour after dark.

Our casualties were Killed No 841 Hav Alta Ullah, No 1608 Sepoy Barhat Ali, No 1000 Sepoy Sur Bir. Severely Wounded No 1129 S Ali Sher, No 873 S Khalgit, No927 S Dhojbir, No 746 S Dalsur, No 1319 S Puran Singh, No 1047 S Hastbir, No 765 Sutbar, No 12021 African machine gun porter Uthuoma. Slightly wounded Sepoy No 258 Kalu [2nd time. He was wounded at Tanga].

The regiment had marched 25 miles chiefly by night & had been on foot 17 hours before the action began, with very little food & what water they could carry on their person. Ammunition expended by MG 1840 rounds and by men 12800 rounds.

Jemadar Chuha
1st Kashmir Infantry.

Lt Cooke's private account of the action itself adds little, but the narrative of the immediate aftermath is of interest:

...as I passed through the village at the top of the ridge it was a shambles –the dead and dying were lying about amidst overturned guns and ammunition etc – I could not stop to pick up anything at the time though I might have got a rifle etc – there was one Britisher on guard over a wounded German who was just about finished. The Punjabis continued to let them have it for some time after we had finished with them – on the ridge we captured 2 machine guns and one MG tripod, one pom pom the whole of No1 and part of No3 Field Companies so far about 20,000 rounds of ammunition MG belts, boxes etc and some parts. In one of the huts we found Col Vallings shoulder straps which we returned to 29 Punjabis – as far as we know we killed 3 white huns and captured wounded and unwounded 16. Killed about 80 Askari and captured about 25 – we picked up quantities of ammunition etc in the bush below the ridge – the men and the porters who had little or nothing to eat for about 24 hours did themselves awfully well there was a ready cooked meat meal for the porters and quantities of rice etc for the sepoys. One or two chef boxes were brought in which made welcome additions to our mess – among other things we got a German sausage which we enjoyed while the Hun was having his way with his 4.1" which he started at 4.30 and continued vigorously until 8pm doing a little damage...

Lyall's regimental War Diary continues:

25 June 1916, Lukigura
Regt in bivouac. Rations received in the morning & food cooked. Men left behind at Kangata rejoined. Search parties sent out all day to recover German stores etc & search the bush.

26–28 June 1916, Lukigura
Camp entrenched. 2nd Line transport rejoined. Half rations.

29 June 1916
Regiment marched at 5.15 am and rejoined 1st brigade under Gen Sheppard. Marched Makindu 11 miles advance guard driving in enemy contact patrols, bivouac north of the stream. Half Rations.

30 June 1916, Makindu
4 Coys under Capt Kerr reconnoitred 3 miles south of stream. Rest of Brigade crossed stream by ford & entrenched & formed camp. Health of the regiment beginning to suffer from hard work, exposure & short rations.

The 2nd Kashmir Rifles' diary then finishes. Makindu is the crossing point and the camp some 8 miles further on was initially called Misha and then Shell. Smuts' army collapsed in this camp, exhausted. It had been over-worked, it was totally under nourished and most of the men had malaria with dysentery.

Anderson writes 'by the third week in July 1916, the supply situation was far from good. The third Division had three weeks' supplies, the force reserve one weeks' and the First Division, (Kashmir Rifles) the effective fighting force, none'.

The problem was that Smuts had put insufficient priority to this aspect of war. The first train to reach Korogowe was on 17 August, so right now the supply chain stretched back beyond Kilimanjaro 217 miles away; the Tanga line to Buiko was reopened in July and the available transport moving along the recently cut tracks could only achieved some 50 percent of the 1st Division's needs. The forced halt at Misha Camp was therefore essential before a further advance to Morogoro and the River Rufigi could take place.

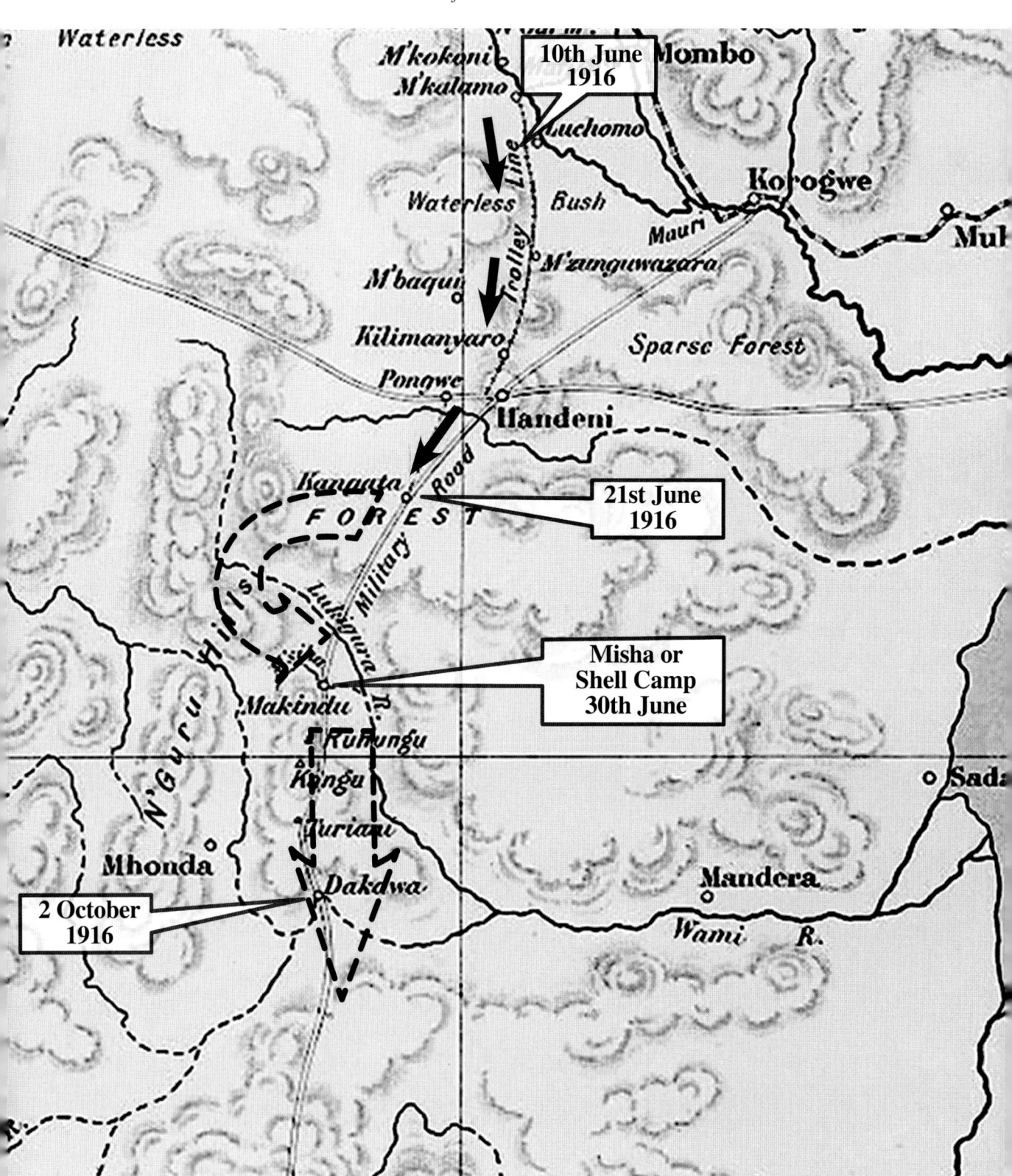

The Battle of Lukigura: 24 June 1916.

'I Can Never Say Enough About the Men'

8

Collapse and Disintegration July 1916 to January 1917

'They never failed me, what ever I asked of them. Their conduct has been excellent through out, and they have never given any trouble. They have felt the malarial climate severely, and suffered a good deal from sickness; but their spirit and esprit de corps have been splendid, and have kept men going long after they ought to have gone sick...'
Brig. Sheppard (writing in April 1917 as 2KR's Brigade Commander)

Smuts had pushed his forces way beyond their endurance and the limits of supply. There was an unscheduled cessation of operations with the wholesale collapse at and beyond the Lukigura River, which lasted throughout July and for some units well into August. It was not just confined to Sheppard's lead brigade in which 2nd Kashmir Rifles served, but spread across all the divisions. Even Smuts, with his tough constitution, went down with malaria at Luchomo, on the River Pangani just north of Handeni.

The army was paying the price for a charismatic leader, who either did not recognise the importance of supply or choose to ignore it. Marching 250 miles in four weeks on very short rations now took its inevitable toll. After so many earlier operations with inadequate supply, poor water, exposure to malaria and the disastrous effects with the Tsetse fly one would have thought Smuts and the high

In two days the pionners had made dug-out accomodation for all the patients.

command would have learnt! Military operations virtually ceased apart from reconnaissance south to assess the way to Morogoro and the Central Railway Line and some defensive measures.

Of course Smuts was able to present a story of success back to London and Pretoria, reporting in glowing and victorious terms how they now occupied the largest and wealthiest portion of German East Africa. Casualty figures in terms of deaths didn't look great, especially by comparison to the Western Front or Gallipoli and the scale of collapse of his troops was obscured by time and distance. Later on in the autumn of 1916 the returning troops to South Africa, to rest and recover, were to cause him considerable embarrassment as 'they told it how it was' but as so few troops from Great Britain had been used his reputation there remained untarnished. The contrast in the management of logistics between General Haig's Western Front and Smuts' march south could not be greater, but it is perhaps not surprising when their different military pedigrees are considered – they were from opposite military experiences, traditions and, of course, fought each other in the Boer War. Interestingly though they were products of Oxford and Cambridge!

Brett Young writes on p.235 of this moment in *Marching on Tanga*

> on every side the campaign seemed to stagnate. Britts, the long awaited Britts of rumour, had reached Luchmo with his Mounted Brigade, and was encamped there, loosing as we heard an average of 50 horses

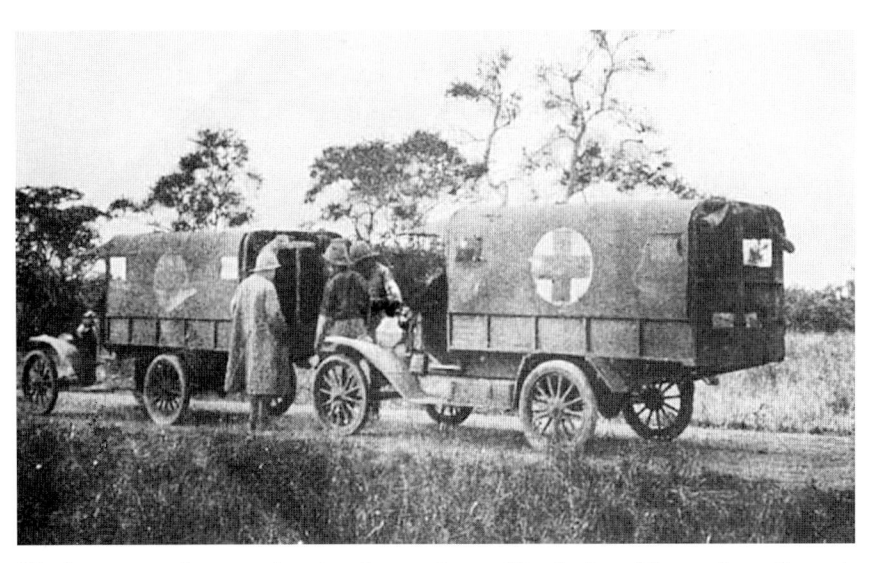

The journey to the casualty clearing station at Handeni on 'Jiggers' ran through a gauntlet of potholes and rocks which smashed the axles and springs. Along the road in bloated heaps swarming with flies lay the stinking cadavers, the remains of the South African Horse – 'Brits' violets'.

a day from fly alone. It was always a puzzle to us that he should have been left for two long periods of inactivity in places which were not only found to be full of fly, but known to be fly infested from the German charts, long before they came to be occupied.

The Kashmir Rifles were amongst the first into Misha (also called Shell or Makindu) Camp on 29 June and Capt Alec Kerr wrote:

A few days later we continued the pursuit as far as Makindu on the Misha River and there we had to halt as the line of communications had become so stretched out that the ration difficulty was becoming very serious. Also there were scattered parties of the enemy wandering about behind us threatening our communications. We spent the whole of July at Maikindu and had a very rotten time. The enemy had a strong position about 6 miles away and they brought up a couple of 4" naval guns and dropped their blasted HE shells all over the camp. Their shooting became almost perfect but the damage done was very slight – in fact out of about 600 shells which they put into the camp only 3 really did much harm. Occasionally people got knocked out with odd splinters but on the whole the damage was more moral than material – what made it so annoying was that we had nothing big enough to hit back with. The only officer in the whole force to be touched was Walshaw, one of our attaches, who got a chunk through his right shoulder blade and will be hors de combat for some months.

In fact the British did hit back with aeroplanes, if that is what you can call the incredibly unreliable 60mph BE2C's with their 50lbs bombs, they didn't hit anything but were incredibly good for morale. It was said that some pilots never flew when sober.

Another story of the camp was the inspection visit of South Africa's Prime Minister Botha, when the men toppled over in their scores while trying to stand to attention during a formal inspection. The photographs in Brett Young's book *Marching on Tanga* show troops huddled under blankets or dug into the hillside in homemade hospitals.

Whilst the Kashmir Rifles did not suffer the total collapse of the South Africans, Rhodesians, the Lancashires, the Fusiliers and the other Indian troops – exact comparison figures are difficult to acquire but the Lancashires were now reduced to just a single machine-gun company, the Fusiliers strength numbered 200, and the Rhodesians were falling off rapidly at 150 on route, to just fifty-three 'on duty' in October, and the 9th South African Infantry were to dwindle to 116 by October.

With the troops dropping like flies it was essential to get the worst of them away from the shelling of the camp. And Brett Young records in *Marching on Tanga* how he travelled with another doctor to set up a Casualty Clearing Station at Handeni (50 miles north east) in a converted German jailhouse, whilst suffering from Malaria himself. The 'hospital' was dreadfully poorly equipped with space for only fifty patients and virtually no beds, drugs and dressings – morphine was used to treat Malaria! Many thousands, including many hundreds of men from the Kashmir Rifles, passed through largely heading back along the broken supply chain to Buiko, and all the way back to Nairobi before evacuation home via Mombasa.

Charles Miller writes in the Battle for the Bundu

> The Indians [he is referring to the 29th Punjabis], reduced in numbers by two-thirds, were even worse off psychologically. Having proved themselves incomparable fighting men, they now showed an almost total incapacity to cope with sickness, succumbing to a peculiar – perhaps oriental – lethargy and fatalism which sabotaged recovery and confounded medical officers.

'They had no more interest in life', wrote Brett Young, 'their souls were as sick as their bodies' and he added, 'why not?' After all, 'it mattered nothing to them whether this detestable country, the scene of their exile and purgatory were ruled by German or British'.

Cooke recorded in his diary on 8 August that the battalion had orders to leave Makindu Camp for good, he notes that 'Kerr was sick and we left him behind', he was in a bad way. Using the information gleaned from Brett Young we can surmise at the possible pattern for Alec's and many thousands of others' evacuation journey.

It would have started with 'jigger truck' from Misha Camp to Handeni (see photo), a two-day journey, followed by three days' wait, truck to Korogoro, one-day wait, train to Buiko for four days, train to Mbuyani for six days, and then finally on to Nairobi where he wrote his letter to MacBrane on the 9 September (see Appendix A):

> My groggy leg seems to be getting on all right and now the other leg has gone wrong and I am practically crippled. The fact is I am bung full of malaria and have had 15 attacks in 8 months and there is some talk of me being invalided to England before it turns into blackwater fever.

Rhan Khan was captured at Jasin and survived the mal treatment of the Germans - 55 made it back to the Regiment two years later out of the 135 that were trapped at Jasin.

He was eventually shipped back to Kashmir (Jammu) in December.

The bugs were to shortly start work on Cooke who on 12 August writes in his diary of his first attack:

> I felt pretty bad with a rotten throat and fever [he goes on later that day to say] ...my fever was now getting the better of me and I felt rather cheap with a temperature of 103.8 so I got some quinine and reported to hospital – the Doctor, Granger, was in the same state they threatened to send me back if I was not better in the morning. Had a bad night and was very sick.

This is where Cooke's diary is at its most interesting as there is no battalion diary and he records and describes the malaria attacks as they develop over the coming weeks and which, as like virtually everyone, hospitalise him. As his illness unfolds so too does the gradual disintegration of the 2nd Bn Kashmir Rifles. Somehow a rotating hardcore of about 350 men just keep going, although clearly debilitated by cycles of malaria attacks and partial recovery.

The Kashmir Rifles reached the River Wami by 13 August and Cooke continues to describe himself as having low fever all day. On the 15th they were counterattacked and during the skirmish, where the listening piquet had been sited he found himself speaking to a German on the telephone before the wire was cut! By the 16th Cooke was sleeping without fever. The following days he mentions the success of the Baluchis and Punjabis crossing and holding the Wami.

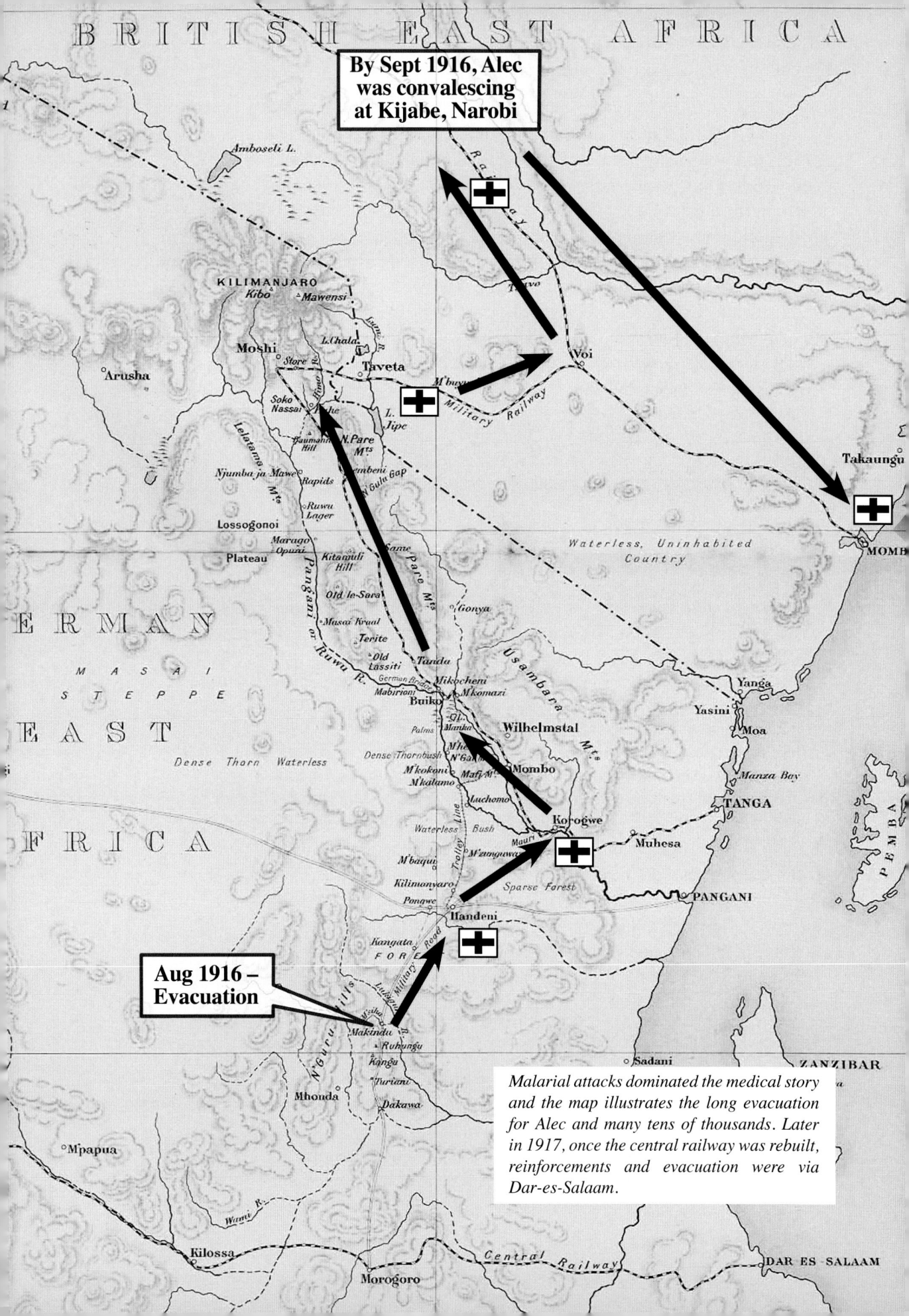

By Sept 1916, Alec was convalescing at Kijabe, Narobi

Aug 1916 – Evacuation

Malarial attacks dominated the medical story and the map illustrates the long evacuation for Alec and many tens of thousands. Later in 1917, once the central railway was rebuilt, reinforcements and evacuation were via Dar-es-Salaam.

Morogoro and the Central Railway were the next goal, however the British forces were again at the end of their broken supply chain and exhausted, whereas the Germans were withdrawing into prepared and supplied positions.

Cooke's diary gradually increases in critical remarks, as he becomes more exhausted, on the fairness of matters especially in carrying the fighting load. On 31 August he wrote with the news that 'after leading the way from Mbuyani some 350 miles we have given way for the 2nd Brigade – certainly they are stronger and fresher but there are no troops in the country to equal those of the old Voi Brigade for good sound work'.

Major Hashial Singh 2KR.

On 2 September his fever returns and he recorded of being on a court martial for the Baluchis where Lyall sentenced a Baluchis' soldier, who had run amok and tried to shoot his comrades, to fourteen years' rigorous imprisonment with three months' solitary confinement with forfeiture of all his pay and allowances. There are no mentions of such breakdowns within the Kashmir Rifles and this must be yet another credit to the personal qualities of the men.

By the end of September the troops were back on half rations and carrying out rear area duties like road repairs and prisoner guards. Lt Col Lyall's regimental diaries restart from 1 October. The first interesting entry is for 31 October when Lyall states that 50 percent of all ranks are unfit. Cooke reveals to the diary on the 10th that 'his nerves are not what they were after two years in this god forsaken land'.

Lt Col Capell, who was the Commanding Officer of 2nd Rhodesia Regiment (also part of the Voi Brigade), describes in his history of the regiment their continuing disintegration and of particular interest is his graphic portrayal of a scene on the road south of Morogoro in October:

> From Mwuha river onwards the low-lying country was clothed in forest and tall elephant-grass, that sprung from swamps and quagmires, across which it was necessary to corduroy the road for miles. Thousands of dead transport animals shared the sides of the road with thousands of dead horses of the SAMR [South African Mounted Regiment], whose saddles were being carried back to the rear by hundreds of porters. The whole road stank insufferably; every few yards lay a putrefying carcase, every few yards a moving, wriggling, seething mass of maggots. Men spat and smoked and held their breath and noses but nothing could deny that abominable stench – miles and miles of it. Tsetse flies that had caused this shambles, this indescribable road of nastiness, bit man and beast incessantly as

The casualty clearing station was a converted German jail house, literally thousands of patients were to pass through this chronically ill-equipped building. Miller comments 'No British soldier would soon forget his Handeni convalescence.'

they marched in the steamy heat. No domestic animal or bird lived in this afflicted land; natives kept no fowls nor goats nor cattle, the fly ruled supreme.

More revolting and disgusting than the stench or the tsetse fly was the great blue blood red headed blow fly in its millions, hatched from the putrid masses that choked the road. As a worn out man lay and slept in sun or shade these dreadful things would buzz and buzz round him, settle on his hair, his moustache, his clothing, and there lay their dirty cream white eggs – flyblown – which in an hour of the fierce heat would be turned into little wriggling maggots. Fly would follow fly and deposit its ova in the same spot, until the waking man, passing his fingers through his hair, would find inch high clumps of fly blow and maggots in it, adhering closely, and see the mass on his clothing and his blankets, and the millions of red –headed horrors still humming round him. Even in murky night a sleeper's unconscious movement would awake that dreadful buzzing and cause the waking man to shudder and squirm in disgust and nausea. But it was war – red, savage and infinitely brutal, sparing nether man nor beast.

The Rhodesians had fought alongside both Kashmir Rifle battalions and each held the other in high regard. In Appendix 1 of his book, Capell records the battalion's medical statistics: 1,038 men served with a typical daily frontline strength of about 300, many of the remainder would be laid up recovering in hospital or in the lines of communications. The statistics are: killed thirty-six, died of wounds or disease thirty-two, wounded eighty-four, admissions to hospital 2,272, total cases of sickness 10,626 of which malaria at 3,127 was the largest, blackwater forty-one, and dysentery 925.

On 4 November Cooke states 'that the Brigade now consisted of the Fusiliers at about 50 strong out of 1100 and the Rhodesians about 25 strong out of 800 – the Baluchis and ourselves with about 25% of our men fit – the wastage is as great as in Gallipoli'. The Regimental Diary makes no comment on manpower. Cooke goes on to say the sickness has returned for him and that they are now out of tobacco and cigarettes. On the 15th he recorded that another fifteen Kashmir Rifles had escaped from the Germans and rejoined them, making the total of escapees fifty-five[*].

By 16 November Cooke writes that 'two months in a decent climate would save me but it will not be I must carry on'.

On 26 November Cooke provides evidence of German maltreatment of prisoners 'Sub Rahn Khan who was captured at Jasin in Jan 1915 returned – he has had a fearful time – he says some of the sepoys legs were allowed to rot off before they got attention - they were beaten and their clothes were taken from them – they were worked for 36 hours without food or rest'.

Cooke reports in his diary a conversation with a supply officer called Hazlerigg who had been with Britts' 3rd South African Division: 'in some of the units men were actually dying of starvation while other units stole the rations, there was not sufficient discipline to stop it. The 5th and 6th SAF killed their donkeys and ate them'.

By the 20th December at Duthumi the fever had returned and Cooke writes:

> by this time I had a temperature of 103 and was again very sick... Nand Jal gave me some asprin which brought the temperature right down, he gave me two injections in the bottom a rather painful procedure – had a rotten night our sick list has been over 100 a day for the last few days. The whole regiment is sick practically – now we are to lead the advance while the precious South Africans who have been reorganising and recuperating for the last three months after some six months service – we have been at it for over two years – will come along behind to reap the glory eat the rations and will fight if they have to.

Nowal Singh Capt Alec Kerr said that Nowal Singh who came out with one of the later drafts that he was too old to keep up and they left him at the depot.

---

* **These were the men captured at Jasin.**

'We lay in an iron truck on heaps of sisal flax piled above the rotten droppings of mules the bed was soft enough but full of fleas.'

Cooke is now so sick that Lyall sends him back and he can't join the operation to cross the Megata River, the Battalion Diary reports the strength as 350 and that they march in heavy rain for three days until the operation is called off from wet exhaustion. On 31 December 1916 they successfully cross at Kiderengwa–Behobeno, as part of the Kiruru Column (2nd Kashmir Rifles, 2nd Nigerian Regiment, with sections of Artillery, Cables and Intelligence).

Cooke reports in his diary of the journey to the Buko-Bucko in a 'Jigger' ambulance, how they got stuck in the mud and how the Jiggers were sent back to collect the 124 other sick Indians in relays. He wrote in his diary from the hospital:

> for the first time in 13 years I have had anything to alter my days programme in spite of 3 years in the plains of India and 2 ¼ years campaigning out here – I think I hold the health record for this campaign anyway. The hospital at Mikesse is an old planters bungalow above the station surrounded by acres of rubber trees have had nothing but tea and toast for days and very little of that.

On 4 January he is moved by train to another hospital in Morogoro, where there are nurses and other comforts including eggs, champagne and beds with sheets:

took 2 grams of caramel and 10 grams of quinine – had a rotten night and the caramel gave me a bad time about 4am – had a dose of salts in the morning and felt generally rotten. The doctor came round about 11am and kept me on a light diet with champagne, two bottles today.

Back with the battalion, Lyall reports a series of long, very hot waterless marches, a few skirmishes with casualties and a growing sick list that he deals with by leaving them behind in rearguard detachments. There was the success of capturing with the Nigerians a howitzer and about eighty prisoners. On 9 January he recorded what must be the lowest point, 'the 2nd Kashmir Rifles are now reduced to 1 BO, 5 IO's, 80 R&F, 1 Follower. No officer or NCO's remain with the machine guns'. Later on he was to say the machine guns were reduced to just two fit men. They reached Mssambassi on the 19th and boarded a train that returned them to Morogoro:

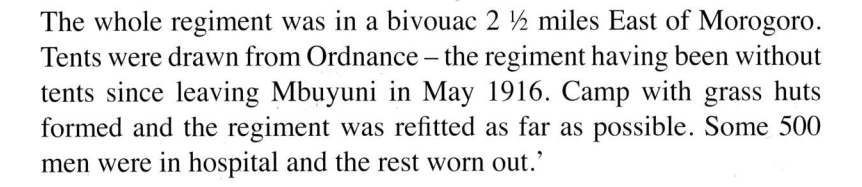

Lt Col Hakim Khan 3rd Kashmir Rifles.

> The whole regiment was in a bivouac 2 ½ miles East of Morogoro. Tents were drawn from Ordnance – the regiment having been without tents since leaving Mbuyuni in May 1916. Camp with grass huts formed and the regiment was refitted as far as possible. Some 500 men were in hospital and the rest worn out.'

Cooke when reflecting on this moment in a letter to his mother in January 1918 (see Appendix C) was to write of Brett Young's book *Marching on Tanga*:

> It is a pity Brett Young was invalided five months before the Brigade came back – he left when we were comparatively healthy – if he had seen the remnants barely 10% strong struggle back into Morogoro last January he might have had some reason for his fear of fever.

Cooke states the Baluchis were seventy-two strong on 5 February 1917. They spent the remainder of January, the whole of February and March, and most of April, near Morogoro in a permanent camp and built a connecting road to the town. Lyall states on 9 February that the regiment was inspected by a Medical Board and about 90 percent were found unfit. The following day he reports that 1st Brigade was broken up and that the regiment would come under command of OC Troops Morogoro and Lt Col Dyke of the 130th Baluchis.

Cooke's diaries make some interesting points on rumours circulating about their likely return to India and on his health, there is more on quinine and a return to eating his food. On 11 January he is taken off quinine and put on tonic. He reports the jigger fly in his toe getting painful and that he had it 'formented and probed'. There follows on the 14th a note that Col Lyall and the remains of the regiment, about thirty rifles, is on its way back to Morogoro. On the 17th he says 'the Doctor cut across the back of my toe nail to bring it off, I hardly felt it as the toe is more or less dead – he said if it were not he would give me chloroform before doing it', he rewards himself by going to what he calls a 'movie show' which was provided free by the YMCA on a sheet stretched between two adjustable telegraph poles.

On the 18th he hears that Smuts is to leave the country and Hoskins is to take over, stating that there have been seven C-in-Cs. He then comments:

> I do not think Smuts is much loss now – his strategy has been good but strategy alone will not win campaigns – the ordnance, supplies and cavalry have been a dead failure – you can starve an army for a week when successful but you can not do it consistently for months in an unhealthy climate – in addition Smuts has never let the South African troops fight for every man lost meant the loss of a vote for himself – Smuts has been too bound up in Politics to be a good C in C. It is a pity for he is a man with a wonderful brain and incidentally a bad staff.

On 21 January Cooke rejoined the regiment from the nearby hospital and also visited the ordnance to claim the machine gun that the regiment had captured at Lukigura.

The final twist in the tale for this exhausted band of brothers was the attempt during March to resurrect a 300-strong rifle force from a combination of the 2nd and 3rd Kashmir Rifles because 'they fight', however this was to come to nothing as, in spite of the prolonged rest at Morogoro, the Kashmiris just did not get well quickly enough and so followed the British, the Rhodesians, the South Africans and the other Indians out of theatre and returned home after 30 months.

Brig. Sheppard's letter 31.1.17 to the Kashmir Rifles' Commanding Officer

My Dear Lyall

The chief has offered me the BGGS and looks as I am to leave the 1st Brigade, I feel that I can perhaps be of more general use on the staff, especially as the 1st Brigade will be 'laid up' for some considerable time.

And it will undoubtedly be to the advantage of the Indian Troops to have me on the HQ staff so I have accepted the Chiefs offer.

I want to thank you and the 2KR for all you have done for me. No Brigadier could possibly have had a better or more loyal brigade – and I have enjoyed my year as Brigadier immensely.

I think that the way your men 'stuck it' in that beastly Dutumi marsh was quite wonderful – and I want you to thank them all, in my name for their cheerful and willing work.

I most sincerely hope we may serve together again. Write to me freely if there is anything I can possibly do for you. I like keeping in touch with the troops and especially with my own lot.

Good luck and au revoir

Yours v sincerely

Jemadar Shak Wal Capt Alec Kerr was mostly complementary about the competence of his brother officers he was also forthright with criticism too – he did not find this officer competent and described him as a congenital idiot!

'I Can Never Say Enough About the Men'

Lt Col Lyall leads the exhausted few - here crossing the Central railway near Morogoro. The final decision to send them home takes an age to make because the GOC wants to retain them because they fight...at the end of January 500 men were in hospital and the rest warn out. The medical board was to find only 20 fit men left in the 2nd Battalion.

The camp near Morogoro where the Kashmir Rifles were sent to recuperate and spent three months before departing via Dar es salam for Kashmir in April 1917. Lt Cooke said it was their first night in tents since the spring offensive of May 1916. The Royal Flying Corps airfield was immediately below them.

'I Can Never Say Enough About the Men'

3rd Kashmir Rifles at Satwari, 12 June 1917 on their return from East Africa
Present are: Nan Bir, Summo, Loola Carrim Bir
Karrim Bir, Sunsa Singh, E J D Money, Durga Dat, Boldiv Singh
Lal Bir, Hanam Singh and Surgeon Singem
(names from Lt Cooke's diary)

9

Return to Kashmir and Reflections on the Campaign

'I feel like one who having lived on the brink of Hell for two and three quarter years is suddenly lifted into fairy land'
Lt Cooke writing about the Vale of Kashmir to his mother on 21 June 1917

Lt Col Lyall's private papers reveal some essential facts concerning the return of the Kashmir Rifles, whereas Lt Cooke expresses both opinion and feelings in great detail, there are no Battalion War Diary records for this period.

The 3rd half Battalion departed from Dar-es-Salem on 22 May 1917 on the SS Palamcotta. Lyall gave their strength as one British officer (Capt. Money), thirteen Indian officers, and 328 rank and file. There were twenty-four Indian followers and two Rears. A total of 342!

For the remains of the 2nd Battalion he states on 1 May the following distribution and numbers:

At Ssingino:	1 x BO, 7 x IO, 165 Rank and File
At Beaumonts Post:	3 x IO, 116 R and F
At Smuts' camp:	1x IO, 26 R and F,
At DSM:	2x IO , 35 R and F
At Mombasa:	5 R and F
At Morogoro:	2 x Rand F

375 men of 2nd Kashmir Rifles embark on the HT Purea at Dar-es-Salem on 27 April 1917. The months between February and April were spent in tented camps recovering. The Generals had hoped to recover 300 'fit' Rifles and pleaded with the Indian Office for more time.

A total of perhaps 375 personnel, this tallies with an indicative count taken from the battalion photograph, when back at Satwari, near Jammu. He states that they were camped near the lookout towers above Dar-es-Salem from 1 May and that they embarked on 19 May on the HT Purea. They arrived at Tanga harbour on 25 May and 3rd Kashmir Rifles joined them on the Palamcotta. They were at Aden by 1 June and they arrived at Bombay on 11 June, where they entrained for Jammu immediately. They were reminded that they were not out of the war yet when their escorting cruiser HMS *Exeter* hit a mine coming into the harbour.

At Jammu on 14 June they 'found a fair crowd awaiting' them before catching another train to Satwari Camp. Alec Kerr and a small party had come to greet them. The major celebrations were a feast given by Rajah Hari Singh in the Regimental Lines on 15 June. On the 16th Lyall comments that the captured machine gun was paraded on an elephant and that the captured colours were upside down.*

On the 17th the British officers, Lyall, Kerr, Cooke and McBrayne, caught a train for Lahore and Lyall finally presented the official letter

---

* **This is an Indian tradition to make the point that they have been captured.**

Being met off the train at Tawi Railway station near Jammu on 14 June 1917, the celebrations were led by the Maharaja and his son.

of thanks and praise from the C-in-C (Hoskins) to the Maharaja at Srinagar on 26 June.

Cooke in a long letter to his mother on 21 June described both the events and his feelings. He had never been to Kashmir before:

> We travelled up via Surat, Delhi and Sialkot arriving at about 4pm on the 14th – here we were met by General Rose the Inspecting General of Imperial Service Troops, the Rajah Sahib and all the state officials and given a reception. The officers went up to the Residency and were the guests of the state as long as we were in Jammu.
>
> The first night the men were entertained by the Maharaja, on the 15th by the C in C of the Kashmir Army [the Rajah Sahib] who is the heir and the 3rd day the 16th they went in procession through Jammu with the captured machine gun and the Hun flags we had captured upside down – they were then formed up and addresses were read to them – this was the worst ordeal of them all as Maj Lyall and I had to sit on the platform with the Rajah Sahib while miles of addresses were read to the Dogras, Gurkhas and Mohammedans – the men were afterwards entertained by the people of Jammu. Jammu is the capital of Jammu State and is built on a low spur of the Himalayas running out into the plains – the view is simply magnificent but it was very hot. We spent a lot of our time in the Rajah Sahib swimming bath.
>
> On Sunday the 17th we said good bye to all the Indian Officers and left Jammu – Col Lyall went up to Simla and I came onto Srinagar

2nd Kashmir Rifles have some 375 men on parade. All that is left of the 715 that started and the further 600 that were drafted out as reinforcemnts. In January 1917 the medical board passed only 20 men fit to fight.

with Kerr and MacBrayne the Inspecting Officers. We left Jammu at about 6.30 pm and had dinner at Wageribad arriving at Rawalpindi early on Monday the 18th morning –there we had two cars and started off for Kashmir – soon after leaving we began to ascend the Himalayas the beauty of which surpasses anything have ever seen – we were soon among fine crested hills rising out of deep ravines the sides of which are cultivated in terraces. The scale of the hills are just a mass of terraces some emerald green and some full of water...

...Muree was a mass of fine trees covered with climbing wild roses in full bloom – here we had breakfast and I brought a little kit as I had nothing but what I stood in and that was pretty shabby. From Muree we descended to the valley of the Jhelum which we crossed at about 2.00pm – from here onwards we ran up the left bank of the Jhelum the road being cut out of the precipitous mountain side above the raging torrent and in many places to run off the road means a sheer drop of 500 to 600 feet into the river – we ran into a heavy storm in the afternoon and the road became very bad. Boulder dropped down from above and land slides threatened to block the road – we reached Ghasi that evening and stayed the night in the Dak Bungalow – the following day Tuesday the 19th we started off again and after a little engine trouble went steadily up the valley of the Jhelum – the scenery became more magnificent as we proceeded – I saw many things I had

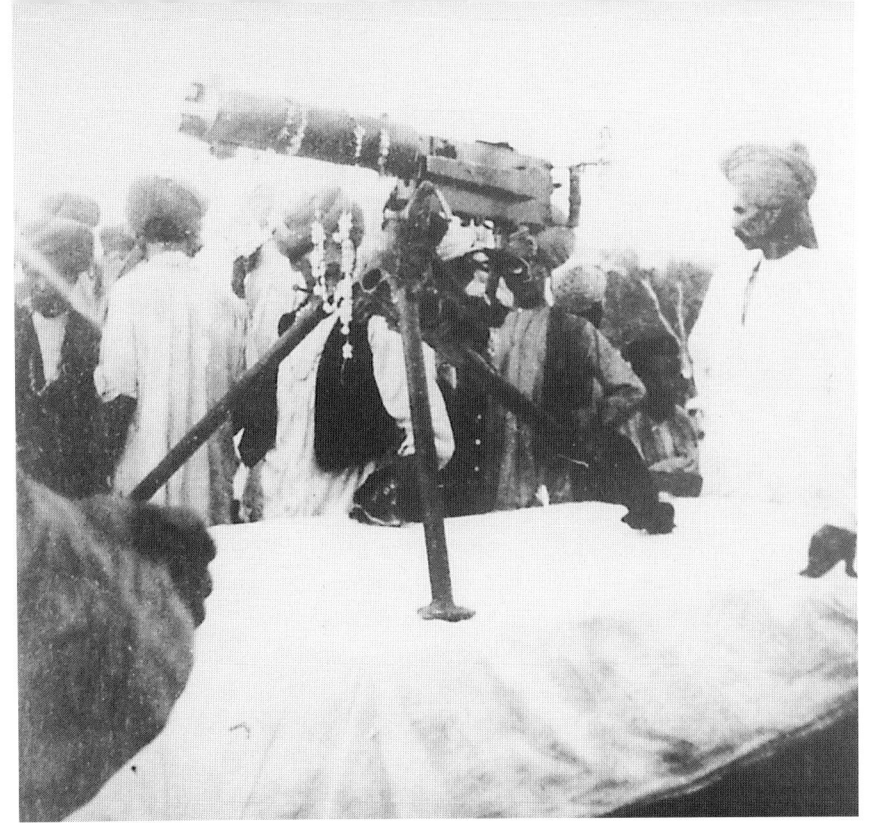

The Kashmir Rifles celebrate their return.

Above: The machine gun captured at Lukigara.

Right: The celebrations continue with the captured banner.

not seen for six years Elm, Walnut, apple and cherry trees – we ran through fine forests and enormous mountains all day until we emerged into the Kashmir Valley where the Jhelum ceases to be a raging torrent and becomes a slow navigable river covered with houseboats etc. Our petrol ran out about 12 miles from Srinagar but we managed to borrow some from a passing car and got in about 6.00pm.

Srinagar is too lovely to describe with its lakes, rivers and canals in a deep hollow of the Himalayas – if you can imagine a verdant terrace ringed round with loft snow clad peeks with a climate like that of a bright sunny day at home and between the waterways emerald green foliage fruit and bright coloured flowers you may gather some idea of what it is like – it is all so wonderfully beautiful that I cannot realise it – I feel like one who having lived on the brink of Hell for 2 3/4 years is suddenly lifted into fairy land. There are quite a lot of people up here women and children with pink cheeks and even after two days I am turning from green to a natural colour. However I would give it all for a month of home in sunny Devon.

The Maharaja asked us all up as his guests but at present I am not on leave but duty – Gen Rose is trying to keep all the special service officers and I hope to get a month or two leave very shortly...

Brahma Singh in the Regimental History makes several significant points about administration, public perceptions, financial compensation, health care and war memorials. He also goes on to describe the 1st and the 3rd Battalions' operation to Palestine and Egypt. To the reader today back in Britain, or indeed in India with its army of over a million men, the military contribution of a few battalions may sound like small beer but to a small and poor country these were significant commitments and the youthful Maharaja Hari Singh as C-in-C had to press hard within the Durbar to achieve financial concessions and compensation for those returning and especially the widowed, the sick and the wounded – many thought the grants were too lavish.

It would be useful to try and gauge the casualty levels and compare them with the respected military author John Keegan's overall analysis where he states in his recent history of the First World War 'in this campaign [East Africa] disease killed or incapacitated 30 men for every man killed in battle on the British side'.

Given that during the entire campaign there were 2,018 Kashmir Rifles deployed with the two battalions this would suggest about seventy killed in action. The tally from the incomplete and sometimes differing records is possibly as follows, totalling about fifty.

The Kashmir Rifles

4/5 Nov. 1914:	17 killed and 42 wounded at Tanga
19 Jan. 1915:	16 killed and 8 wounded at Jasin, of the 155 prisoners (90 escaped and 15 died of wounds and maltreatment)
22 Mar. 1915:	11 killed or captured at Epiron
12 Apr. 1915:	2 killed 1 wounded at Mzima
10 Jun. 1916:	2 killed at Makalamo
25 Jun. 1916:	3 killed and 9 wounded at Lukigura

Niak Arant Narain Nagarkoti 2nd Kashmir Rifles.

Given that this is incomplete and that many of the wounded may well have died subsequently a figure of seventy does seem about right, especially as there do not seem to be any records of the number invalided out, and this may be significant as Cooke on 5 January 1918, twelve months after their withdrawal from the African frontline, wrote 'that a great number of men who returned from Africa are still unfit'.

It is probably unlikely that there were many riflemen from the 2nd Bn who landed at Tanga and were still amongst the fit 'rifles' at Dar-es-Salem thirty months later, it is more likely for the 3rd Kashmir Rifles, who were not used operationally quite so much and who in January 1917 had just ninety-six sick in hospital, compared with the 505 from 2nd Bn, who at the same time also had 235 present in the battalion that were declared unfit.*

This is almost certainly the same moment where the figure '90% unfit' was declared by the Medical Board. This would suggest a nominal battalion strength of 750, which is close to the original establishment of 1914.

The 2nd Bn can lay claim to a casualty rate of greater than 98 percent, an extraordinarily high level of disintegration – the calculation is as follows. The battalion started in 1914 with 715 men. On the basis that they received two-thirds of the reinforcement drafts (a conservative estimate) this would be 600 of the 909 making a total of 1,315 men who served with the battalion. On 28 February 1917 the War Diary states that there were 280 men still standing and that the Medical Board declared 90 percent of these unfit – they were therefore left with just twenty fit men from a possible 1,315 – a 98 percent casualty rate. This is a truly extraordinary feat of military endurance.

From a modern day, British perspective, these are remarkably high

---

* p.123 Brahma Singh History of the Jammu and Kashmir Rifles

casualty rates, caused by the commander's combination of over ambition and a complete disregard for logistics, and would likely be deemed negligent. Smuts would be brought before a House of Commons Select Committee and made to account for this tragic state of affairs. Judging Smuts by today's morality and ways of thinking is an interesting intellectual exercise because he too would have been able to counter in the same vein with, he had never been trained and did not have the experience of 'management or staff work' for high command and that he was first and foremost a leader – and of course his political masters in making such an appointment were therefore negligent too.

However, this was a different age and one that was very much characterised by heroes and leaders and this of course is Smuts' great quality; he was undoubtedly totally inspirational figure. Brett Young, who was not slow to criticise and who had to treat the consequences of his general's negligent supply decisions, says in *Marching on Tanga* (p.238), just after giving Smuts' ADC some arsenic and iron pills for the general as he was going back to the Front having been laid out with malaria:

> The more I think of it the more I realise how the personality of that one man dominated the whole conduct of the war in East Africa. And I sometimes wonder what would have happened if fortune had not carried him safely through the risks he faced daily, for though his divisional generals or brigadiers might well have carried out in detail the broad strategic movements with which he quartered that wide country, we should have lacked the enormous psychical asset which his masterful courage gave us, and I think we should have endured our deprivations and our sickness with a less happy confidence.

The next question then is, could Smuts have developed and effectively led any other strategies that might have defeated Lettow-Vorbeck (remember he and a greatly diminished force was never caught and that they did not surrender until two weeks after the Armistice of 1918)? Whilst the answer is likely to be yes –as to what that might be in detail and the merits of one course of action versus another is something of an endless debate. However, the crux of the matter is to identify, at the highest level, the limitation of Smuts' leadership as demonstrated in East Africa.

This seems to have been a grave inability to learn from his experiences and to ask the basic questions – what has gone well? What hasn't gone well? What can we do differently? Instead he continues in a blinkered fashion and so remains locked into a dysfunctional

Above: This picture of the 2nd Battalion was taken on 16 June 1917 at Satwari Camp near Jammu on their return from East Africa. The officers are named below and had all served in East Africa.
Back row: Jemadar Shadi Wali, Subedars Bhagrun Singh, Parsidh Singh, Randir Singh, Jemadar Kaalu, Subedar Marden Ali Khan Sub. Ass. Surgeons Abdul Kadir and Mahumedin, Jemadars Ran Khan, Naran Si, Bal Singh
Middle row: Subedars Nowal Singh, Umah Puthi, Maj. Hashial Singh, A.N. Kerr, Lt Col Haidar Ali Khan, Maj. R.A. Lyall, Lt G.H. Cooke, Nand Jal, Sub. Sher Ali Khan
Front row: Jem Fagir Din, Naram Singh, Lal Singh, Sub. Jekram Singh, Milkha Singh, Jem Mahdu, Sub. Kessi Singh.

Below: Lt Col Haidar Ali Khan now firmly back in command following the dual leadership of operations, Lt Col (local) Lyall reverts to the Inspector of State Forces and after the war is back to a Major! Interestingly the administration never caught up, so he was not paid throughout the war. Note the Eagle on the banner is upside down, to denote the fact that the enemy were defeated.

repeating cycle. This is in marked contrast to Lettow-Vorbeck who, following his victory at Jasin, recognised that he could not win in a long campaign, sustaining casualties at such a high rate and so changed his strategy.

Smuts' mind is so totally set on his concept of manoeuvre and outflanking, hoping to force a decisive engagement that he repeatedly ignores the military advice from his staff (Ross Anderson, *The Forgotten Front* p.187). He does this to both his fighting groups – in April to the 2nd Division with van Daventer's cavalry advance on Kondoa Irangi, and then again in June and finally on the Central Railway in August; for the 1st Division (and therefore the Kashmir Rifles) there are also three collapses that have been described in this book, each progressively worse than the one before and finally resulting in total disintegration (Buiko in May, Misha in August and on the Megata River in December). His staff officers already knew of the challenges of tropical campaigning and its consequences from their own experiences of 1914 and 1915.

Effective leadership often demands a certain firmness of hand, fixity of purpose or perhaps that wonderful expression 'the courage of your convictions', but there comes a point when the evidence for change is overwhelming. For Smuts the alarm bells were screaming by August, Ross Anderson writes (p.139 *The Forgotten Front*) in June 'the third Division had three weeks supply, the Force Reserve one weeks and First Division, the effective fighting force, none', he goes on p.151 'First Division had not received full rations since 27 May some four and a half months ago'.

Yet Smuts did not learn nor did he try or countenance different approaches and so responsibility for the disintegration of his command must reside with him alone.

The Brigade Commanders executed Smuts' commands and for much of the time the Kashmir Rifles were under Brig. Gen. Sheppard and he developed a high regard for their capability, endurance and performance (see Appendix C).

Leadership within the Kashmir Rifles was exercised through a dual chain of command – the battalions were led by a series of their own Indian commanding officers who distinguished themselves as both brave and capable: the 3rd Bn, Lt Col Durga Singh Indian Order of Merit (IOM) First Class for Bravery and invalided back to India wounded at Tanga, then by Major Gandharab Singh who was killed on the Tsavo river line and awarded the Order of British India (OBI) 2nd Class, the 2nd Bn by Lt Col Raghubir Singh killed at Jasin, and then Lt Col Haider Ali Khan OBI 1st Class. The other

The Kashmir Rifles

chain of command was through the attached British officers, acting Lt Col Lyall, Capt. Alec Kerr MC and Lt Cooke for the 2nd Bn and Capt. Money for the 3rd Bn.*

The relationship between the few attached British officers and their Kashmir Rifle brothers is worth considering; at Tanga the British officers report in the battalion diaries on the leadership performance of their commanding officers in a way that reflected their training and peace time supporting role, Capt. Money states: 'So I informed Col Durga Singh to retire his regiment to the railway cutting' and 'I should like to take this opportunity of saying that all through the actions up to the time of his being wounded he handled his regiment very ably and skilfully and with much personal bravery'.

This form of words changed with the death or departure of the Kashmir Rifles' commanding officers and during 1915 'command' transfers to the British officers. Certainly for the advance south in 1916 the 2nd Bn's diary entries express command from the British officers. Lyall signs himself in the diary as R.A. Lyall Major, Local Lt Col Commanding Kashmir Bn, and certainly he attends the Brigade Commander's Orders Groups and Conferences to receive the battalion orders, at Lukigura the diary entry states 'Capt Kerr commands the advance guard' and again 'Capt Kerr was ordered to make good the ridge with the advance guard'.

One would like to imagine the relationships were good and there is no evidence from the diaries and letters of anything other than high levels of mutual respect – Alec Kerr's letter in Appendix A is particularly useful in this regard as very clear opinions on military competence and incompetence are expressed in a totally matter of fact way, as well as support for welfare issues. But perhaps the most illustrative example of this complex relationship are the group photographs at Satwari Camp upon their return in 1917 with Lyall back in the rank of Maj. and Lt Col Haider Ali Khan centre stage in the combined officer group, clearly as the commanding officer.

The test of course is did this 'shared' command work on the ground and in practice: were the Kashmir Rifles more or less competent than other battalions? The answer, as I hope this book reflects, is self evident for the Kashmir Rifles held together on active service for longer than any other battalion and of course actually achieved Smuts' enveloping strategy with the overnight march and assault at the Battle of Lukigura.

Ass. Surgeon Mahunedin

Given the casualty levels all would have suffered terribly from tropical diseases. Sub. Ass. Mahumedi spent eighteen months as a German prisoner and he provided evidence of German brutality towards Indian POWs.

---
* **Whilst the peace time establishment was one per battalion during the military operations this seems to have increased to a maximum of four.**

The Kashmir Rifles today at more than twenty battalion strength and known as the Jammu and Kashmir Rifles (the only surviving element of State Forces and the only part of the Indian Army that has always been officered by its own) seen here at the regimental centre Jabalpur 2006.

The JAK Rifles maintains close links with its great history, here is Dr Karan Singh opening the museum at Jabalpur in 2006, he is the direct descendent of the Maharaja of Kashmir and is a member of the Indian Upper House.

The Kashmir Rifles

> *Major (retd) Brahma Singh writes...*
>
> " It may be of interest to note that the institution of the Special Service Officers(SSOs) that appeared to work so smoothly during WW I ran into trouble right at the out set of WW II when its functioning was sort of challenged by none other than an Officer of the J&K State Force, Major (later before the highest military authority in the theatre, his own military training and qualification as an Officer to match with those of his SSOs, to lay his claim to his right to command his unit without interference. It goes to the credit of the British authorities that, after the initial hesitation, their response was pragmatic and practical and as a special case the SSOs were withdrawn and Major Bhagwan Singh was allowed to enter battle in independent command of his unit. Two years later into the War the SSOs were withdrawn from all the units of the State Forces even while they served outside their States. "

Perhaps the lasting and enduring outcome of the campaign for the Kashmir Rifles was their wider recognition as first-class fighting troops. It gave their officer corps a head start in the process to come of 'Indianisation', as they merely carried on being officered and led by their own. Perhaps they were in the ideal position to build their subsequent expansion as the new Indian Army developed thirty years later. Today the Jammu and Kashmir Rifles are twenty battalions strong and can claim to be the only survivors from the private armies of the Maharajas – they are thus amongst the oldest regiments of India and certainly can boast of a wonderful tradition of selfless and honourable soldiering fully justifying Capt. Alec Kerr's words 'I can never say enough about the men'.

******

Appendix A

Alec's letter to MacBrayne (the British Officer back at the Satwari Camp/Depot, near Jammu) on 9.9.16. He had been a captain with the Jind Infantry that at Jasin had taken 50 percent casualties when trying to relieve the pressure on the fort by crossing the heavily defended Suba River. (see Horden, p.126)

My Dear Mac B

I forget when it was that I last wrote to you but it must have been long ago as I have written no letters for ages.

I have been in hospital now for over a month with malaria, and some complication called "phlebitis" due to a clot of blood in the leg. I don't know when I shall manage to get about again and I am afraid it will be some time before I can rejoin the Regiment.

We left Mbuyani on the 18th May forming part of the 1st East African Brigade under Shepherd and took part in everything that happened during the advance down the Usambara Railway, then across to Handeni, and the final advance on Morogoro. We had a lot of hard marching, short rations, and bad water and I can never say enough about the men. Fighting was never very severe and was usually a desperate effort to cut off the enemy's rearguards as they never attempted to really stand up to us. The first scrap was at Mkomazi where the Rhodesians did all the fighting there was – we had nothing to do but had our own first taste of artillery, the enemy using a 4.1" naval gun and some field guns. The next bump was at Mkalamo where we tried to round up the garrison who had retreated from Mombo. The fight took place in the afternoon after an 18 mile march, and in attempting to get round the flank and cut off their retreat the Brigade succeeded in getting hopelessly entangled

The Kashmir Rifles

in dense bush. The 130th Baluchis had all the fighting and most of the casualties; we ourselves had only 1 Coy engaged who lost about 3 men. The total casualties were about 60 and prisoners reported the enemy loss as 135. The enemy made good their escape during the night and next day we followed up, and the pursuit continued for a fortnight. We nearly succeeded in cutting off part of the garrison of Handeni and two of their Coy's were badly knocked about and dispersed by a contingent of S. Africans who formed the reserve of our force. Two days later these same S. Africans followed up the enemy and walked straight into an ambush and the Huns more than got their own back.

The next stand was made at the crossing of the Lukigura River where the enemy's rearguard was located in a strong position covering the bridge. Shepherd Column did a frontal demonstration to occupy attention while the rest of the force did a night march round the back of the position. We were detached from the Brigade and detailed as advance guard in this flanking attack. I think we marched a good 35 miles and fetched up at noon next day plum in the rear of the enemy's position without a soul knowing of our arrival. Unfortunately the staff had very poor information and no one knew exactly where the enemy were nor the lie of the ground – otherwise we could have blasted the whole b..... However we knocked spots off the swine and finished off with the bayonet, capturing two maxims, a pom pom, lots of ammunition and baggage. With any luck we should have got their artillery and trebled their casualties. We did practically all the fighting that day and Hoskins the Divisional Commander was awfully pleased with the Regiment. At the critical moment just before the final charge we got hung up and I could not get the men on – there were only 2 weak Coy's with me and we were being pasted by 2 maxims and at least 100 rifles at a range of not more than 100 yds, and the air was fairly buzzing with bullets. Luckily we had about 100 men of the Royal Fusiliers supporting us and they came up and started the charge – once started, our lot went in great style, but it was the tommies who got us going. Amongst the stuff we collected was the office box of the 1st Field Coy and in it I found an official account of the part played by that Coy in the capture of Jasin.

A few days later we continued the pursuit as far as Makindu on the Misha River and there we had to halt as the line of communications had become so stretched out that the ration difficulty was becoming very serious. Also there were scattered parties of the enemy wandering about behind us threatening our communications. We spent the whole of July at Maikindu and had a very rotten time. The enemy had a strong position about 6 miles away and they brought up a couple of 4" naval guns and dropped their blasted HE shells all over the camp. Their shooting became almost perfect but the damage done was very slight – in fact out of about

600 shells which they put into the camp only 3 really did much harm. Occasionally people got knocked out with odd splinters but on the whole the damage was more moral than material – what made it so annoying was that we had nothing big enough to hit back with. The only officer in the whole force to be touched was Walshaw, one of our attaches, who got a chunk through his right shoulder blade and will be hors de combat for some months.

Early in August the advance recommenced, but Smuts' effort to round up the main enemy forces at Turiani, in front of Makindu, failed to come off and the wily Hun slipped away. There was a stiff fight with a strong rearguard on the Wami River and they escaped again, but I missed that as I had collapsed and was on my way back to base. I don't know where the regiment has got to but presumably they entered Morogoro with Shepherd.

I don't know how long this show is going on for – the enemy have any amount of ammunition as unfortunately a small ship ran the blockade last April and landed some howitzers, maxims, and tons of rifle ammunition. Apparently they have got clean away south of the central railway and it may take months to round them up.

I have seen nothing of the Jinds, but I heard that they distinguished themselves in a scrap near Koragwe, and I rather fancy that they were with the force that occupied Dar-es-salam.

Some of our people have been invalided back to India – among them are 2 N.O.'s (Native Officers) – Subaders Chabilal and Hakam. A year ago Chabilal was probably the best N.O. in the Regiment but he is an old man and hard work, bad food, and fever have knocked all the stuffing out of him – I believe he has served his time for a full pension and he has thoroughly deserved it. If he had stayed on out here he would have died in a month or so, Lyall took the first opportunity to get him back to India alive. The same applies to Hakam who is one of the survivors of the sisal factory at Jasin – the only thing is that he has not yet earned a Subadar's pension and I think he might be allowed to serve his full time at the depot unless the Durbar can see their way to let him have a special pension. Subadar Lal Singh has also been invalided – he is a useless rotter who has shirked every unpleasant duty and is not worth keeping – a rotten Coy Commander suffering from cold feet. He got a lot of kudos for a patrol affair near Makatau last year but the truth is that two Havildars, Naran Sahai and La Singh, took charge and ran the whole thing. He really should have been tried by Court Martial for the regrettable incident at Laitokitok in March 1916, when he lost 12 men out of his Coy. [Alec has his year wrong, this is 1915 and is referred to as Epiron in the Regimental Diary and Official History; the area of Laiokitok is south west of Epiron, just to the north of Kilimanjaro].

I hope you won't have to send out any more Officers with drafts from India as Kalu Dalbahadur and Amin Khan will make better Coy

Commanders than anything you are likely to send from Satwari. Of the last lot of N.O.'s from India Sub Narwal Singh is an old man who would have done better on pension, he is physically incapable of hard work and has been seedy ever since he arrived so he has been left at the depot. Jamadar Shak Wali is a congenital idiot and useless – if we can only get him to do something really bad we might get him pushed out. Jamadar Bal Singh of the 1st KR who arrived last year is turning out well – he is not brainy but is full of guts and in the Lukigura scrap he led his Coy in the charge yelling like a banshee. The whole of that draft of the 1st KI have done well and I always meant to write to Ishar Singh to tell him what a good lot they are – one of them L.NK Guranditta is an exceptionally fine scout who has put in some really top hole work.

I don't know that there is much else to write about – at present I am in the Convalescent Home at Kijabe near Nairobi. My groggy leg seems to be getting on all right and now the other leg has gone wrong and I am practically crippled. The fact is I am bung full of malaria and have had 15 attacks in 8 months and there is some talk of me being invalided to England before it turns into blackwater fever.

Give my love to Cala, and write soon

yours

A N KERR

Appendix B

Cooke's letter discussing the book, *Marching on Tanga*

Satwari Camp
Jammu
13 -1 - 18

My Dearest Mother
...etc

Marion's parcel arrived a few day's ago with 'Marching on Tanga' in it for which heaps of thanks – Brett Young's account of East Africa is certainly the most truthful I have read though he is wrong in some places with the names of units and what they did – for instance he says the Fusiliers bore the brunt of the Lukigura fight as a matter of fact they did not come up to our support until we had been at it for quite a long time – I do not know how long, one has no idea of the time under these circumstances it seems like a lifetime sometimes when it is only an hour or two but they certainly only came up just before we charged – that they played a very big part in the charge there is no doubt and unless they had gone through with us I do not think we would have got through – it is a pity Brett Young was invalided five months before the Brigade came back – he left when we were comparatively healthy – if he had seen the remnants barely 10% strong struggle back into Morogoro last January he might have had some reason for his fear of fever.

    The book to me is extremely interesting as I know every incident he mentions and everyone to who he refers – his photos are good too and I noticed our men in many of them. In one he must have just missed me because he has the men of my machine gun section in it.

You probably noticed that he mentions the Kashmir's being sent ahead to cut the road – that always fell to our lot as we carry Kukris – (I always carried one too as being a more useful weapon than a revolver at close quarters and I always had to go forward with the road cutting parties as we had no other British Officers to take a turn.

...etc

Appendix C

Letter from Brig. Sheppard, who had been Kashmir Rifles' Brigade Commander and later Chief of Staff to the GOC. It is an unofficial letter (D.O, Demie Official?) intended for Maj. Gen. Rose (the Inspector of all British Imperial Service troops) to show the Maharaja. It is dated 18 April 1917 and is from Dar-es-Salaam. The Kashmir Rifles were returning to India.

My Dear Rose

The 2nd and 3rd Kashmir Rifles will be leaving us shortly. Only the C-in-C can, of course write officially about their services; and therefore I (as their Brigadier) send you a D.O. – which you are welcome to show to the Maharaja, which must not be officially published.

They have done well from the very start.

I have had the 2nd under me for a year past; and the 3rd at frequent intervals. I have seldom had command of units that I trusted so much. They never failed me, what ever I asked of them. Their conduct has been excellent through out, and they have never given any trouble. They have felt the malarial climate severely, and suffered a good deal from sickness; but their spirit and esprit de corps have been splendid, and have kept men going long after they ought to have gone sick. Very great credit is due to their Commanding Officers and Special Service Officers, who have worked most loyally with me through out. I feel quite distressed at parting with the regiments – and feel that I am losing not only most reliable soldiers, but real personal friends.

I hope the Maharaja will allow me to renew my acquaintance with them, when I get back to India...

Appendix D

Malaria

As the story of the Kashmir Rifles in East Africa was being written it became clear that a greater understanding of Malaria and its impact on the individual would be an essential part of assessing the story and its significance as a or possibly even the determining factor for the military campaign. Digging into medical dictionaries produced massive amounts of information much of which is difficult for the lay person to understand and also fails to convey the human suffering. What follows is taken from Wakipedia, and Sir Arthur Hurst's Medical Diseases of War (1941).

Whilst the illness had affected man for tens of thousands of years it was not understood until scientific studies on malaria made their first significant advance in 1880, when a French army doctor working in the military hospital of Constantine Algeria named Charles Louis Alphonse Laveran observed parasites for the first time, inside the red blood cells of people suffering from malaria. He therefore proposed that malaria was caused by this protozoan, the first time protozoa were identified as causing disease. For this and later discoveries, he was awarded the 1907 Nobel Prize for Physiology or Medicine.

However, it was Britain's Sir Ronald Ross working in India who finally proved in 1898 that malaria is transmitted by mosquitoes. He did this by showing that certain mosquito species transmit malaria to birds and isolating malaria parasites from the salivary glands of mosquitoes that had fed on infected birds. For this work Ross received the 1902 Nobel Prize in Medicine. After resigning from the Indian Medical Service, Ross worked at the newly-established Liverpool School of Tropical Medicine and directed malaria-control efforts in Egypt, Panama, Greece and Mauritius.

The first effective treatment for malaria was the bark of cinchona tree, which contains quinine. This tree grows on the slopes of the Andes, mainly in Peru. This natural product was used by the inhabitants of Peru to control malaria, and the Jesuits introduced this practice to Europe during the 1640s where it was rapidly accepted. However, it was not until 1820 that the active ingredient quinine was extracted from the bark, isolated and named by the French chemists Pierre Joseph Pelletier and Joseph Bienaimé Caventou.

Owing to its extensive geographical distribution and almost epidemic concentrations in all warm countries malaria is much the most common of all human disease. Where ever warmth and water exists together malaria is found, provided there are mosquitoes in which the parasite can develop its full cycle and there are people suffering from malaria who can be bitten by the suitable mosquito. The usual limits of the area are between 63 degrees North and 35 degrees South.

In the war of 1914-18 of all the deceases responsible for casualties malaria easily took first place. In the British Army alone the admissions to hospital for malaria were almost half a million. The two severest campaigns were in Macedonia and East Africa. Sir Ronald Ross on Macedonia Campaign states 162,000 admissions with a mortality rate of 1% – on East Africa there were 100,000 admissions for 1917 alone.

It is not that malaria in war time is more severe than in peace-time it is merely that exposure, exertion and fatigue magnify its effects. Preventative measures and personal protection are frequently difficult if not impossible owing to the tactical situation. Troops exposed can not be immediately released as they are needed to complete the operation consequently the sick rate of those infected escalates the longer they are in theatre and are untreated. In addition these men who remain at duty when infected gradually deteriorate in physical fitness.

The development of the malarial parasite can take place only in the female of certain species of anopheline mosquito – 95% never become infected because they have not bitten an infected person. There are three well defined species of human malarial parasite that produce fever – Plasmodium vivax producing a benign tertian malarial fever sometimes known as B.T.(about 80% of cases) – Plasmodium malarice producing a fever known as quartan – and Plasmodium falciparum producing a fever sometimes known as M.T. (about 15% of cases and 90% of the deaths) The parasites multiply within red blood cells over a period of days.

Symptoms of malaria include fever, shivering, arthralgia (joint pain), vomiting, anemia caused by hemolysis, hemoglobinuria, and convulsions. There may be the feeling of tingling in the skin, particularly with malaria caused by P. falciparum. The classical symptom of malaria is cyclical occurrence of sudden coldness followed by rigor and then fever and sweating lasting four to six hours, occurring every two days in P. vivax and P. ovale infections, while every three for P. malariae. P. falciparum can have recurrent fever every 36–48 hours or a less pronounced and almost continuous fever. For reasons that are poorly understood, but which may be related to high intracranial pressure, children with malaria frequently exhibit abnormal posturing, a sign indicating severe brain damage. Malaria has been found to cause cognitive impairments, especially in children. It causes widespread anemia during a period of rapid brain development and also direct brain damage.

Severe malaria is almost exclusively caused by P. falciparum infection and usually arises 6–14 days after infection. Consequences of severe malaria include coma and death if untreated—young children and pregnant women are especially vulnerable. Splenomegaly (enlarged spleen), severe headache, cerebral ischemia, hepatomegaly (enlarged liver), hypoglycemia, and hemoglobinuria with renal failure may occur. Renal failure may cause blackwater fever, where hemoglobin from lysed red blood cells leaks into the urine. Severe malaria can progress extremely rapidly and cause death within hours or days. In the most severe cases of the disease fatality rates can exceed 20%, even with intensive care and treatment. In endemic areas, treatment is often less satisfactory and the overall fatality rate for all cases of malaria can be as high as one in ten.

Chronic malaria is seen in both P. vivax and P. ovale, but not in P. falciparum. Here, the disease can relapse months or years after exposure, due to the presence of latent parasites in the liver. Describing a case of malaria as cured by observing the disappearance of parasites from the bloodstream can therefore be deceptive. The longest incubation period reported for a P. vivax infection is 30 years. Approximately one in five of P. vivax malaria cases in temperate areas involve over wintering by hypnozoites (i.e., relapses begin the year after the mosquito bite).

A malarial attack consists of stage of coldness or rigor, a stage of heat and a stage of sweating. These are followed by a period of interval between attacks, the duration and intensity of these attacks varies enormously. Sometimes they will come on slowly sometimes very rapidly.

The cold stage usually lasts one and a half to two hours. There is shivering, amounting in many cases to a rigor, the face is pale and pinched, the patient covers himself with everything he can lay his hands on, the skin is blue and cold looking. Vomiting may occur and also headache and aching limbs. The feeling of cold is entirely subjective; if the temperature is taken, it is found to be several degrees above normal and rapidly rising.

The hot stage usually lasts between one to six hours. The shivering abates and gives rise to feelings of warmth growing to intense heat. The headache increases and the temperature rises and may reach 106*. The pulse is rapid, full and bounding. Respiration is hurried. The skin is dry and burning, the face flushed. The clothes that were piled on in the cold stage are now tossed off and the patient is very thirsty.

The sweating stage lasts fro two to four hours. The patient generally begins to sweat on the forehead, then all over the body. The sweating is profuse and may even soak the mattress. As soon as the skin becomes moist the temperature falls. It may become subnormal and the patient feels relieved but exhausted and often sleeps. He may feel quite well after sweating has ceased and be able to go about his work. The spleen becomes enlarged to a greater or lesser degree during the attack.

Every day or two there is a fresh attack of the same kind unless effective treatment is instituted the attacks recur for ten to fourteen days, when they get less severe and soon cease for a few days. Spells of a few days of intermittent fever may alternate with spells of freedom from fever for several months during which the patient becomes weaker and more anemic, the spleen and often the liver increase in size. Eventually the attacks become less frequent and less severe. Natural recovery takes place unless the weakened patient is attacked buy some other current disease such as pneumonia or dysentery.

This rapid review of malaria and especially its effects make the achievements of the Kashmir Rifles all the more remarkable. Sustaining military operations and performance is always challenging especially when the physical elements are running against the military intention – but in addition to acute shortages of water and food that would have taxed the endurance of even the most robust constitution to have had to endure repeated attacks of malaria defies belief.

The First World War experience in East Africa was truly horrific and it is no wonder that Lt Lewis wrote to his mother in late 1916 'I would rather be in France than here' – he should have known as in 1914 he had witnessed the slaughter of every single man in his half battalion on the Western Front and had experienced all the horrors of trench warfare.(p.7 *Tip and Run* by Edward Paice).

Notes on Sources

Horden, *Military Operations in East Africa*
This is the official history – it was painstakingly researched and very factual. First published in 1941. It is the essential and authoritative reference.

Brett Young, Francis, *Marching on Tanga*
The author was the regimental doctor with the Rhodesians, he must have treated many soldiers from the Kashmir Rifles. His story is compelling and has some great descriptions of the challenges he and the troops on the ground faced. He states strong opinions and the book is essential reading. First published in 1917.

Meinertzhagen, Army Diary
The author was on the British East African Staff (intelligence) during 1914, 1915, and early 1916. He tells his story in 1960 from his diary. It is full of strong opinions and it certainly captures some of the challenges of the campaign and benefits from being controversial. It is very complimentary about the Kashmir Rifles, whilst lambasting many other units.

Crowe, *General Smuts' Campaign in East Africa*
The author was in command of General Smuts' Artillery. Written in 1918 it is a general history and background.

Paice, Edward, *Tip and Run*
The most recent history of the Great War and its impact across Africa. Published in 2007. Throws new light on many issues – it is especially strong but don't expect to see mentions of the Kashmir Rifles.

Anderson, Ross, *The Forgotten Front*
The author, who has served in both the Canadian and British armies, has constructed a fully researched and objective history of the war. Published in 2004. It is essential reading for its analysis and new thinking – especially strong on its view of the German commander Lettow-Vorbeck and the general breakdown of logistics.

Anderson, Ross, *The Battle of Tanga*
The must-read book on the Battle of Tanga, beautifully researched and illustrated. It was first published in 2002.

Pocock, Geoffrey, *Legion of Frontiersmen*
The author spent twenty-five years researching this history of a truly unusual regiment – in East Africa it fought alongside the Kashmir Rifles as the 25th Battalion of the Royal Fusiliers. At the Battle of Lukigura they came up into the line and provided vital support and reinforcement for the bayonet charge.

Capell, *The 2nd Rhodesian Regiment in East Africa*
The author commanded the battalion as it fought alongside the Kashmir Rifles – he is very complimentary but there are only a few mentions. Some good descriptions and narrative of the hardships endured during this campaign.

Fendall, *The East African Force 1915–1919*
A general history, written shortly after the First World War, from personal experiences of a non-fighting senior officer.

Miller, *The Battle of the Bundu*
First published in 1974, the author brought together in wonderfully readable chapters the agonies of the war in East Africa. A must read – there are a few positive words on the Kashmir Rifles, but it is an overview.

Singh, Brahma, *The History of the Jammu and Kashmir Rifles*
Very thorough and the only complete history of the JAK Rifles. Another history was written in the 1960s by Maj. Gen. D.K. Palit, entitled *Jammu and Kashmir Arms*, however this was not formally 'adopted' by the regiment, although some of the material was used in Maj. Brahma Singh's book.

Buchanan, *Three Years War in East Africa*
The author describes his soldiering in East Africa with the Legion of Frontiersmen.

Corrigan, Gordon, *Sepoys in the Trenches*
This book investigates and records the bravery of the Indian Corps in France during the First World War. It effectively counters any criticism of the regiment and positively sets the record straight on their performance. Its value in relation to East Africa is its descriptions of how the Indian functioned and its culture.

Trevelyan, *The Golden Oriole*
A great read for those wanting to understand the British perspective of the Raj and snap shots of its culture. Especially useful for its description of the journey to Gilgit and the way the Presidency operated in 1930.

Barua, *Gentlemen of the Raj*
A study of the Indian Army Officer Corps, 1817–1949. It researches and describes the evolution and especially clear on the 'Indianisation' process

Regimental Diaries

The Imperial War Museum has the private diaries of both Lt Col Cooke and Lt Col Lyall. These are available on appointment through the reading room.

The National Archives at Kew have the incomplete Kashmir Rifles' battalion diaries.

Opposite: Gulmarg.

Followed by Alec winning the Duncan Vase at Gulmarg.

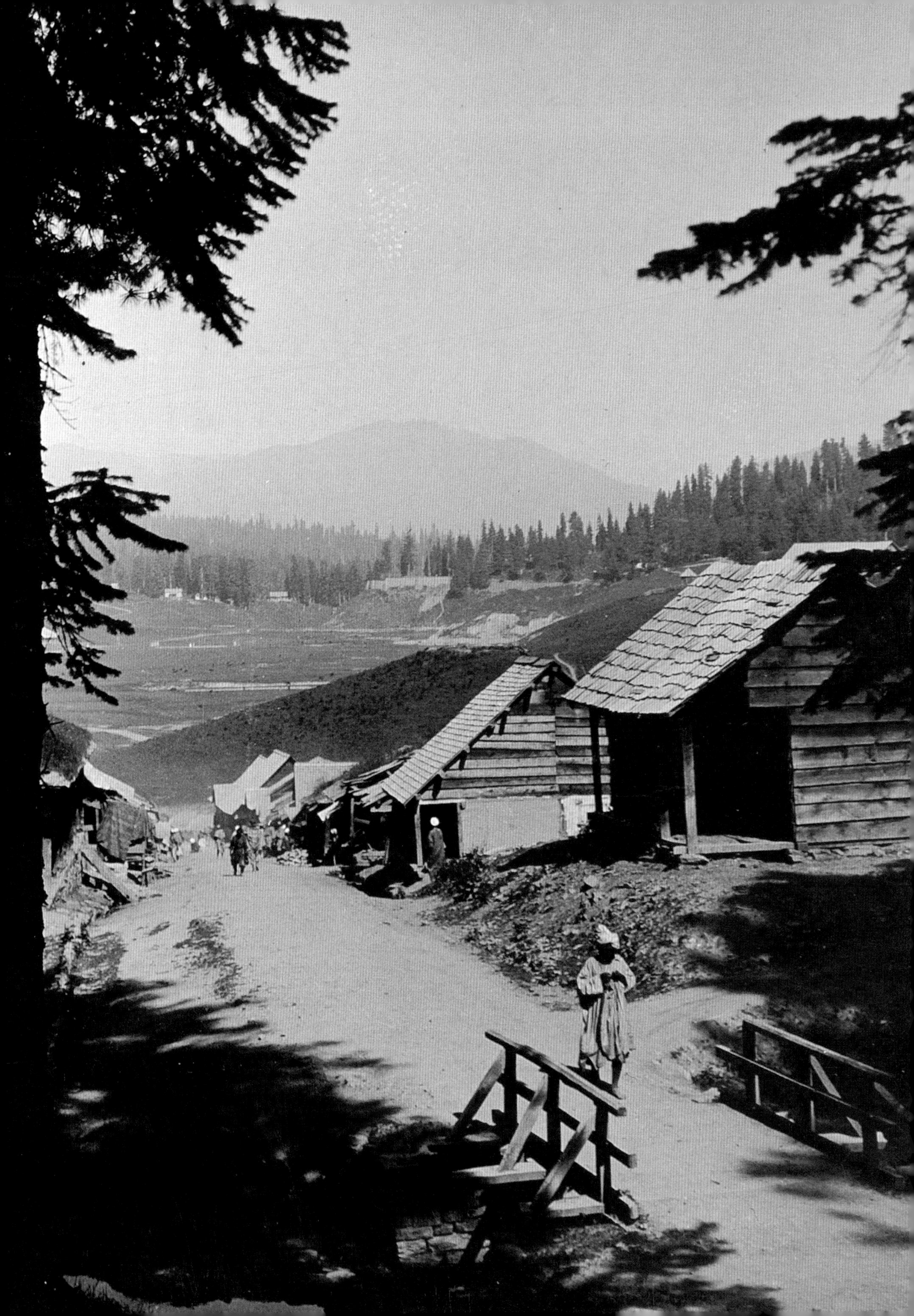

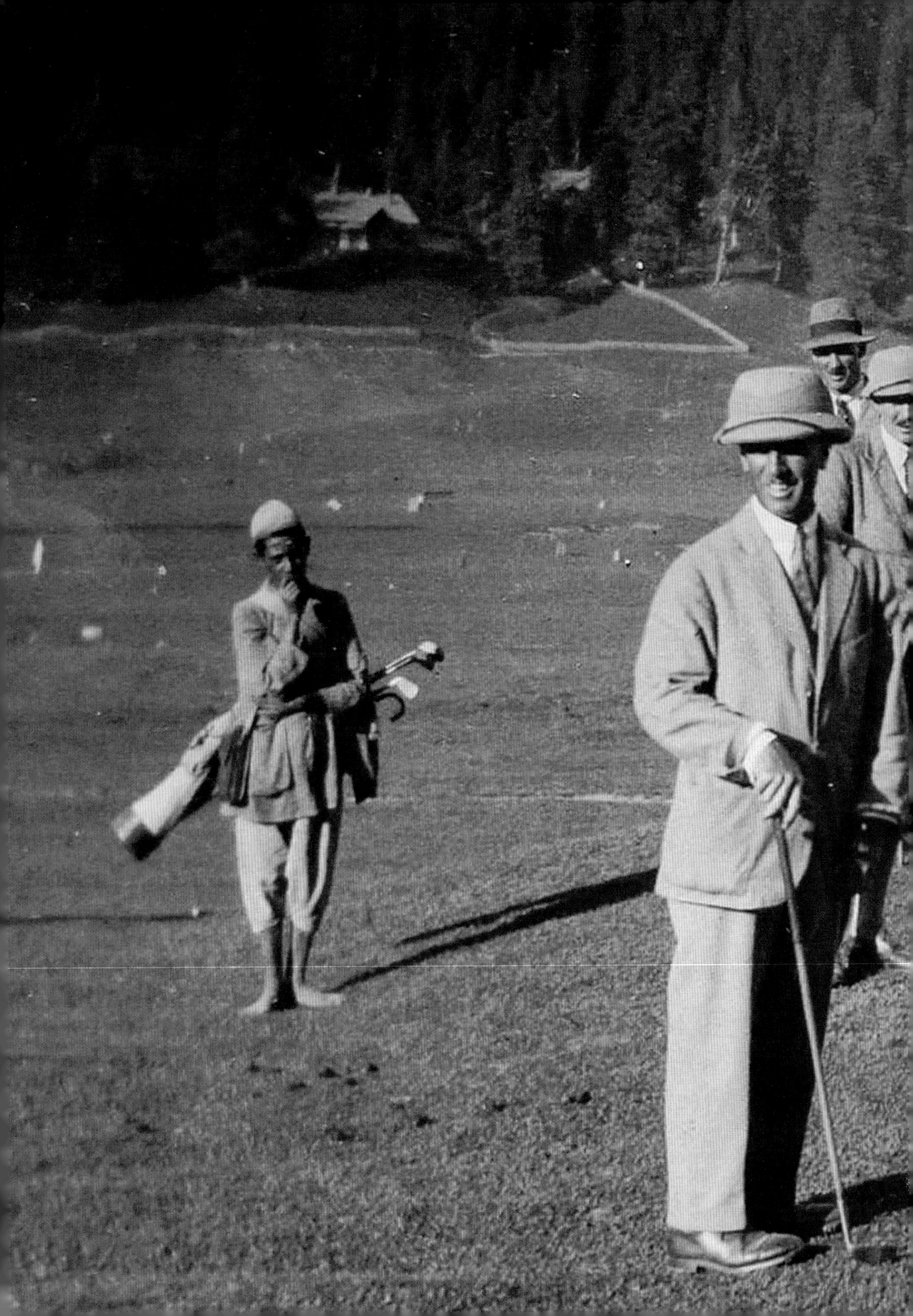

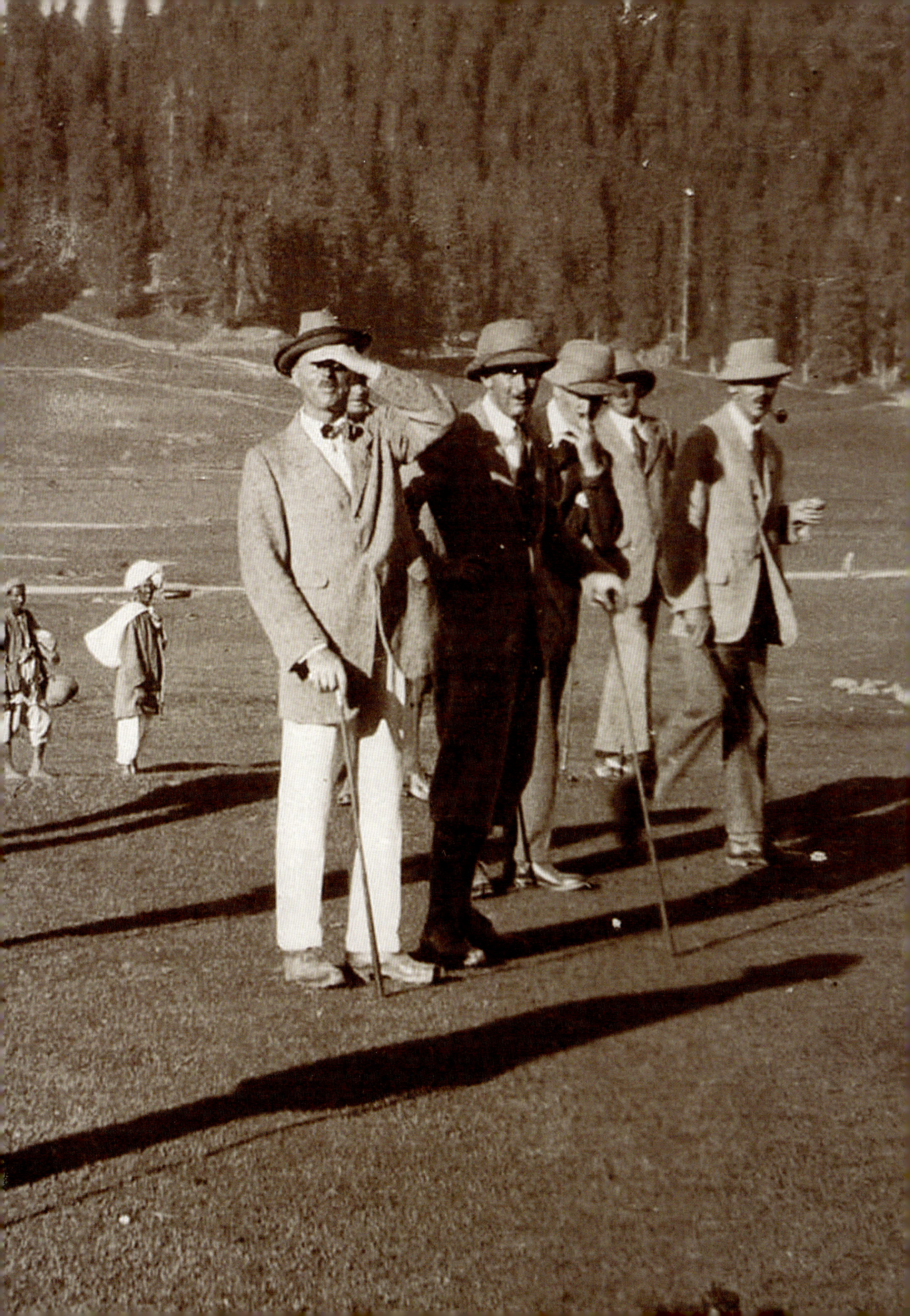

'I Can Never Say Enough About the Men'

Alec Kerr's Military Cross which recognised the Kashmir Rifles success at Lukigura He led the Advance Guard through much of the march south.

Alexander Kerr's MC Citation and Mention in Despatches

Conferred Military Cross EG9 499 of 1917 The Citations reads
"For conspicuous gallantry in action. He assisted to organise and led an attack against the enemy displaying great courage and determination. He has rendered most valuable services through out"

The two 'mentioned in Despatches' (opposite) are signed by Winston Churchill as secretary of state for war and dated 8th May 1916 and 22 November 1916.
Alec served with the Kashmir Rifles form 1912 to 1920. He was the attached British Officer and whilst he spent most of his time with the 2nd Battalion he also served with the the 1st and 3rd Battalions.

Indian Army
Capt. A. N. Kerr, 38th Dogras, attd. 2nd Kashmir Rif.

was mentioned in a Despatch from
Lieutenant General The Honourable J. C. Smuts
dated 8th May 1916
for gallant and distinguished services in the Field.
I have it in command from the King to record His Majesty's
high appreciation of the services rendered.

Winston S. Churchill
Secretary of State for War.

War Office
Whitehall, S.W.

The War of 1914-1918.

Indian Army
Capt. A. N. Kerr, 38th Dogras, attd. 2nd Kashmir Rifles.

was mentioned in a Despatch from
Lieutenant General The Honourable J. C. Smuts
dated 22nd November, 1916
for gallant and distinguished services in the Field.
I have it in command from the King to record His Majesty's
high appreciation of the services rendered.

Winston S. Churchill
Secretary of State for War.

War Office
Whitehall, S.W.
1st March, 1919.

Alec's Photo of 1912

The nearest we can get to Alec's photograph of Minimarg and Haramukh ...from the Tragbhal
See page 20 for Alec's original photograph.

The Kashmir Rifles lead the Advance south from Kilimanjaro through the Pare Hills.

Looking North over the Wular Lake towards the Tragbhal Pass.

The Kashmir Rifles

Buiko today, the railway was the axis of advance.

The Railway sidings where the Askari reinforcements detrained and tipped the battle of Tanga in Germany's favour.

The Railway Cutting at Tanga which the Kashmir Rifles took and captured their first German MG Inset: The photograph from Chapter 3.

The site of Misha Camp today where many thousands of Gen Smut's soldiers collapsed.

The Lukigura Battlefield and the Kanga Mountains behind - where German 4.1" shellfire was directed onto Misha Camp it was renamed Shell Camp.

The banner in the JAK Rifles museum captured at Lukigura. There is no mention of this in either Lt Col Lyall's Battalion Diary or Lt Cooke personal one – However in a note in Horden's official military operations "some amusement was caused by the capture of a German wearing part of the Konigsberg's ensign made up as an under-garment."

Sunset over Lukigura Battlefield.

Kilimanjaro remained in view on the long March south for well over a week.

Pangani River at Buiko in low season – in 1916 it was the source of life and death – water and malaria.

The Beach at Tanga where the Kashmir Rifles landed.

The Camel Bridge on the Dal Lake from the Shalimar Gardens.

Romance of Kashmir.

The 2nd Bn BodyGuard on UN Operations Congo 2010 – The Commanding Officer Col Lakhbinder Singh Lidder and 'Mr Andrew'.

Lt Col Dogra checks out the Jasin Battlefield and finds no sign of a walled fort only mud and sisal.

The Author addresses the BodyGuard in the Congo nearly 100 years after their first African Expedition.

*A completed section of the Army's new road on the Tragbhal Pass.
Note the snow in this photograph taken in June proving that in Alec's day it was only passable in the summer months.*

'I Can Never Say Enough About the Men'

The Commonwealth War Grave at Tanga where the Kashmir Rifles dead are remembered.

The Kashmir Rifles

A special and final thank you to the Regiment . General Jaswal, the Colonel of the JAK Rifles for encouraging me to complete the mission when publishing challenges seemed overwhelming and Brigadier Rodrigues, the Centre Commandant for hosting and making my wife Tance and I so welcome at the 2010 Reunion Jabalpur.

A Shrike in the Shalimar Gardens